Interactive Storytelling
for Video Games

Interactive Storytelling for Video Games

A Player-Centered Approach to Creating Memorable Characters and Stories

Josiah Lebowitz

Chris Klug

Routledge
Taylor & Francis Group

LONDON AND NEW YORK

First published 2011 by Focal Press

2 Park Square, Milton Park, Abingdon, Oxon OX14 4RN
711 Third Avenue, New York, NY 10017, USA

Routledge is an imprint of the Taylor & Francis Group, an informa business

First issued in hardback 2017

Library of Congress Cataloging-in-Publication Data
Application submitted

British Library Cataloguing-in-Publication Data
A catalogue record for this book is available from the British Library.

ISBN 978-0-240-81717-0 (pbk)
ISBN 978-1-138-42746-4 (hbk)

Contents

Special Thanks

First off, I'd like to thank Laura Lewin and Anais Wheeler at Focal Press for all their help during the proposal and preparation of this book, Chris Klug for his excellent contributions, and Beth Millett for her editing.

I'd also like to thank the entire teaching staff at the University of Advancing Technology for all they taught me and for their help when I was researching the material for the papers that eventually became the basis for *Interactive Storytelling for Video Games*. Extra-special thanks to Michael Eilers, Ken Adams, and Derric Clark for their knowledge and advice on game design; Sharon Boleman, for information on story structure, clichés, and archetypes; and Kathleen Dunley, for helping with my research, introducing me to some new types of interactive stories along the way, and coming up with the perfect subtitle.

And I can't forget the great licensing, marketing, and legal staff at the various developers who helped me obtain permission to use so many great screenshots in this book. In particular, I want to acknowledge the extraordinarily helpful folks at Don Bluth Games, Nippon Ichi, XSeed, Game Arts, Konami, and Square Enix, who really went above and beyond the call of duty.

Finally, I'd like to thank everyone who participated in my research surveys and, of course, all the writers, designers, artists, programmers, and the rest who created the many excellent games mentioned throughout this book.

One

Game Stories, Interactivity, and What Players Want

The Importance of Stories

Since the dawn of time, people have been telling stories. What started out as retellings of hunts and tales of their ancestors soon expanded, bringing forth myths and legends. Some stories sought to teach, others to warn. Some attempted to solve the great mysteries of the world; others strove purely to entertain. All across the world, all throughout time, no matter how they lived or what language they spoke, every race, every culture, and every tribe has created and passed on a wealth of stories. And while some stories have slowly faded away, others have been told and retold for centuries, shaping our thoughts, religions, philosophies, and the very world itself.

Looking back at our history, few things have had as much influence on human development and civilization as stories. They've driven us to explore, to fight, to hope, and to dream. They've been the inspiration for art, music, technology, and, of course, more stories. Today, thanks to powerful printing presses, TVs, and the Internet, we have access to a nearly endless supply of stories covering every subject and genre imaginable. No matter what your interests are, there's a story out there for you – probably hundreds or even thousands.

Unsurprisingly, having so many different stories at our disposal has made many of us rather picky. If a story isn't well written or if it features characters or situations that we don't like, why should we spend time reading, watching, or playing it? After all, there are lots of other stories out there waiting for us. Because of this overabundance of stories, modern writers often work hard to attract an audience. Many carefully study what people already like and tailor their settings, plot, and characters to match. Others work hard to perfect their writing and master the many nuances of language, pacing, and character development. Some simply write what they enjoy and hope that it will find a suitable audience. And then there are the brave few who strive to create new and different types of stories and storytelling methods. They push forward with new media and new ideas, many of which challenge the very foundations of storytelling itself. Only time will tell which, if any, of these approaches is the best. Perhaps there is no best method. As long as the author enjoys creating the stories he or she writes and his or her audience (however large or small it may be) enjoys them as well, does anything else really matter?

My name is Josiah and, like most others, I was introduced to stories at a young age. Fairy tales, fables, history ... when I was a child, they filled my imagination and inspired me to create stories of my own. Because my family lived far out in the country, I often wasn't able to spend a lot of time with other kids, so I threw myself into my favorite stories. I read them, acted them out, and dreamed up new ones. Over the years, I created hundreds of stories, many of which stretched into epic sagas of exploration and adventure. Perhaps that in and of itself isn't so unusual, but – unlike most kids, who grow up wanting to become an astronaut or a fireman – I wanted to be an author.

Over the years, that desire waxed and waned as I grew and learned about other people, places, and things. But throughout all that time, I never lost my interest in stories and I always returned to writing. There were two things in particular that drew me back and brought me to where I am now. The first was a book I read long ago. Looking back, I no longer find the story all that different or exciting. I don't even own a copy of it anymore. But I'll always remember that book and be grateful to it for introducing me to one of the most important elements of writing: the plot twist. Today, that simple twist would likely elicit no more reaction from me than a nod or an "I thought so," but back then it was enough to make me put the book down and pause in wonder, thinking back over the rest of the story and how that one shocking revelation had changed everything. Since then, I've come across countless other plot twists, created some of my own, and become rather good at predicting them long before they take place, but that first simple revelation was where it all began.

After that, looking for more stories with shocking plot twists and big reveals, I gravitated toward mystery and fantasy novels while simultaneously trying to work those elements that so intrigued me into my own writing. Due to a series of unrelated incidents, I also became interested in video games, primarily due to the sheer fun and creativity of Nintendo's early *Super Mario Bros.* games. Though much different from the stories I loved, games also attracted me, and I began to dream up and draw out plans for my own colorful platforming games. It wasn't until much later that those two separate interests – games and storytelling – collided, all thanks to a game like nothing I had ever played before: a game called *FINAL FANTASY VII.*

FIGURE
1.1

FINAL FANTASY VII: the game that changed my life. © Square Enix Co., Ltd. All rights reserved.

My Life as a Game Designer

I have been a professional writer/designer in the game industry since 1981, and my stories have been enjoyed by the gaming public from almost the beginning of that career. For a very long time, I did not consider myself a writer, but simply a game designer who happened to use stories in his game designs.

Like many, I had been the GM (game master) in my own fantasy role-playing campaign for years, and, truth be told, it was the fact I was running that very campaign that got me my first game job. I had no inclination to go into the game business at all, as I was making my living as a lighting designer in the NYC theater. I was passionate about games, especially role-playing games, mainly because they were much akin to improvisational theater. I had recently switched the role-playing game I was playing to a new one, called *DragonQuest*, which was published by a game company in New York called Simulations Publications, Inc. (SPI). One Friday night, I had gone into NYC to test one of their new games, as they held open public testing of their new titles every Friday night. I sat down to play a game (a game about the battle of New Market in the Civil War), and at the end of the night, a staff designer came over to chat with me about the experience. His name was Eric Lee Smith. "Well," he began, "what did you think?"

I described in great detail what I thought worked about the game and what didn't. Little did I know, but the more I talked, the more Eric became impressed. I suppose I demonstrated knowledge of games and design with my descriptions. Or maybe I just showed him I was more mature and literate than his average tester. Or maybe Eric was exhausted after a long week at SPI. I may never know.

He furrowed his bushy red eyebrows. "What kinds of games do you play?" I told him that I had just switched my fantasy role-playing campaign to his company's *DragonQuest*. I went into why I liked it and why my group had switched from AD&D.

"That's fascinating. So you really like *DragonQuest*?" I assured him that I did indeed. I asked him if the designer of that game were in the office that evening. Maybe I could talk about the game with him a little bit?

"Well, funny you should ask. He just resigned from the company this week and we're looking for someone to replace him." I was stunned. That particular designer was well known, his games were popular, and the people who played SPI's games had bought many copies of that designer's games.

"It seems like you know the game very well, and we need someone to write adventures for the game. Might you be interested in a job as a freelancer writing a *DragonQuest* adventure?" I was stunned again. I had never been to SPI to test their games, they didn't know me, Eric certainly didn't know me at all, and here I was being offered a job. Sort of. I told Eric I was interested and came back the next week to meet with Eric's boss, David Ritchie, who indeed gave me a freelance job to write a *DragonQuest* adventure.

But, see, at that point, I didn't consider myself a writer. Not at all. My friend Bob Kern, who played in my campaign, now *he* was a writer, and so I asked him to join me in this assignment. Bob and I wrote the adventure (me coming up with the story structure and Bob coming up with the words); we submitted it, they accepted it, and I got a co-author credit.

That was my first taste. I was hooked.

Later on I joined the staff of designers at SPI, helped write the game fiction for their new science-fiction game *Universe*, and then got to head up an effort to redesign *DragonQuest* for a second edition, wrote more adventures (this time on my own), then moved on to a new company called Victory Games, where I won awards for both my role-playing games and my role-playing adventures – all story-based gaming.

Since then, I have written many game stories, been lead writer on a number of titles, and been Creative Director on two MMOs – and all these games have been story-driven. My reputation in the industry is that of a content-centric designer, and if you need a game that has a deeply rooted engrossing story, you should really consider me, Chris Klug, for the job.

That introductory experience mirrors how I got involved in co-authoring this book with Josiah. I will bring to light how the theories Josiah mentions are applied in the "real world" of game writing. I might use examples of my work; tell how we managed sometimes to screw things up;

and reveal how, on our better nights, we managed to make things a little bit better. It's possible that Josiah and I might disagree on certain points, but hopefully the ensuing discussions will give the reader a deeper understanding of the process of making a story work for the audience, because, after all, that is the only thing we writers should care about, making the audience feel something at the end of the day.

—Chris

Stories in Video Games

Unlike books and film, which can be considered mature forms of media, video games are relatively new, with the first arcade machines appearing in the early 1970s, and are still growing and evolving in nearly every way. Every few years, new game consoles are released promising more realistic graphics, higher-quality sound, and a bevy of new features. On the PC side, changes happen even faster, with newer and better hardware being released every few months.

But gaming hardware isn't the only thing that's changing. Games themselves are evolving as well, with new control schemes, gameplay elements, and genres appearing on a regular basis. Like all other aspects of video games, their stories are in a state of change as well. Game stories have evolved from the simple kidnapped-girl plot of *Donkey Kong* to the complex novel-length tales of modern RPGs. In addition, the ability of the player to interact with and affect the story has created many new and different types of stories that are difficult if not impossible to portray in other kinds of media.

Although games are an excellent medium for many types of storytelling, their interactivity makes them far different from more traditional media such as books and film. Interactive stories themselves have many unique and challenging issues that aren't encountered when writing a more traditionally structured tale, which we'll be discussing all throughout the rest of this book. Game writers also need to think about many other factors, such as the synthesis between the story and gameplay and how to maintain a proper pace when the story's progression is, at least to a certain extent, controlled by the player (a subject we'll explore in depth in Chapter 4).

Old Media and New Media

Although it is true that interactivity creates a new art form, it is crucial to understand that stories in games are *dramatic stories* (akin to film, television, and theater), unlike novels and short stories, which I'll call *fiction*. All these stories are fictional; they are just consumed in a different way. Dramatic stories are performed for the audience; novels and short stories are "read." Drama = performance; fiction = read. Games, though interactivity does indeed change things, work in the player's mind in a fashion much closer to screenplays, television, and live theater, and not much like fiction at all. I will talk more about this as we get deeper into the book, but keep it in mind. In fact, it would be useful for you to think about what makes things different between novels and drama. How do you experience both kinds of stories?

—Chris

Make no mistake: whether you're a novice or an experienced writer, writing for games is a very difficult and challenging experience, though it can also be extremely rewarding. If you're new to game writing, this book will help you learn about proper story structure, the types of storytelling methods used, and the particular problems and challenges you'll encounter when creating your stories. Even if you're already an experienced game writer, the breakdown of different story structures may help you more clearly define the types of stories you're called to write and the later sections on the pros and cons of highly interactive stories and the types of stories that players like best should provide some interesting food for thought.

Writer as Emotional Architect

We will, of course, ultimately focus on what the players want, but let us not forget the role of the writer/designer as it meets these desires of the audience. At the end of the day, what any consumer of any kind of entertainment is paying for is to be manipulated into feeling something. Consumers (especially gamers) may not like to admit that they are paying to be manipulated, but that's the truth. The worst thing you can do as a designer/writer is to create something that leaves the player unaffected emotionally. In other words, the last thing you should be is boring. It's better, honestly, for you to create something that makes the players angry than to leave them unaffected, because at least if they are angry, they'll be talking about you, and they cared enough to want something from the story in the first place. Think about the reaction when David Chase ended *The Sopranos* midscene – how the switchboards at the cable companies lit up with complaints at the abrupt ending. Regardless of whether they liked the ending, all people were talking about the next day was how he ended the show. His did his job in spades.

Entertainers are paid to make the audience feel something. This is a foundational concept to understand what I try to do as a writer. It is not only our job; it is our mission.

—Chris

We'll be starting out in Chapter 2 by exploring the history of storytelling in games and how the different storytelling styles appeared, grew, and evolved over the years. We'll also be examining some of the games that helped define the storytelling styles of their generations and how they've affected current storytelling trends.

In Chapters 3, 4, and 5 we'll delve into the basics of any good story: the structure and character development. Important topics include common story themes, maintaining proper flow and pacing, and creating interesting and believable characters. Throughout all three of these chapters, we'll also be looking at a variety of different games to help get a better idea of how these elements work in practice and the different ways they're used in games. If you're new to story writing, pay close attention to the material in these chapters and you may be able to avoid many of the common mistakes made by beginning writers. If you're already an experienced writer (for games or any other medium), think of these chapters as a refresher and a look at how the story elements you're already familiar with are adapted for use in games.

My Approach to the Job

Game stories are drama, and drama is about structure first and foremost and character secondarily. What this means is that unless you are paying a writer to help design the sequence of events in a game, you are only getting a small piece of what he or she can bring. The real work of a writer is to design the setups, the payoffs, the reversals, and the surprises – to design the "gap between expectation and result," as Robert McKee said.

—Chris

Chapter 6 builds on the previous chapters by explaining what elements really make stories interactive and/or player-driven – things that even many experienced writers have trouble properly defining. It will also provide a brief overview of the different story types and structures used in games, giving you a hint of the things that will be covered later on.

You Can Have Both

We'll talk about how you resolve the conflict inherent in designing a story that makes the players feel something, that manipulates them, and that can be player-driven at the same time.

—Chris

Once you know the basics of story writing and have a grasp of the different types of interactive stories and their histories, it's time to move on and learn how to actually create those stories. Chapters 7 through 11 each take a particular interactive storytelling style and examine it in depth, explaining how that type of story should be planned and structured, its unique advantages and disadvantages, and any unusual challenges you may come across. Throughout these chapters, we'll also be studying a wide assortment of games that use these styles. Those games will show the many different approaches that game writers take with their stories as well as give you a sense of which elements do and don't work well and the things that may need to be improved upon in the future.

Though you'll probably be familiar with many of the games discussed, there will likely be a few that you've never played or possibly never even heard of. Keep in mind that to properly explain and discuss the stories of these games, I'll often have to summarize many different parts of the plot, including big twists, endings, and the like. Naturally, the best way to become familiar with a game's story is to play the game for yourself. Even though I'll be pointing out the occasional flaw or problem section in some of these games, they're all excellent titles and, if you have time, I highly recommend playing as many of them as you can. Although I may have to give away some parts of a game's plot for the sake of discussion, there will always be plenty of surprises left untold. So even if you've already read about a game here, don't be discouraged from picking it up and giving it a try for yourself, even if it's a type you don't usually play. You never know, you may find out that you enjoy that kind of game a lot more than you thought.

As I said before, game stories are an evolving art form and, like any art form, there are a variety of opinions on which styles and methods are the best and which should be discarded, which brings us to the last part of the book.

Interactive Stories vs. Traditional Stories: The Great Debate

The first big game storytelling debate was centered on the question of whether games even needed stories to begin with. However, at this point that debate has all but ended. The answer? Yes, no, and maybe. In the end, it all depends on the game. Sports and puzzle games, for example, focus primarily on their core gameplay. As long as the gameplay holds up, little need is seen for a formal story. On the opposite end, even though people often do enjoy the gameplay in adventure games and role-playing games (RPGs), many fans of those genres have little interest in titles without interesting characters and deep storylines. In the end, games don't "need" stories. If a game is fun, people will play it. However, nearly any game can be improved – often significantly – by a good story. Although it's taken time, the majority of the game industry seems to have finally realized this fact, as evidenced by the rising amount of story-focused games in genres that were once known for having very basic stories (first-person shooter [FPS] and action games, for example) or even no stories at all (like puzzle games).

There's a Story Behind Every Game

Man's natural desire to make sense of his world is so strong that if game designers abdicate all authorial responsibility and try to create a game without a story, players will impose a story upon the game anyway, regardless of whether the designers had one in mind. Because of this reality, designers must make story-related decisions (even if it is simply on the level of what the game pieces look like or what the background music sounds like) in such a manner that supports all the other game elements and forms a coherent whole. To do that successfully, they must understand how story works in the audience.

—Chris

However, with the debate on the need for stories over, a new one has sprung up to take its place. Now that it's been decided that stories have their place in games, the question is what types of stories are best? Unlike books, TV, and movies, games are designed to allow the player to take an active role in the story, be it the hero, a group of heroes, or an undefined guiding force. At first, the player's role in the story was only to help his or her heroes succeed by fighting monsters, solving puzzles, jumping over gaping pits, and the like. Assuming that the player successfully got the heroes from Point A to Point B, the story would continue the way it was supposed to and that was that. But it wasn't long before game designers and writers started experimenting with the familiar formula. They sought to give the player control of not only battles, exploration, and puzzles, but also of how the story itself played out. In real life, if the princess were locked in a castle waiting to be saved, the brave hero doesn't really have to save her. He doesn't even have to try. Maybe he'd rather stay home and drink, hook up with her younger sister, or even defect and join her kidnapper, the evil vizier (which is a redundant title, because – in the world of video games clichés – it can generally be assumed that all viziers are evil). In a book or film, that type of interaction is extremely difficult and inconvenient to create. In a video game, however, which is built around interactivity and player choices, the technical limitations all but disappear (though other problems, which will be discussed throughout Chapters 7 through 14, still remain), allowing designers and writers to create many different paths for the player to take.

Over time, there's been a stronger and stronger drive to create games that give players more choices and more control over the story itself. Some of these games have been fairly successful; others have not. Many people in the game industry champion these highly interactive player-driven stories as the ultimate form of storytelling and as the way in which the industry as a whole must head if it wants to continue to grow and evolve as both a medium and an art form. There are others, however, who insist that putting too much control in the hands of the player is a mistake and that more traditional forms of storytelling are still the best. But, in the end, no matter how much freedom is given to the player, he or she still experiences the story in a linear fashion (even if the player gets to choose which line to pursue).

The debate is ongoing and complex, with proponents on both sides weighing in on a large number of different factors in an effort to prove that their form of storytelling is superior. To get a better understanding of this important debate, Chapter 12 looks at the argument from the point of view of the pro-player-driven storytelling group, carefully summarizing their key statements and points as to why a high degree of player control makes for a better story.

Chapter 13 will do the same for the traditional storytelling supporters, providing a detailed look at their primary points and arguments. If you've yet to seriously explore this issue, these chapters will give you a solid summary of both sides' viewpoints and help you start to form your own thoughts and opinions on the matter. If you're already firmly on one side of the storytelling debate, I recommend that you read through both chapters with an open mind and carefully consider the arguments made not only by your side but by the opposing group as well. Perhaps you'll even find your own perspective shifting when all is said and done.

Although the opinions of the game design and writing community are of course very important, something just as important – if not more so – is the opinions of the players themselves. In the end, games are made for and supported by ordinary gamers, so their opinions need to be taken into account. Many industry professionals claim they know what players want, but how can they be so sure? Having been unable to find any serious research on the subject, I set out on a mission to dig deeper and try and discover just what it is players want from a game story by conducting a set of national surveys on the matter. Do players want freedom to do as they please or do they want a tightly controlled experience? Do most of them even care? And how do these preferences affect which games they buy? The results of my research are in Chapter 14 and provide answers to these all important questions. Whether my discoveries put an end to the debate is up for you to decide, but no matter which side of the issue you're on, I'm sure you'll find some interesting things to think about.

Finally, in Chapter 15 we'll be taking a look back at all the things we've covered and use them to peer ahead and consider what the future is likely to hold for storytelling in games. Only time can tell whether those theories will be true, but either way, it's bound to be an interesting ride. Whether you want to write for games or just play them, and no matter which side of the debate you're on, it's an exciting time for video games, stories, and everyone who enjoys them.

Summary

Stories, whether read in books, watched in movies, played in games, or heard about from another person, are an important part of our lives. They've inspired us and shaped the ways we act and look at the world since the dawn of mankind and will continue to do so for as long as we exist. Games may be a new and different form of storytelling, but that doesn't make them any less important.

Writing stories for games is challenging and requires thinking about and dealing with many issues and challenges that other writers never have to consider. And although adding a high degree of interactivity significantly increases those challenges, it can also allow the player a unique opportunity to take an active role and shape the progression and outcome of the story, though whether or not giving players that much control is a good thing is a complex issue that is frequently debated by those in the industry. Being a game writer can be fun, but there's also a lot of difficult work involved, so let's get started.

Things to Consider

1. What key events in history have been influenced by stories?

2. How have stories influenced your life? Which stories have had the greatest impact on you?

3. What makes writing for games different from writing for books or film?

4. How much control do you think players should have in game stories and why? Keep a copy of your answers and see if you still feel the same way once you've finished reading this book.

Two

A Brief History of Storytelling in Games

Before we start seriously looking at the nuts and bolts of game storytelling, I think it's important to pause and take a look at the past. Games have come a long way since the days of *Pong* – and it's not only the graphics, sound, and gameplay that have improved, but the storytelling as well. It's interesting to trace the history of game stories as they evolved from a few lines of text or a couple of pixelated cut-scenes to the complex high-definition multimedia experiences of today and look at the titles that helped shape the eras in which they were released. Of course, a complete study of game history would require an entire book of its own, but we have time to take a look at a few of the highlights. In the end, no matter how much games continue to grow and change, they'll still be partially shaped by the events and titles of years past. As the saying goes, "To understand the future, one must first look to the past."

The Beginnings of Game Stories

In the earliest days of video and computer gaming, there were no such things as stories. Beginning in 1962 with the creation of *Spacewar!* (which was later renamed *Computer Space* and released as one of the earliest arcade games in 1971), the first wave of video and computer games could do little more than move a few dots and lines around a screen. Not only could they not display long lines of text, but they lacked the memory required to store it. The explosion of the arcade market following the release of *Pong* in 1972 did little to improve the situation. Due to serious hardware and memory constraints, any story was limited to a few of lines of text printed on the side of the arcade cabinet. Though some arcade games managed to fit in a few words or a short cut-scene or two, it wasn't until the late 1970s (for computer games) and the early 1980s (for arcade games) that things began to change.

Case Study: *Donkey Kong*

Developer: Nintendo
Publisher: Nintendo
Designer: Shigeru Miyamoto
System: Arcade
Release Date: 1981 (US)
Genre: Platformer

Nintendo's *Donkey Kong* was a game of firsts. It was the first game designed by industry legend Shigeru Miyamoto (who also created many other Nintendo series, including *Super Mario Bros.*, *The Legend of Zelda*, and *Pikmin*), the first game to feature the iconic Mario (then named Jumpman) and Donkey Kong, the first platformer game (or possibly the second, depending on whom you ask), the first game to include multiple level types – and Nintendo's first big hit. It was also the first game to use cut-scenes to visually portray a complete story. Though *Donkey Kong* wasn't the first game to tell a complete story (it was predated by early computer text adventure games, which we'll be discussing shortly) or the first game to use cut-scenes (a few other arcade games came first), it was the first to combine the two elements and marked the beginning of a gradual movement toward more story-based games in the arcade market.

Donkey Kong's story is told over the course of four levels. As the game begins, we see the giant monkey Donkey Kong grab a woman (originally known simply as Lady but later renamed Pauline) and climb to the top of a tower. Mario (Jumpman) gives chase but Donkey Kong damages the structure and proceeds to sneer down at him. At this point, the level begins and the player is tasked with guiding Mario to the top of the tower while dodging rolling barrels thrown by Donkey Kong. Throughout the course of the level, Pauline frequently cries for help, adding to the urgency of the situation. Should the player manage to reach her, Mario and Pauline stare into each other's eyes and a heart appears above their heads. However, that heart is soon broken as Donkey Kong grabs Pauline and makes off with her. Levels 2 and 3 are similar, with Mario pursuing Donkey Kong and Pauline across increasingly complex and difficult areas. In the fourth and final level, Mario is able to remove the supports from the building, causing Donkey Kong to plummet painfully to ground and allowing Mario and Pauline to finally reunite.

Although Donkey Kong's story may seem simple by modern standards, it was the first arcade game to add any sort of background information or story to the game itself rather than just printing it on the cabinet. It was also the first game of any kind to tell a story using a series of cut-scenes. It would still be a few years before stories started becoming an important part of arcade and console games, but *Donkey Kong* was the game that started it all.

FIGURE
2.1

Dirk the Daring is off to rescue the princess in *Dragon's Lair*. Image courtesy of Bluth Group, Ltd. (1983), Don Bluth.

Two years later, in 1983, *Dragon's Lair* took things considerably further.

Created by former Disney animator Don Bluth, *Dragon's Lair* used movie-quality animation to tell its version of the classic princess-in-distress story with players helping bumbling knight Dirk the Daring on his quest to rescue Princess Daphne from an evil dragon. The use of laser discs for storage, combined with beautiful prerecorded video sequences and voice acting, allowed *Dragon's Lair* to achieve a level of audiovisual quality and storytelling that it would take other games years to reach. However, the heavy reliance on prerecorded video did limit *Dragon's Lair*'s gameplay. With each obstacle Dirk faced, players could do nothing more than choose from one of several prompts and then watch the predetermined outcome, boiling the gameplay down to a combination of luck and memorization and severely limiting replay value. Despite its flaws, *Dragon's Lair* remains an important title in the history of game storytelling and allowed gamers a very early glimpse at what the future of gaming could hold.

FIGURE
2.2

Dirk vs. the Lizard King. Image courtesy of Bluth Group, Ltd. © (1983), Don Bluth.

Text Adventures and Interactive Fiction

In 1976, a few years before *Donkey Kong*'s debut, computers saw their first story-based game with the creation of *Colossal Cave Adventure* (also known as *Colossal Cave* and, more commonly, *Adventure*), the first text adventure or IF (interactive fiction) game. Though the original version ran only on a massive mainframe computer, rapid advancements in technology soon allowed *Colossal Cave* and other IF games to reach the consumer market.

Text adventure titles were, as their name suggests, entirely devoid of graphics. Areas, items, and characters were described to the player via blocks of text and the player interacted with the game by entering simple words or phrases such as "go east," "open door," and "use sword." As computers of the day lacked the power and memory necessary to spell-check or otherwise verify multiple variations of phrases, they could usually understand only one or two versions of each command. So although "use sword" might produce the desired result, "swing sword" would instead display an error message, leaving the frustrated player to try and figure out why a seemingly reasonable action wasn't recognized. Many text adventures were also famous for their difficult gameplay, which was often based around complex maze-like areas and tricky inventory-based puzzles. Character deaths also tended to be a frequent occurrence, often as the result of seemingly benign actions, and in some games it was even possible to unknowingly perform a wrong action and render the entire game unwinnable, something that the player might not discover until hours later. All of these elements are frowned upon in modern gameplay, but at the time, they were not only acceptable but expected.

The stories in text adventures varied wildly, covering many different genres and writing styles. Though most cast players as a nameless generic hero who has to explore a strange area, others placed more of a focus on character development and plot-driven stories. From an interactivity standpoint, interactive traditional stories, multiple-ending stories, and branching path stories were all frequently employed, and a few titles even neared the level of freedom and choice available in open-ended stories (a summary of the differences between these storytelling styles can be found in Chapter 6, with in-depth explanations in Chapters 7 through 11). Text adventures enjoyed a brief golden age during the late 1970s and early 1980s, but as computer technology continued to advance, they were soon replaced by more visually pleasing graphic adventure games. They retain a small but dedicated fanbase that continues to make new text adventure games under the IF moniker.

The first computer RPGs also began appearing in the early 1980s starting with *Ultima I: The First Age of Darkness* in 1981. Though their stories initially lacked the depth of those found in the better text adventures, they evolved quickly, offering better sound and graphics along with deeper gameplay and more complex storylines, eventually helping inspire famous console RPGs such as *DRAGON WARRIOR* (1986) and *FINAL FANTASY* (1987).

Case Study: *Colossal Cave Adventure*

Designers:	William Crowther, Don Woods
Publisher:	CRL
System:	PDP-10 (later ported to a variety of other computers)
Release Date:	1976 (original version), 1977 (updated version)
Genre:	Text Adventure

Created as a hobby by caving enthusiast William Crowther and significantly expanded the following year by Don Woods, *Colossal Cave Adventure* marked the start of the adventure game genre and was the first game to feature a full in-game story.

> >You are standing at the end of a road before a small brick building. Around you is a forest. A small stream flows out of the building and down a gully.

And so it begins. The story itself is pretty simple. You play as a generic hero (or yourself, if you prefer) who finds himself standing in the woods (described in the previous text quote). Exploring the building will turn up an all-important lamp and several other useful items; after a little more wandering around, you'll come across the entrance to a cave. Loosely based on the layout of Kentucky's Mammoth Cave, the cavern is a vast maze of twisty little passages and strange rooms. An assortment of dangerous creatures roam the area, ranging from the realistic (a bear) to the fantastical (dragons, dwarves, and so on), but there is also a plethora of fabulous treasures to be found. Of course, many of the treasures (as shown by the following quote) are either guarded or otherwise difficult to obtain.

> >You are inside a barren room. The center of the room is completely empty except for some dust. Marks in the dust lead away toward the far end of the room. The only exit is the way you came in.
>   >There is a ferocious cave bear eyeing you from the far end of the room! The bear is locked to the wall with a golden chain!

The solution to this bear room involves using some food (which you may or may not have picked up earlier) to feed and pacify the bear, unlocking the golden chain (if you previously found the keys), taking the chain (it's a treasure), and then getting the bear to follow you, as he'll come in handy later on.

Though *Colossal Cave* almost fits the mold of a fully player-driven story, just turning you free to explore and do as you please, there's a loose plot thread strung throughout the game about the mystery of the caves and why all these strange things are inside. Also, although the game doesn't tell you exactly what your goal is other than exploration and survival, there is an ending, trigged by collecting all the treasures and solving a final puzzle. However, as your character has very limited inventory space and is hounded by treasure-stealing pirates and other hazards, the treasures have to be safely stored in the building from the start of the game (another thing that the player must figure out on his or her own).

As with many other text adventures, it's possible to make the game unwinnable by accidentally losing or destroying important items. Completing *Colossal Cave* without the use of a guide requires playing and restarting the game many times while making a map of its vast and confusing tunnels. The game also features a point system with a maximum possible score that can be obtained only by collecting and keeping every treasure with no deaths before your lamp runs out of power (which puts an end to your explorations, unless you previously traded a certain treasure for extra batteries), a feat that requires detailed knowledge of the cave and some careful planning to achieve.

Many modern gamers may scoff at the lack of graphics and find *Colossal Cave*'s unforgiving gameplay frustrating, but it provides a fascinating look at the start of the adventure game genre, and its twisty passages and imaginative chambers are just as engrossing now as they were over 30 years ago. If you're interested in exploring the roots of PC gaming, you can find out more about *Colossal Cave Adventure* and download many different free versions of the game at http://www.rickadams.org/adventure/. (I recommend the Windows version of *Adventure 3*, which, aside from being based on the most popular release, also runs well on most current computers.)

RPGs, Adventure Games, and the Growing Importance of Stories

Today, games with deep stories can be found in every genre, but from the late 1980s until the mid 1990s, the stories in most games tended to be simple variations of the "rescue the princess" or "save the world from the evil villain" themes. Though there were exceptions, deep, complex stories were mostly limited to American RPGs and adventure games (on the PC) and Japanese RPGs (on consoles).

On the PC side, newer and better hardware allowed text adventure games to transform into graphic adventure games. Though originally nothing but text adventures with simple static artwork, adventure games soon grew to include detailed animated graphics and more user-friendly point-and-click interfaces. The so-called golden age of PC adventure games featured many excellent titles but was primarily dominated by two developers. The first was Sierra, with popular series, including *King's Quest*, *Space Quest*, and *Leisure Suit Larry*. The second was LucasArts, with games such as

The Secret of Monkey Island, *Sam & Max Hit the Road*, and *Day of the Tentacle*. Many of these titles are still as fun and hilarious as they were when first released and are available in various classic game bundles and from downloadable game services.

Adventure games from this era were often characterized by bright, colorful graphics and humorous storylines. The gameplay tended to emphasize a mix of conversations, item collection, and inventory-based puzzles. Though interactive traditional stories were the most common, some multiple-ending and a few branching path stories were used as well. Though far less frustrating than many text adventures, point-and-click adventure games often featured at least a few puzzles with highly illogical solutions and frequently forced players to engage in a "pixel hunt," which refers to the process of moving and clicking the mouse all over a screen in hopes of finding a missed item or other important "hotspot." Although early point-and-click adventure games also retained the frequent deaths and unwinnable scenarios that plagued text adventures, they soon began to move away from that (led by LucasArts), eventually reaching the point at which it was impossible to become permanently stuck and there were few, if any, ways to die.

The genre later underwent another significant change in 1993 with the release of Cyan Worlds' classic adventure game *Myst*. In a significant change of style from the games that had come before it, *Myst* used a first-person perspective and made the player (instead of a developed character) the hero. It also replaced the cartoon-like 2D graphics with highly detailed 3D scenes, emphasized ambient sounds rather than a full musical score, and made its puzzles environmental in nature rather than inventory-based. *Myst* also took a much different approach to its story. After being transported to the island of *Myst* by a strange book, the player is given free rein to explore and try to solve the island's many tricky puzzles. The story is, in contrast to most adventure games of the time, very serious and told primarily through a series of notes and journals scattered about the islands, leaving players to track down and piece together the clues and determine why the island of Myst and the other ages it links to are deserted and how the two brothers Sirrus and Achenar have become trapped inside a pair of unusual books.

Myst's sharp departure from the formula used by past adventure games was a surprising success, making it the bestselling PC game of all time until 2000 (when it was unseated by *The Sims*, which we'll discuss in Chapter 11) and spawning several sequels and a massive number of clones and copycat games. The *Myst* style continued to dominate the PC adventure game genre for several years until the steady rise of FPS, MMO (massively multiplayer online), and strategy games took over the PC market and forced the adventure genre into near dormancy.

Throughout all this, PC RPGs continued to evolve as well, led by the *Ultima* and *Might and Magic* series, though the changes were nowhere near as drastic as those seen in the adventure game genre. Primary improvements included better graphics, the switch to a first-person perspective (for some but not all titles), and increasingly complex gameplay systems, many of which were based heavily on the classic tabletop RPG *Dungeons & Dragons*. From a story perspective, the increase in available memory allowed for more text, which led to longer in-game conversations and branching dialog systems in which the player could frequently choose between multiple responses to questions and inquiries posed by nonplayer characters (NPCs). An interesting thing to note is that although console RPGs (which we'll be discussing in a moment) focused primarily on character-driven stories featuring well-defined heroes and villains with complex personalities and backstories, PC RPGs tended to feature generic heroes and focus more on exploration and character building with broader yet simpler storylines.

Meanwhile, as personal computers were still relatively new, complicated, and expensive, consoles continued to dominate the game market. The NES (Nintendo Entertainment System) and later Super NES and Sega Genesis were vast improvements over earlier systems such as the Atari 2600, allowing for games with better graphics, more varied gameplay, and longer and deeper stories. Though most of the popular genres of the time, like platformers and action games, kept their stories short and simple, the storytelling in RPGs rapidly improved. Unlike PC RPGs, which were developed in the United States, console RPGs were primarily developed by Japanese companies such as Square and Enix (which eventually merged to form Square Enix). No one would call the stories in RPGs such as the first *DRAGON WARRIOR* or *FINAL FANTASY* masterpieces, but their epic quests and twisting tales stood in stark contrast to the brief cut-scenes and scattered lines of dialog found in other games of the time. In addition, some games such as *Castlevania II: Simon's Quest* began to introduce multiple-ending storytelling, allowing players to have a say in how their stories ended.

When the Super NES and Sega Genesis began their battle for living room dominance, RPG makers took advantage of the increased power and memory to hone their craft and tell increasingly rich stories. Square led the charge, creating many classic titles such as *FINAL FANTASY VI* (originally released in the United States as *FINAL FANTASY III*), *CHRONO TRIGGER* (which we'll talk about more in Chapter 8), and *SECRET OF MANA*, which are still considered by many to feature some of the best gameplay and stories the genre has ever seen. *FINAL FANTASY VI* in particular is known for its diverse and interesting cast of characters (including fan favorite villain Kefka) and deep story, which touched on many mature issues such as death, suicide, and teen pregnancy. Other notable titles include Nintendo's *Earthbound* and *Super Mario RPG*, Enix's *Illusion of Gaia* and *Ogre Battle*, and Sega's *Phantasy Star* series. Although interactive traditional stories still dominated the period, *CHRONO TRIGGER* used multiple-ending storytelling to great effect and *Ogre Battle* featured a complex branching path story.

Unfortunately, though console RPGs were huge hits in Japan, with new Square and Enix titles frequently resulting in long lines of fans camping out to await their release, they remained a niche market in the United States. Whether this was due to a lack of advertising, their complexity, or their radically different gameplay styles when compared to the market dominating platformer games is hard to say. Regardless of the reasons, this situation led to many Japanese developers refusing to release major RPGs, even extremely popular ones, in the United States (such as *FINAL FANTASY II, III,* and *V, FRONT MISSION, STAR OCEAN,* and *DRAGON WARRIOR V* and *VI*). Others (such as *FINAL FANTASY IV*) were significantly edited or scaled back to make them "easy enough" for American gamers. Fortunately, the stories mostly remained intact (aside from occasional translation issues) and began to show U.S. gamers that game stories could contain the same depth and complexity found in novels and films, though it would be a few more years until gaming's story revolution truly began.

Case Study: *FINAL FANTASY IV*

Developer: Square Co., Ltd.
Publisher: Nintendo of America, Inc.
Writers: Hironobu Sakaguchi, Takashi Tokita
System: Super Nintendo
Release Date: November 23, 1991 (US) (originally called *FINAL FANTASY II*)
Genre: RPG
Other   PlayStation (included in *FINAL FANTASY CHRONICLES*, 1997),
Versions: Game Boy Advance (2005), Nintendo DS (2008), Wii Virtual
                 Console (2010)

FIGURE
2.3

The cast of FINAL FANTASY IV (from the DS version). © Square Enix, Co., LTD. All Rights Reserved.

Square Enix's *FINAL FANTASY* series is one of the most well-known RPG franchises the world over. Unlike its biggest competitor *DRAGON QUEST* (also by Square Enix), which focuses on traditional old-fashioned RPG adventures, the *FINAL FANTASY* series has always striven to push the envelope, try new things, and advance the genre and the game industry as a whole. Many of the gameplay elements that were first introduced in *FINAL FANTASY* games have gone on to become standard features in hundreds of other titles. *FINAL FANTASY* games (especially the numbered "main series" entries) have developed a reputation for cutting-edge graphics, sweeping musical scores, new and innovative battle and character development systems, and – most importantly – memorable characters and deep, complex storylines. Because of their reputation and the impact many of their stories have had throughout the game industry, we'll be discussing several *FINAL FANTASY* titles throughout the course of this book.

Originally released in the United States as *FINAL FANTASY II* (due to *FINAL FANTASY II* and *III* not being released outside Japan), *FINAL FANTASY IV* was a groundbreaking RPG that paved the way for many future titles. Notable new features in *FINAL FANTASY IV* included a longer quest and larger world than past games, an Active Time Battle system (now standard in many RPGs), and a far longer and deeper story with a wide cast of unique and fully developed characters.

It should be noted that the original U.S. release featured significantly reduced difficulty in an effort to better appeal to U.S. gamers and had all religious references removed to comply with censorship requirements. Due to space constraints, certain minor plot and backstory elements were removed as well. Later rereleases and remakes, however, are truer to the game's original Japanese version.

FINAL FANTASY IV tells the story of Cecil, a dark knight serving the kingdom of Baron. Recently, the king of Baron has been behaving extremely erratically and attacking other nations for reasons that are flimsy at best. Cecil questions his motives, only to find himself stripped of his rank and sent along with his best friend Kain to deliver a package to a nearby village. The package, however, turns out to be a trap that destroys most of the village. Horrified by what he has done, Cecil leaves Baron, setting off with the last survivor of the village, a girl named Rydia. Upon learning that the king of Baron is trying to collect the world's elemental crystals, Cecil decides he must do his best to protect them. Along the way, he is joined by numerous companions (many of whom later sacrifice themselves to save the rest of the party), is forced to confront his own dark past, and discovers that both the king and his friend Kain are being manipulated by a man named Golbez, who is using them to further his own evil schemes. And that's just the beginning.

FIGURE
2.4

FINAL FANTASY IV's plot can get a bit melodramatic (from the DS version). © Square Enix Co., Ltd. All rights reserved.

By modern standards, *FINAL FANTASY IV*'s plot is a bit on the melodramatic side, with all the mind control, heroic sacrifices, and "I am your father"–type moments. However, many fans still consider it to be their favorite entry in the series. Also, in terms of both length and scope, *FINAL FANTASY IV* greatly surpassed previous console RPGs and also featured characters with far more developed personalities and backstories, making it a truly groundbreaking title in the history of game storytelling.

The Cinematic Evolution of Game Stories

Video game storytelling started to first hit its stride in the RPGs and adventure games of the late 1980s and early 1990s, but it wasn't until the late 1990s that story-based games began to break out of their niches and spread across all genres. Due to the efforts of several groundbreaking titles, a far wider variety of gamers started to appreciate and desire games that had not only good graphics and gameplay, but good stories as well.

Though the late 1990s and early 2000s were a great time for storytelling in console games, PC gamers weren't so lucky. With the rise in popularity of FPS, RTS, and sim games (none of which were well known for their stories), adventure games and RPGs lost quite a lot of their popularity. Adventure games were hit particularly hard, though a few good titles, such as *Myst III*, were released during that period. Meanwhile, Bioware and Black Isle managed to keep the PC RPG genre alive with classic games like *Baldur's Gate*, *Neverwinter Nights*, and *Planescape: Torment*, and begin to move the genre more in the direction of open-ended stories. There were also a handful of good story-based games released in other genres, such as the cult classic action game *Dues Ex*, but they were more the exception than the norm.

While story-based games were losing ground on the PC, the exact opposite was happening in the console market. With a new generation of consoles warring for supremacy, games were once again evolving at a rapid pace. There were many great games released on both the Sega Saturn and Nintendo 64, but it was newcomer Sony's PlayStation that won the fight and helped advance game storytelling toward its current state. Armed with a stronger processor and far more storage space than anyone could have dreamed of back in the days of cartridge-based systems, developers were able to make many groundbreaking titles for the PlayStation, two of which in particular revolutionized the way game stories were told.

The first was Square's *FINAL FANTASY VII*. No longer content with appealing only to a niche market and armed with the most graphically impressive game of its time and a massive marketing budget, Square was determined to replicate their success in Japan in the United States. Due to a combination of amazing graphics, excellent review scores, and the massive media blitz surrounding its launch, *FINAL FANTASY VII* was a runaway success, selling millions of copies. It also introduced many U.S. gamers to RPGs, effectively bringing the genre into the mainstream and paving the way for a steady stream of Japanese RPGs over the following years. We'll be discussing *FINAL FANTASY VII*'s story in depth in Chapter 7, but for now know that it continued to evolve the formula used in past titles and featured an epic globe-spanning quest filled with one of the most memorable casts of characters to be found in the entire series.

In addition to greatly increasing the popularity of RPGs and providing one of gaming's best-loved stories, *FINAL FANTASY VII* also introduced many gamers to full-motion videos (FMVs). As opposed to normal in-game graphics, FMVs are computer-animated movies that are created and rendered ahead of time. Although they can't be interacted with, they allow for a far greater level of detail than is otherwise possible. Though *FINAL FANTASY VII*'s FMVs seem rather crude by today's standards (or even when compared to those of its sequel, *FINAL FANTASY VIII*), they were cutting-edge for their time and allowed the artists to show important story scenes in far more detail than would have otherwise been possible, allowing players to accurately read the characters' body language and facial features, making them feel far more real and alive, and adding considerable impact to the game's biggest moments.

FMVs proved so popular and effective that many developers began incorporating them into their own games, starting a trend of highly cinematic game storytelling. Even now, FMVs continue to remain an important part of game storytelling, though as graphic quality continues to improve, the line between normal in-game graphics and FMVs is rapidly shrinking.

Though FMVs were an important part of the puzzle, game storytelling was still missing a crucial element required for cinematic storytelling: voices. Voicing acting had been used sporadically in video games for years, but the limited memory capacity on cartridges, discs, and arcade boards made it highly impractical. Even with the launch of the PlayStation and Saturn, with their high-capacity CDs finally offering enough storage space for voice-overs, most early game voice acting was brief and amateurish. It took another big game (*Metal Gear Solid*, which we'll discuss momentarily) to show the industry how much quality voice-overs could add to a game.

Multiple-ending stories began to become increasingly more common during this time as well, with games like *Metal Gear Solid* and *Blood Omen: Legacy of Kain* (which will be covered in Chapter 8) helping to popularize the concept. Developers also continued to experiment with branching path stories in games such as *FRONT MISSION 3* (covered in Chapter 9).

Case Study: *Metal Gear Solid*

Developer: Konami
Publisher: Konami
Writers: Hideo Kojima, Tomokazu Fukushima

System:	Sony PlayStation
Release Date:	October 21, 1998 (US); June 18, 2009 (PlayStation Network rerelease)
Genre:	Stealth Action
Other Version:	*Metal Gear Solid: The Twin Snakes* (GameCube, 2004)

Designer Hideo Kojima's games are known for several things, including their excellent gameplay, clever boss battles, deep twisting stories, numerous hidden jokes, and infamously long cut-scenes. His most popular work is the long-running *Metal Gear* series. Though it began in 1987 on the MSX2 and NES, it wasn't until the release of the third entry, *Metal Gear Solid* (*MGS*), that the series became particularly well known. Featuring a complex and mostly believable near-future plot with full voice acting and unique gameplay with an emphasis on stealth and cunning over straight-up action, it become a huge hit and went on to inspire many other stealth action games.

Kojima worked very hard to make the world of *MGS* as realistic and believable as possible. Though it lacked the FMVs and prerendered backgrounds of *FINAL FANTASY VII*, an enormous amount of attention was paid to the graphics to ensure that everything from the buildings to the characters came across as realistic and believable.

Aside from a couple of super-powered villains, the story is also very firmly rooted in the real world. The tale begins with Solid Snake, a retired government special forces agent, called in for one last job. The new members of Snake's old unit (Foxhound) have gone rogue, taking over a remote Alaskan military base and with it, one of the government's most secret weapon projects, the bipedal-nuclear-equipped tank dubbed Metal Gear Rex, while also securing several high-ranking hostages. Foxhound is using Rex to blackmail the government, demanding the remains of the legendary soldier Big Boss (a.k.a. Naked Snake from *Metal Gear Solid 3*, which we'll talk about in Chapter 5). Due to Snake's past connections to both Big Boss and Metal Gear, and his skill at infiltrating and destroying enemy bases single-handedly, the government sees him as their only hope of stopping Foxhound. However, there are a number of important events going on behind the scenes, and over the course of his mission, Snake is faced with a complex web of plots within plots that could put even the best spy novels to shame. Featuring deep themes including love, war, and the dangers and potentials of nuclear weapons and genetic engineering, the story of *MGS* remains both emotionally moving and intellectually intriguing.

Despite being on a stealth mission, Snake meets many characters along the way, including allies like the captured soldier Meryl Silverburgh and Rex's designer Hal "Otacon" Emmerich, and enemies including Russian spy Revolver Ocelot and the mysterious Foxhound leader Liquid Snake. He's also backed up by a radio support team that he can contact at almost any time to learn more about his mission, weapons, and surroundings, or just to chat. The sheer

FIGURE
2.5

Don't get between a wolf and its prey!

Snake's radio support team is always ready to provide useful information and/or witty comments about the current situation.

number of these mostly optional conversations is so enormous that the average player will hear few, if any, repeats. In addition, every line of dialog in the game from important conversations to minor radio banter was recorded by a superb cast of voice actors. The emotions that couldn't be shown in the character models (as impressive as they were for their time) found full expression in the voices. Though far from the first game to use voice acting, *MGS* featured one of the best implementations then seen in gaming, which – when combined with its diverse cast of interesting characters – went a long way toward pulling players into the story and making it feel as real and believable as Kojima wanted.

Although it would still be a while before a large percentage of games adopted full or near-full voice acting (even on CDs, voice files required a very large amount of disc space), *Metal Gear Solid* set a standard for both the amount and quality of voice acting and brought about a change in the industry, showing that a character's voice was just as important as his or her 3D model.

Game Stories Today

In the 2000s, successive generations of PCs and gaming consoles allowed drastic improvements in graphics, to the point of surpassing many of the best FMVs of past generations. At the same time, DVDs and Blu-ray discs have increased the amount of available storage space so that it's no longer impractical for games to include hours of voice-overs and prerecorded music. With technological limitations fading rapidly, game designers and writers have begun to focus more heavily on improving their gameplay and stories while also experimenting with new and different types of games.

On PCs, FPS, real-time strategy (RTS), and simulation games retained their popularity but increasingly began adding stories and RPG elements to complement their traditional gameplay. Retaining the PC RPG genre's strong focus on exploration and character development, many of these new games such as *Fallout 3* (which we'll talk about more in Chapter 10) and *Borderlands* strive to provide open-ended stories with expansive worlds and a large amount of freedom for players to explore and do as they please. Even more traditional FPS and RTS games, with linear campaigns and few if any RPG elements, frequently contain epic stories with well-developed characters, marking a significant change from the majority of earlier titles.

Traditional PC RPGs also continue to be made by companies like Bioware, though the genre is increasingly shifting online with MMORPGs (massively multiplayer online role-playing games) such as the immensely popular *World of Warcraft*. Most MMOs use a form of fully player-driven storytelling, though some have used open-ended and even interactive traditional stories as well (we'll be talking in depth about MMOs and their storytelling styles in Chapter 11).

Of particular interest to longtime PC gamers, the point-and-click adventure game genre was revived almost single-handedly by Telltale Games. Staffed by many former LucasArts employees, Telltale brought back classic series such as *Sam & Max* and *Monkey Island* while also creating adventure games based on a variety of popular licenses.

While retaining the genre's classic gameplay, tricky puzzles, and hilarious stories, Telltale's games have updated the style with easier controls and inventory management, a discrete hint system (where characters will voice a suggestion as to what to do next when the player appears to be stuck), and a more robust and user-friendly conversation system. Another change that Telltale has brought to the genre is the concept of episodic games. Rather than release one big game every year or so, Telltale games are divided into seasons consisting of between four and six monthly "episodes" (games), each containing several hours of gameplay.

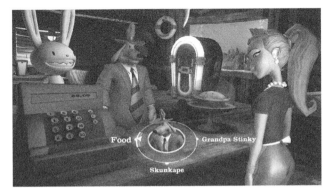

FIGURE
2.6

Sam and Max, freelance police, in their third season of episodic adventure games, *Sam & Max: The Devil's Playhouse*.

FIGURE
2.7

Aliens, psychic powers, floating brains, and elder gods? Just another day on the job for Sam and Max.

This approach has allowed Telltale to release a steady stream of new games and also made it easy for gamers to try out a single episode for a low price before deciding whether they wish to buy the entire season. Depending on the particular season, the episodes can be anything from a series of self-contained though loosely connected adventures to chapters of a single full-length story. Though many companies have expressed interest in episodic games, Telltale is widely considered to be the only developer to get it right, and their hard work has introduced the PC adventure game genre to an entirely new generation of gamers.

Rapid growth also happened in the casual PC game market. Focusing on games that are simple to pick up and can be played easily in short sessions, many early casual games had little to no story, but as the genre has grown and matured, casual game developers have begun adding a wide variety of different stories (mostly using interactive traditional storytelling) to their games, such as *Plants vs. Zombies* and the *Samantha Swift* series of hidden picture games.

Another recent development in PC gaming is the sudden popularity of social networking games. Centered around social network sites such as Facebook, social networking games offer players a chance to work with (or sometimes against) their friends in a variety of different tasks. However, despite their meteoric rise to popularity, social networking games are still in their infancy and the majority of titles, such as the well-known *FarmVille*, focus primarily on attracting and retaining players with assorted mini-games and item collection systems, with little to no story to support the gameplay.

On consoles, the techniques that developed during the cinematic era have been expanded and refined, making game stories even more epic and filmlike in their presentations. As on PCs, RPG-style gameplay elements and stories have steadily spread to other genres, leading to the explosion of story-driven games of all types.

RPGs continue to be at the heart of game storytelling. Japanese RPGs such as *FINAL FANTASY XIII* and *THE WORLD ENDS WITH YOU* (which we'll examine in depth shortly) still provide highly structured cinematic stories in many different styles and genres. In addition, ports of popular PC RPGs (such as *The Elder Scrolls* series and assorted Bioware games) along with a few specifically made for consoles (such as *Fable 2*, which we'll discuss in Chapter 10) have given console gamers a taste of open-ended storytelling.

Meanwhile, a variety of action, adventure, platformer, and FPS games have been released that feature deep, well-done stories of their own. Interactive traditional storytelling still remains the dominant form, but multiple-ending, branching path, and open-ended storytelling have all been used in many games as well, creating a wide diversity of titles that are sure to contain something for every type of gamer.

A console development that has had surprising effect on game storytelling is the addition of online stores and downloadable games and content. The easy access to downloadable games has encouraged developers to release new and innovative titles such as *Flower*, which have experimented with many different types of gameplay and storytelling. It's also allowed console gamers to experience some of the best casual and adventure games, which were formerly available only on PCs. At the same time, downloadable retro games have introduced many new gamers to now-classic titles such as *FINAL FANTASY VII*, *Metal Gear Solid*, and *Ogre Battle*, increasing interest in their stories, characters, and storytelling styles. This has also led to a trend of creating new retro-style games that make use of not only old-style graphics, music, and gameplay, but storytelling techniques as well.

Another change brought about by online stores is the concept of downloadable content (DLC). DLC is extra content released after a game has shipped that can be downloaded (often for a small fee) and added to an existing game. Though DLC usually comes in the form of new costumes, weapons, or playable characters, some companies have experimented with using DLC to expand a game's story, including new areas, levels, and plot elements. Generally shorter and less expansive than the expansion packs familiar to PC gamers (which were frequently closer to complete sequels than simple add-ons), often costing several dollars and containing only a few hours at most of additional gameplay, DLC has been used in many games to expand on the setting and backstory (as in *Grand Theft Auto IV* and *Heavy Rain*) and/or to provide an epilogue to bridge the gap between a game and its sequel (as in *Prince of Persia*).

Perhaps the most important change in current game storytelling is the ongoing effort to integrate the story more tightly with the gameplay. In many older games, the storylines can feel rather tacked on, as if they were written after the game was already near completion and forced to fit into a preexisting level structure and gameplay style – which was, in fact, often the case. Though it's still an ongoing process, more and more developers are realizing the importance of bringing writers in during the early planning and development stages to ensure that the story and gameplay are better matched. Developers are also experimenting with making tutorials and other fourth wall–breaking gameplay elements fit more naturally into the world. In *Prince of Persia*, for example, the player learns the basics of exploration and combat by following and mimicking the movements of a person he's chasing, along with some unobtrusive text prompts, rather than having someone break character by telling the prince that he has to use the X button to jump. Other "gamey" elements – from health bars to healing potions – are also having their presence and functions modified or worked into the story, becoming less obtrusive in the process. Although many of these experiments have met with mixed success, they show the growing realizations throughout the industry that games are a strong storytelling medium and that it's important to make an effort to fit the other elements of the game (gameplay, graphics, music, and so on) with the story rather than just forcing the story in at the last moment.

Case Study: *THE WORLD ENDS WITH YOU*

Developer:	Square Enix Co., Ltd./Jupiter
Publisher:	Square Enix, Inc.
Writers:	Tatsuya Kando, Sachie Hirano, Yukari Ishida
System:	Nintendo DS
Release Date:	April 22, 2008 (US)
Genre:	Action RPG

FIGURE
2.8

Neku and Shiki find themselves forced into a deadly game. © Square Enix Co., Ltd. All rights reserved.

When creating *THE WORLD ENDS WITH YOU*, the team set out to make a game that would take full advantage of the DS's unique features – a goal at which they clearly succeeded. However, what really sets *THE WORLD ENDS WITH YOU* apart is the way it merges together its gameplay, graphics, music, and story into a single unified whole, with every single element of the game fitting with and supporting the others.

The game takes place in Tokyo's trendy Shibuya district, the heart of Japanese fashion and teen culture. Featuring many fully recognizable streets and shops from the real Shibuya, *THE WORLD ENDS WITH YOU* uses its setting to exceptionally good effect. The sharp Japanese comic–style graphics fit and enhance both the setting and the focus on Japanese teen culture. The soundtrack – which is made up primarily of a fusion of musical influences from hip-hop to rock to electronica – does the same, providing the same type of listening experience you'd be likely to find in the stores of the real Shibuya. Character development is similarly setting appropriate. The characters' stats are based primarily on their clothing, with new items being available for purchase from a wide variety of stores, all of which cater to fans of different Japanese fashion trends. Stats can also be permanently raised by eating at various restaurants and fast-food stands (in a realistic nod, characters can eat only so much every day before becoming full).

Store clerks start out impersonal and at times even rude, but grow more friendly and helpful as the player returns and continues to shop with them over the course of the game, offering special discounts, off-menu specials, and tips about various outfits' secret abilities. Continuing the fashion theme, Neku's attacks and special movies in battle are determined by which collectable pins he's wearing. There are several hundred pins in the game, each with their own ability, and many are able to grow stronger and evolve into new and different pins as they're used. Finally, depending on the day and particular part of Shibuya the player is in, different clothing and pin brands will be in and out of style. Tailoring your outfits to match the current fad will grant a nice stat boost in battle; wearing unpopular items will result in reduced stats, making for far more difficult fights. But, as any follower of fashion can tell you, fads are very prone to change. Showing your style by fighting while wearing a certain brand's clothing will cause its popularity to slowly but surely rise, allowing determined players to work the trends to their own advantage. Though many of these elements may sound slightly gimmicky on their own, when combined, they go a long ways toward making the game's virtual Shibuya feel almost as alive and dynamic as the real one.

The story begins when the teenage hero Neku wakes up in the middle of a crowded street with his memories a jumbled mess. Before he can figure out what's going on, he's attacked by a group of strange monsters. While trying to escape, he meets a girl named Shiki, who informs him that the monsters are called Noise and can be defeated only if the two of them form a pact and work together. As it turns out, Neku and Shiki are only one of many pairs being forced to compete in the Reaper's Game. The Game challenges players to survive for seven days while completing a set of riddle-like missions (sent via cell phones, the one thing no Tokyo teenager goes without). If they're defeated by the Noise or fail to complete any challenge within the allotted amount of time, they'll be erased from existence. Neku, like many teenagers (in Japan or elsewhere), is a recluse who has trouble understanding other people and just wants to be left alone. As such, he isn't at all happy about being forced into the Game or being teamed up with the upbeat and outgoing Shiki. However, as he is frequently reminded, one of the most important rules in the Game is to trust your partner.

FIGURE
2.9

Noise must be fought simultaneously on both screens of the DS. © **Square Enix, Co., Ltd. All rights reserved.**

The main reason necessitating this trust and the Game's partner system is the Noise. Noise are monsters that exist simultaneously in two separate zones or planes of existence. The only way to defeat them is to fight them in both zones at once – hence the need for a partner. *THE WORLD ENDS WITH YOU* shows this by using a unique battle system in which the player uses the DS's lower touchscreen to control Neku while simultaneously using the D-pad to control his partner on the top screen. Enemies exist on both screens and also disappear from both, regardless of which character finishes them off. Similarly, Neku and Shiki share a single life gauge, so ignoring one character in favor of the other generally results in a quick death. Though a bit difficult to master early on, the battle system is unique and extremely fun once the player gets used to fighting on two screens at once. It also strongly enforces the story theme of trusting and working with your partner. As the game progresses, and the player becomes more skilled at controlling both characters in battle (in essence, forming a stronger team bond between the two), Neku slowly begins to open up and trust Shiki as well, creating a perfect mirror between the character's growth in the story and the player's growth in the game.

Later on, a major plot twist forces Neku to team up with a new partner, Joshua. Unlike Shiki, who was relatively easy to like, Joshua acts smugly superior and seems to be up to something behind Neku's back. As much as Neku knows that he needs to trust Joshua, his personality makes it very difficult to do so. These mixed feelings are mirrored on the gameplay side. In battle, Joshua plays much differently than Shiki, completely throwing off whatever rhythm the player had established during the first part of the game. Once again, however, as time passes, the player will grow used to Joshua's fighting style and come to appreciate his skills, much as Neku and Joshua start to put aside their differences and become friends.

FIGURE
2.10

Tokyo's vibrant Shibuya district is expertly re-created. © Square Enix, Co., Ltd. All rights reserved.

Neku and his friends' growth is conveyed in other ways as well. Though contestants in the Game can't interact directly with most of Shibuya's residents, they're given the ability to read their minds. Aside from being very useful on certain missions, it also helps to show Neku that other people aren't really so hard to understand and have their own problems and uncertainties, just like he does.

Another concept that plays a large role in the story and gameplay, aside from trust and friendship, is that of bravery. It requires a certain amount of bravery to trust and open up to others – and the more dark or embarrassing some part of your past or personality is, the more bravery is required to share it. Neku's growing bravery can be clearly seen throughout the story, but like the rest of THE WORLD ENDS WITH YOU's elements, it's mirrored in the gameplay. I already talked about how clothing and fashion play a role in the game; if you're at all familiar with Japanese fashion, you won't be surprised to know that some of the available outfits are extremely over the top. The interesting thing about the clothing in THE WORLD ENDS WITH YOU is that, with a few exceptions, any character can equip any item. If you want to put Neku in a frilly pink dress and combat boots with a skateboard and a stuffed cat, you can do it ... provided that he's brave enough to pull it off. Each piece of clothing has a minimum bravery rating required to wear it. A T-shirt or pair of slacks isn't a big deal; a maid outfit can only be worn by the truly brave. As with other stats, the characters' bravery can be raised throughout the course of the game, but gradually, just as their bravery slowly increases in the story. Bravery is also demonstrated during battles, which feature a strong risk vs. reward factor. When fighting, players can choose to chain a large number of battles back to back, without a chance to rest or heal in between. Though risky, it significantly increases the chance that enemies will drop money or pins. The player can also choose to increase the game's difficulty, allowing him or her a chance at receiving rarer items, and/or fight at a significantly reduced level, which will provide an additional boost to enemy drop rates. Early in the game, fighting with a high difficulty setting, reduced level, or in a long chain is likely to result in a "game over" screen, but as the game progresses and the player grows more confident with the battle system and more trusting of Neku's partner, he or she will become braver and will end up fighting long chains of high difficulty battles at a reduced level in order to claim the best prizes.

In the end, THE WORLD ENDS WITH YOU succeeds on many levels with its stylish graphics, catchy soundtrack, deep enjoyable battle system, and engaging story. But it's the way these elements combine while strengthening and complementing each other that makes the game far more than the sum of its parts.

The Limits of Storytelling in Games

With the memory and processing power of modern computers and game consoles, there's no type of story that can't be told in games. Some types of stories don't lend themselves as easily to games as others (something we'll talk about more in Chapter 3), but with enough planning and creativity, there's no reason stories in any genre or style can't be made into good games. Games even allow for stories that give the player a significant amount of freedom and control over the progression and outcome of the main plot. However, it's when working with high levels of player control and interactivity that we encounter the limits of game storytelling.

The most important thing to realize is that in any game, the player can do only things that the designers, programmers, writers, and other creators accounted for when crafting the game. Similarly, the game can respond to the player only in a set of predetermined ways. Though artificial intelligence (AI) can be used to allow computer-controlled enemies and allies some semblance of thought and planning, any gamer will be quick to point out that even the best AI-controlled enemies and allies can't compare to having a good human at the controls. And that's just one of the simpler forms of AI.

Let's say there's a game using a very open and nonlinear form of storytelling and the hero is sitting at a table talking to a rather dodgy individual. In this game, the hero may have a choice between several different things to say (let's suppose there's a threatening response, a friendly response, and a clever response) along with the ability to bribe the other man, kill him, or get up and leave. That seems like a lot of options. But what if the same situation were occurring in real life? The hero would have all of those options, but there'd be many other things he could do as well. He could offer to work for the other man, talk about the weather, jump up on the table and dance a waltz, or do any of a limitless number of other things. Many of the actions he could take would be pointless, impractical, or even utterly ridiculous, but that doesn't change the fact that he could do them if he wanted to. But in games, no matter how much freedom players are given, if the design team didn't put in a dance option, the player can't dance, and if they didn't give him the option to talk about the weather, he'll be unable to do so. A real-life hero could even decide to ignore his quest entirely, go home, and watch TV. But unless the art team created a model for the hero's home and also made a whole bunch of TV shows for him to watch, that isn't going to happen either.

To put it bluntly, with the infinite number of choices present in real life, there's no way even the best and largest game company could ever hope to account for them all. At present, the only way such a thing is possible is to have a human moderator (like a dungeon master in a game of *Dungeons & Dragons*) who listens to the player's actions and then twists, changes, and even completely rewrites the story as he or she goes. And although that works fine for a few friends sitting at a kitchen table using their imagination, it's obviously impossible to do in a game played by millions of people where a single area or character can take weeks or even months of work to create. The only other option would be to create a computer AI whose knowledge, understanding, and creativity are close enough to those of the human brain that it would be capable of acting as a dungeon master, writing new story sections and creating new game areas and elements on the fly to suit the players' actions.

If you were to ask a collection of computer programmers and tech experts how far away we are from creating such an AI, you'll get answers ranging from a couple of years to a couple of centuries; some will say that it's utterly impossible, no matter how much time is involved. My own personal opinion is that if such an AI can be created, it's most likely decades or even centuries away. However, there's really no way of knowing other than to wait and see what happens. If a fully competent dungeon master AI ever is created, it would drastically change the face of gaming and game writing, but at this point in time, there's little use worrying about how to use or work with a technology that's so far from completion. If and when the time comes, such an AI would probably work far differently than we can imagine today, so there's little reason to speculate. A more interesting question is whether giving players total freedom to do as they please in games would really be a good idea, but that's a debate for later on.

The Rubber Meets the Road

One of the hidden challenges of creating interactive stories is the realities of game production and the limitations imposed upon writers. I've been in many meetings in which the publishers wanted widely branching stories – the kind that allow (and encourage) multiple replays of the game. They adored the idea of adding a bullet point to the back of the box stating "infinitely replayable!" And so did we, the writers. However, the reality of production was our enemy. It has been my industry experience that the single most expensive part of game production is content. By "content," I mean creating the environments, characters, levels, dialog, artwork, and animations in which the player experiences the game, which takes more time and manpower than any other single element of the game, including the software coding. Most inexperienced people looking at games don't fully grasp how cost- and time-intensive these parts are. And, when cost containment begins to enter the discussions, you can often get a great deal of bang for your buck when you begin to talk about cutting story lines, characters, levels, and so on. After all, it's not just the creation of the assets that costs money. The testing, polishing, and debugging of these play areas often cost as much or more than building the assets in the first place.

Because of this, the same people in management who were understandably advocates for multiple branching storylines are first in line to suggest "corraling" the breadth of the game's story possibilities in order to contain costs – especially when it might be mentioned that players may not *see* all the content when the play the game. If you originally designed, say, four endings, it may be obvious to you that upon playing the game the first time, *only one* of those endings can be enjoyed by the player. The other three will be seen only if the player completes the game four times. When management is looking to cut costs, spending money on content that may or may not be seen by the typical player is not viewed favorably.

The dirty secret here is that few gamers (few as compared to the number of copies sold of any title) actually complete a game once, let alone multiple times. So it's often hard to justify the cost and development time for many multiple endings, middles, and beginnings.

I was sitting in a room the other day with a half-dozen gamers, all of whom had played *Dragon Age: Origins*. They were discussing the four main multiple endings amongst themselves as I listened. All these players were big fans. None of them had played the game more than once, even though all of them had played it to completion. When I asked them about the lure of multiple endings, they talked about how cool it was that there *were* multiple endings, but none of them was intrigued enough to play the game again to see how the alternate path felt, as the game had been satisfying enough once through.

Was it worth the money to create the multiple endings? Only EA knows for sure.

—Chris

Summary

Although games and game stories originally faced serious technical limitations, these limitations have all but disappeared over the past several decades, allowing game designers and writers to create nearly any type of game and story that they can imagine. This freedom has also given rise to a lot of experimentation with new and different storytelling techniques. One especially popular trend is to give players more control with branching path, open-ended, and fully player-driven stories (all of which will be explained in depth in Chapters 6 through 11), though there's a limit as to how much freedom they can allow. However, interactive traditional stories continue to dominate the market (as shown in Chapter 14).

The importance of creating games with good stories is also being realized. Once found only in RPGs and adventure games, deep and twisting plots and well-defined characters are now present in games in all genres. The diversity of game and story types means that now, more than ever, there are games that will satisfy any type of player. Perhaps most importantly, game developers are working harder to ensure that all the different parts of their games work together with and support the story, creating far more cohesive and engaging experiences.

Things to Consider

1. What do you consider to be several of the most important and influential games in the history of game storytelling and why?

2. Do you think voice-overs and FMVs significantly improve the way games tell their stories? Why or why not?

3. In what ways do you believe that game storytelling has improved over the last five years? How about the last ten years?

4. Are there any particular aspects of game storytelling that you think still need significant improvement? What are they and how could they be improved?

5. Do you believe that a dungeon master AI would improve game storytelling? Why or why not?

Three

The Hero's Journey and the Structure of Game Stories

If you ask a dozen writers what the hardest part of writing a story is, you'll probably get a dozen different answers. The character development, the ending, the discipline to simply sit down and write: it varies from person to person. But every writer, regardless of style and preferences, has to start in the same place. Before you can write a story, you need an idea.

For many writers, coming up with ideas is easy. In fact, at times the greatest challenge can be deciding which idea to focus on. When working on games, you may not even have to worry about the initial idea. Depending on your position and the team structure, you may have a basic idea or even a full outline given to you by the creative director or lead designer and be tasked with expanding it into a full-fledged story.

"I Think I'm Gonna Write the Great American Game Story"

Since the advent of 3D engines, what most often happens when you talk about story development in games is that either an idea for a certain type of gameplay springs into being and a story is concocted to support that gameplay idea, or marketing wants a game in a certain type of genre, so the team begins to search for a story idea to fit the genre. Those kinds of situations are the most common when the story idea comes along early in the game development process. But if an idea for an original great story

39

pops into someone's head, outside the world of games, I'm not sure the initial way to express that story would be, "I'll tell that story as a game." More likely, the creator of that idea would start to write a novel, a screenplay, a live play, or maybe a pilot for a television series. This distinction is one of the difficulties in the actual development of original game stories. Often the best story ideas take some other form first because games are *not* known primarily for their story, but rather their gameplay. And that makes existing story adaptation into a game (if it ever reaches that point) even more difficult.

—Chris

Either way, taking that basic idea and expanding into a full-length tale that's suitable for games is a very important task and one that, if done incorrectly, can easily turn even the best ideas into dull, uninteresting stories. To help you prepare for this process, we'll start out by examining which types of stories are best suited for games and why, then move on to study a classic story structure that is used as the basis for a wide variety of stories, especially in the game industry. We'll also take a look at some of the common themes and clichés present in game stories and discuss when they should and shouldn't be used.

If you're just starting out as a writer, these guidelines will give you a solid foundation on which to begin your writing. If you're already experienced with creating story ideas and structures, consider this a review and look at the case studies to see how those elements are used in video games.

Types of Stories Best Suited for Games

As a storytelling medium, video games offer many advantages over print and film. Like TV shows and movies, video games provide a full audiovisual experience complete with "sets" (levels), "actors" (digital characters), voices (spoken lines delivered by real-life actors), music, and sound effects. However, unlike film, video games are not limited to short stories or "story chunks" that can be told in thirty minutes or two hours. Depending on the type of game and the resources of the team creating it, a game can span anywhere from several to over one hundred hours. Typical games, however, tend to last between ten and twenty hours for action, adventure, and FPS titles and between forty and sixty hours for RPGs. Of course, only a portion of that time is occupied by the story; the rest is filled with exploration, fighting, puzzle solving, and the like. But their length gives games far more time to set up complex plots and develop characters than the average movie or TV show. In this way, games are similar to books.

Drama as a Unique Story Type

Let's spend a little time expounding on the nature of dramatic stories and how they operate differently in the mind of the player/audience.

Difference #1

Novels/fiction take place in the mind of the reader, and the reader generates all the images for the story (setting, characters, props). All drama has, on the other hand, already generated the "look" of the piece for the audience. The audience sees the locales, the actors/characters, the costumes, and so on, all looking the way the creators want them to. This can be a good thing or a bad thing from the audience perspective, but regardless, it places the brain of the viewer in a different place than a novel does.

Difference #2

Novels can be read over time; in fact, the reader controls the pace at which the story is consumed. The reader may stop, skip ahead, reread, skip to the end and then go back, and so on. The reader is totally in charge of the way the way the story is consumed. In drama, stories happen much more quickly, and always at the pace of the creators. There is no going back to recheck facts, reexamine clues in a murder mystery, or anything like that. The story unfolds in front of the audience, and the audience has to keep up. They must pay attention to get all the information they need. In fact, the authors use tricks to get something to "land" with the audience (meaning that it is understood and remembered), and any information that is crucial must often be told and retold and reiterated many times and in different ways to an audience so that it will stand out in their minds by the time the climax arrives. This balance, between staying one step ahead of the audience so they don't figure out the story too quickly and giving the audience enough reminders of crucial info so they don't forget, is one chief challenge *and* difference of dramatic writing compared to narrative fiction. This is why structure (defined as the sequence of events) is so important in drama – much more so than in fiction. The time-bound nature of drama makes it a very different way of thinking about the writing. It is less about language and more about the way the story unfolds.

Difference #3

The audience is usually aware in narrative fiction of what characters are thinking and feeling. In fact, getting inside a character's head is one of the joys of reading fiction. In drama, the audience can never know what a character is *thinking*. All they know is what the character *does*. Feelings and thoughts are often implied. So characters' emotional states in fiction can be told through their thoughts, but we know characters' emotions in drama only by what they do. Even what they say may be suspect, as the best kind of dialog in drama always layers in subtext, where the intention and meaning may differ from the surface words. This interplay is why actors' performance is so crucial in drama.

This dichotomy leads to many delicious moments in drama, as characters reveal their motivations that they have hidden from us through their actions (think about *Toy Story III* when Lotso the bear revealed that he hadn't "joined up" with Woody and the gang only when he refused to help them escape from the furnace). Hidden knowledge is used quite differently in narrative fiction than in drama. So, in order to use this technique, stories must be structured differently, and characters must behave differently. Thus, the techniques of seeing the visuals, controlling the pace of the story, and showing characters by what they do combine in a way that makes dramatic stories very different for the audience as well as the writer.

—Chris

Games also have other advantages that are uniquely theirs, all of which tie into their interactive nature. As previously mentioned, games create a framework that can be used to let players make important decisions and change the progression and outcome of the story. And even if the main story itself remains unchangeable, interaction has other advantages. The addition of optional side-quests, for example, gives the player the chance to pursue other tasks and quests that although not vital to the main plot can be used to provide additional details and expand on the world and story. In-game books, journals, and the like can serve a similar purpose, allowing players to delve deeply into the details and backstory or simply ignore them and focus on the main plot.

"Dear Diary, Today I Leveled Up"

The tools mentioned so far augment the "show, don't tell" nature of drama and must be used carefully as they affect the pace at which the story is consumed. Too often they can be used as a crutch, as story elements that rightly ought to sit on the screen as player activities or NPC interactions become journal entries instead, owing to time or budgetary constraints. On the positive side, using this technique can pull into the game some of the more enjoyable elements of the narrative style, where we can enjoy what a character we may never have met was or is thinking.

—Chris

For many players, the interactivity also helps them form a close bond with the characters much more easily than in print and film. Regardless of how much control the player has over the story, during the game he or she does, to a certain extent, become the main character, sharing the hero's triumphs and failures. With the player taking an active role in the process, the thrill of defeating a powerful foe or the agony of a being unable to save a dear friend becomes all the more real. We'll be talking more about the unique emotional experiences that can be created in games throughout the rest of this book, especially in Chapter 5.

Despite these advantages, telling stories in games has its drawbacks as well. For example, depending on the type of game and the storytelling method used, game stories can require considerably more time and effort to create than a typical book or movie script. Keeping a strong pace and maintaining player interest can be difficult over the course of a long game (which is discussed in Chapter 4) and interactivity itself provides a host of new and difficult challenges, which is an issue we'll be dealing with throughout this entire book. And, aside from all that, there's the simple and undeniable fact that some types of stories just don't work well in games – at least not without a lot of extra planning and effort.

A Writer's Challenge

Perhaps the biggest difficulty in creating compelling game stories is that the story is really out of the writer's control. What I mean is this: in a film, once the script is greenlit, 99 percent of the time they shoot pretty much what's on the page (lines may change, but whole scenes rarely get altered in a big way). There are exceptions, but not all that much. Now, in the final edit things may indeed change, but I'm saying that for the most part, they shoot what's been written. So if the writer's structure doesn't work, it's pretty much his or her own fault. In games, they almost *never* build the whole story as written; whole levels (which are about the same as an "act" in traditional written media) can be (and are often) cut, mostly at the last minute, after other levels (acts) that occur later in the story have already been built, so you can't go back and fix the issue or smooth it over, and the writer is seldom consulted when these events occur. These cuts occur for mostly good and proper reasons, mind you, but this is not the ideal process for the writer. Thus, even the most artfully crafted story structure can come undone at the last minute as the writer is left to patch together sequences that may not make as much sense as they once did.

—Chris

The "Best" Story Types

Although stories in modern games cover a very wide range of genres and styles, if you look closely, you'll see that some story types that are extremely popular in books or on TV are poorly represented or even entirely nonexistent when it comes to games. For example, games have action and adventure stories written in a multitude of styles and set in nearly every conceivable time and place, but where are the game equivalents of romance novels, sitcoms, and real-world coming-of-age stories? Some say that it's a matter of demographics and that your average gamer simply isn't interested in those types of stories, but the true problem can be found by looking at the basic principle of video games themselves.

When you break video games down to their very essence, you'll see that above all else, they're games. I know: not exactly a shocking revelation. But think about it. What's the one thing every single game from *Monopoly* to *World of Warcraft* has to have, regardless of its style, genre, or platform? The answer, of course, is gameplay. Whether it's practicing cut-throat business techniques or exploring a monster-infested wilderness, a game needs to provide the player with something entertaining to do besides merely watching the story unfold. As a result, video games tend to focus on fighting and strategy, exploration, puzzle solving, or some combination of the three. These types of external conflicts are far easier to portray in a game-like fashion than the more internal emotional conflicts that are often the focus of things like romance novels and sitcoms. Therefore, a "proper" game story needs to support a large amount of external conflict.

It also makes it a lot simpler both for designers and players if the story focuses on only a single character or group of characters. Jumping back and forth between a lot of different people not only requires more design work, but also makes it difficult for the player to get used to playing as any one specific character. This issue can be fixed easily if all the characters play exactly the same, but that tends to annoy players who rightly believe that a teenage girl shouldn't move and fight in the same way as a hardened war veteran. Stories with a lot of character swapping can be done well in games, but it takes a lot more thought and balance on the design side to keep the gameplay smooth.

Who Are You?

The nature of the interactive world is that one player identifies with one character on the screen. Most great designs clearly define who you are in the game. Perhaps that is an overlord controlling a population or a solitary soldier with an automatic weapon. Regardless, the one-to-one correspondence is clearly laid out.

When you allow a player to control multiple identities, the player mentally shifts into a state where he or she starts to feel like a god and actually like none of the characters on the screen.

—Chris

When you look at things from this perspective, the lack of certain story types makes quite a lot of sense. It's only natural for stories about soldiers, mercenaries, and alien invaders to include a lot of battles while stories about detectives and treasure hunters provide many opportunities for exploration and puzzle solving. With stories like those, you don't need to try and force the gameplay to fit with the story or vice versa – they work together easily. From a basic story perspective, a space marine fighting aliens makes perfect sense. Trying to find a good reason for a sitcom dad to be fighting hordes of enemies or making a series of death-defying leaps, however, is much more difficult.

Using Nonideal Stories

Just because some types of stories aren't easy to use in video games doesn't mean that they can't be done – you just need to work a bit harder to create the necessary synthesis of story and gameplay. The passion-filled storytelling style of romance novels, for example, is skillfully re-created in Japanese dating sim ("simulation") games. In dating sims such as Konami's popular *Love Plus*, the player takes the role of a boy or girl (depending on the game) and is tasked with getting through daily life while befriending and carefully building and maintaining a relationship with one or more characters. The gameplay is often dialog-heavy and tends to focus on time management (hanging out with friends, going on dates, studying, working, and so on) and figuring out the right things to do and say to win the heart of your chosen girl or guy. Though dating sims are very popular in Japan, they're rarely, if ever, released overseas.

> Though few pure dating sims are currently being released in English, if you're curious about the genre and can't read Japanese, a few Japanese RPGs featuring a large number of dating sim elements, including some titles in the *Sakura Wars* series and the PlayStation cult classic *Thousand Arms*, have been released in the United States. You can also get English releases of some rather heavily adult-oriented dating sims from Jbox (http://www.jbox.com).

For another example of how to turn a nonideal story into an excellent game, just look at *Flower*. In *Flower*, several potted flowers sit on a windowsill in a dark and dreary city, dreaming of sunny days and grassy fields. As a story, the idea sounds much better suited for something like an experimental film than a video game. Yet *Flower*'s zen-like gameplay, which has the player guiding a cluster of flower petals blowing in the wind in order to bloom more flowers and open up new paths, and simple yet well-done story won over gamers, making it one of the top-selling downloadable games on the PlayStation 3.

These are only two examples; there are many more out there. What games like *Love Plus* and *Flower* prove is that just about any type of story can be made into a good video game. Using nonideal story types is difficult and requires a lot of creativity and careful planning in order to ensure that the story and gameplay make sense and work well together, but it can be done.

The Hero's Journey

Now that you understand a little bit about the nature of game stories, it's time to talk about their structure. The structure can best be thought of as the basic progression or outline of your story. For example, in a romantic comedy the structure usually looks something like Figure 3.1.

FIGURE
3.1

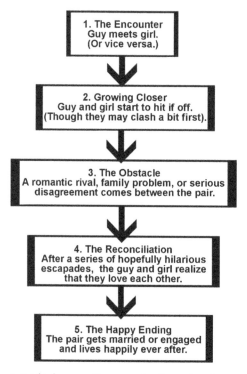

A typical romantic comedy story structure.

Though overly generic, the example in the figure makes for a solid structure around which the majority of romantic comedy stories are based – all you need to do is tweak the details a bit to personalize it and make it stick out. But chances are good that you won't be using the romantic comedy structure very often in video games, so let's take a look at a more useful one.

What Is the Hero's Journey?

The hero's journey is not just a story structure, it's *the* story structure, at least when it comes to certain types of stories, such as those about heroic quests, epic adventures, and journeys of enlightenment. The hero's journey is the story structure on which ancient myths and legends from around the world are based. Many early civilizations' greatest stories such as Gilgamesh, Beowulf, and the *Iliad* and the *Odyssey* make use of the hero's journey, as do a large number of modern stories, especially when it comes to things like fantasy novels and video games. The hero's journey is such a logical structure and so prevalent in literature that even writers with no formal knowledge of it often unknowingly use it in their stories.

The Writer's Journey

The gentleman who "uncovered" the Hero's Journey, Joseph Campbell, has often commented that the journey itself is a kind of proto-story, turning up as much as it does in the mythologies of the world in part because it links us to our essential selves. In other words, it tells the story of what it means to be human. In that manner, he has described the story structure as being embedded in our DNA. I believe that it is, because the journey's structure is found in many stories written by authors who may not be aware of the structure's formal definition. Also, because the structure is commonly found in fairy tales and because most Western authors heard those stories when they were being put to bed as children, the structure is unconsciously echoed time and time again. That is partly why it resonates for us so intently.

—Chris

Be sure to keep in mind, however, that the hero's journey isn't a story in and of itself – it's just a basic framework around which to build a story of your own. If you're having trouble mapping out the progression of your story, the hero's journey can prove to be an invaluable resource, giving you an idea of what events should take place and what elements your story may be missing. It can also give you ideas for characters, pacing, and other vital elements. With enough creativity and imagination, the hero's journey can create an endless array of unique and diverse stories. J.K. Rowling's *Harry Potter* series and George Lucas's *Star Wars*, for example, may seem to have little in common, but they both make use of the hero's journey. Lucas has even publicly acknowledged the influence that Campbell and the hero's journey had on *Star Wars*.

Structure of the Hero's Journey

The hero's journey can be roughly broken down into three general acts: the departure, the initiation, and the return. Those acts can be further broken down into more specific stages. Depending on exactly how you break things down, you can end up with anywhere from ten to seventeen stages. However, it's important to note that many of these stages are optional and therefore don't always appear in stories that use the hero's journey. The following is my own breakdown of the stages, based on a combination of the seventeen-stage version from Joseph Campell's *The Hero with a Thousand Faces*, the twelve-stage version from Christopher Vogler's *The Writer's Journey*, and my own experience with the structure.

Using the Journey as a Guide

It is crucial to understanding the structure that you think of these stages as emotional signposts rather than actual events in your story. That is, you are looking to evoke the feeling of a departure or the feeling of a death in the belly of a whale rather than having a character actually die in the belly of a whale. It is the emotion of the moment that the audience responds to, not the outer wrapper. This is often where young writers become lost as they use the journey's structure.

—Chris

Stage 1: The Ordinary World

The so-called ordinary world is where we're first introduced to the hero, who is living out his or her normal everyday life. Of course, depending on the setting and the hero him- or herself, this "ordinary world" could actually be quite extraordinary. For example, life in a magic academy or space marine outpost is anything but ordinary to us, but if you grew up in that type of environment, there really wouldn't be anything special about it at all.

This time in the ordinary world is a chance to introduce the hero and explain a little bit about who he or she is before the start of the adventure proper. In *Harry Potter*, Harry's ordinary world is life with his unpleasant aunt and uncle; for Luke, it's his uncle's farm on Tatooine. You want to use this stage to show a bit about the hero's background and his or her normal life, such as family, friends, and occupation. You shouldn't give away everything, especially if your hero is really much more than he or she seems, but it's important to convey a sense of who the hero is and what the hero does or doesn't stand for.

One important thing to remember is to not let the ordinary world stage run on for too long. Introducing your hero and setting the stage for things to come is all well and good, but if you spend too much time focusing on the hero's boring everyday activities, players will start to lose interest. Learning that the hero is a farmer in a small town is all well and good, but describing his or her activities on the farm every day for an entire week is probably overkill. Sooner or later, something has to happen!

Stage 2: The Call to Adventure

Naturally, the hero can't continue going about normal life forever. Sooner or later, something has to break the hero away from the ordinary world and set him or her on the path toward adventure. The call can come in many different forms. At times it's an actual call, such as Harry's letter from Hogwarts or Princess Leia's famous "Help me, Obi-Wan Kenobi" message. At other times, it's less direct. Hearing rumors of a long-lost treasure, spotting a suspicious figure in the woods, and dreaming of life in another place can all be calls to adventure. The call is anything that starts to take the hero away from normal life and causes him or her to wonder if he or she really belongs in the ordinary world after all.

Depending on your story, the call could be a sudden and immediate event, such as an unexpected enemy attack, or a slow and gradual thing, such as the hero becoming discontented with his or her life. In video games, however, in which you generally want to get the player into the action as quickly as possible, a sudden call is often the best way to go.

It's also important to think about just what the call is going to be. Usually the call is something related to the main plot like rumors of a treasure or an attack by the main villain, though in some cases the call itself is relatively unimportant, serving only to lure the hero away from the ordinary world and into a position in which later encounters will involve him or her in the main conflict. Sometimes the call is even an attempt to lure the hero into a trap. What the call is and how the hero reacts to it will say quite a lot about the hero's personality and motivation, so be sure not to gloss over it. A retired space marine may be eager to jump into battle during a surprise alien attack, but a young boy is likely to be scared and more interested in survival than anything else. Keeping your characters consistent and believable is a very important part of good storytelling and one we'll be covering in depth in Chapters 4 and 5.

Stage 3: Refusing the Call

Stage 3 is an optional stage that reflects significantly upon the hero's mindset. Although some heroes will accept the call to adventure immediately (removing the need for this stage entirely), others will resist. Maybe they're scared, maybe they don't want to leave their ordinary life behind, maybe someone talked them out of it, or maybe they just don't care. Harry, for example, initially refused to believe that he could possibly be a wizard, as it all just seemed too crazy and impossible; Luke's uncle urged him to forget about the mysterious message and focus on his normal work. Whatever the reason, if heroes refuse the call, something needs to happen in order to make them change their minds. Quite often, this something is a tragedy or disaster brought about by the hero's initial refusal to take action, but at times it's a more benign event, and on rare occasions it even turns out that refusing the initial call was in the hero's best interests. Either way, by the end of this stage the hero must have answered the call and, willingly or unwillingly, taken his or her first steps toward starting the adventure.

Danger, Will Robinson!

I do not believe this stage is optional at all. It is a crucial point in the story to have either the hero refuse the call (or at least doubt it) or have someone close to the hero tell the hero "Don't go" or "Aren't you worried about the danger?" Without this stage, the audience does not appreciate the risk or stakes involved in the journey. The best way to handle this in a game is to have others tell the player how dangerous this path is. The player will never refuse it, of course, but the danger can be made clear.

—Chris

Stage 4: The Mentor

Though some heroes begin their adventure knowing everything they need to know, or at least thinking that they do, others need a bit of information and/or training to help them get started. This is where the mentor comes in. At times the mentor actually provides the call to adventure and/or forces the hero's hand if the call is refused. At other times, the hero and mentor don't meet until the adventure is already underway. The cliché mentor is a wise old person – often a wizard or such – who has come to aid the young hero in his or her task. Following the cliché, the mentor's job is to teach the hero just enough to get by and then die (often in a heroic self-sacrificing way) before having a chance to relay the most important bits of information. Obi-Wan Kenobi is a perfect example of this type of mentor. He teaches Luke the basics of fighting and using the force, but sacrifices himself in the battle against Darth Vader when the adventure has only barely gotten underway.

However, just because it's a common cliché doesn't mean that you have to stick to it. Mentors can come in any shape or form, and there's no law stating that they have to die in the second act. Because the old man mentor is so overused, it often pays to do things a bit differently in order to keep player interest high. In some stories, the mentor is young and only slightly more experienced or knowledgeable than the hero himself like Etna in *Disgaea: Afternoon of Darkness*. In others, such as *Higurashi: When They Cry*, the mentor may, either knowingly or unknowingly, end up giving the hero false information, causing more harm than good. At times, the mentor may even betray the hero entirely. And, of course, there are games like *FINAL FANTASY VII* that don't have a mentor of any kind. I'll be discussing all those games in the coming chapters, so keep the hero/mentor relationship in mind when you read their case studies.

Stage 5: The First Threshold

So the hero has answered the call and met the mentor. Now what? To close out the first act, the hero needs to cross the "first threshold" and begin the adventure in earnest. This stage often serves as both the hero's first big challenge and the point of no return, from which there's no more avoiding the call or returning to the ordinary life. Battles and long journeys are common types of first thresholds, as are people who are determined, for one reason or another, not to let the hero leave (parents, commanding officers, or similar), but there are many variations.

Luke's first threshold was escaping from Tatooine on the *Millennium Falcon*, which involved skill and a certain level of danger; Harry's occurred when he stepped through the barrier on Platform 9¾ and began his journey to Hogwarts, which required nothing more than an act of willpower on his part. The threshold can also be an event triggered by the hero refusing the call (as previously mentioned). Often the hero will have the mentor to help with this stage of the journey, and it's also one of the more common times for the mentor to sacrifice him- or herself to save the hero, but at other times the hero will need to take this first step into the great unknown alone and unaided.

This is a time for heroes to strengthen or affirm their resolve and show what they're really made of. It's also a good time to give the player the first real challenge in the game itself, perhaps in the form of a tricky puzzle or boss battle. With the first threshold crossed, it's time to move on to the second act, which constitutes the majority of the story.

Stage 6: The Journey

Despite the fact that there were five stages leading up to this point and five more still to come, this stage actually takes up the vast majority of the story, spanning from immediately after the crossing of the first threshold until the point when the hero has nearly completed his goals. In game speak, that means that this stage goes until the player reaches the final level, dungeon, or quest.

The first thing that should be focused on is showing just how different this new world and life are from the ordinary world where the hero began. In *Star Wars*, Luke found himself drawn into the battle between the Rebel Alliance and the Empire almost immediately after leaving Tatooine, when his ship was captured by the Death Star. Harry's train ride to Hogwarts was similarly filled with strange sights and magical happenings, showing him and us that he had truly left the ordinary world behind.

Once the world itself has been established, there's still plenty of ground to cover. As this stage makes up the bulk of the hero's journey, it's full of encounters and adventures. This is when the hero travels about, exploring the world and gaining friends, enemies, and rivals. The hero may fall in love, face loss and betrayal, and be forced to deal with all manner of monsters and obstacles. If the cliché old man mentor is still alive when this stage begins, he'll be sure to heroically sacrifice himself at some point (occasionally returning later on in a more powerful form). Throughout their travels and trials, the heroes will learn more about the new world and themselves; grow more comfortable, skilled, and confident; and have numerous encounters (some good, some bad) with other people and creatures. They'll also learn, if they haven't already, what their eventual goals will be and the things they'll need to do in order to accomplish them.

Although the *Star Wars* movies and *Harry Potter* books can actually be broken down into a series of small hero's journeys, each occupying a single entry in the series, when we take them as a whole, the journey stage in *Star Wars* starts when Luke leaves Tatooine and doesn't end until he and the rebels begin plotting the destruction of the second Death Star in *Return of the Jedi* (the third movie in the first trilogy). Harry's journey is long as well, beginning when he boards the train for Hogwarts in the first book and continuing up until the start of the seventh and final book when he begins his search for the horcruxes.

This is your chance to fully take the reins of the story, develop your places and characters, and explore the events that lead up to the final confrontation. Just about anything can happen in this stage, with the only limit being your imagination (and possibly your budget). By the time this stage is complete, the main characters (both heroes and villains) should be known, most mysteries and secrets should have been revealed, and the hero should be almost ready to push forward toward the final battle or challenge and bring the adventure to a close.

Stage 7: The Final Dungeon

My video game–inspired name aside, this stage of the journey doesn't necessarily have to contain a dungeon or anything of the sort. (However, when you're writing for video games, there's a good chance it will.) With the bulk of the quest complete and the goal clearly in sight, this is the stage where the hero makes any final plans and preparations and then goes off to storm the villain's castle, blow up the alien mother ship, challenge his or her greatest rival to a last duel, prove who the murderer is, or the like.

Luke's "final dungeon" stage involves the planning for the assault on the second Death Star, the mission to shut down its shield generator, and then the assault itself. Harry's was his quest to find and destroy the remaining horcruxes in order to strip Voldemort of his near immortality.

The final confrontation itself isn't part of this stage, but everything leading up to it is. In this stage, you should focus on wrapping up loose plot threads (remaining mysteries, character relationships, and the like) and giving the heroes and the player a chance to show off how much they've grown and improved over the course of the adventure. Some of the toughest puzzles, battles, and challenges are usually found in this portion of the story – all leading up to the final confrontation.

That said, it should be noted that you can also create a fake version of this stage at some point during the journey in order to play some mind games and set things up for a big plot twist. In Square Enix's *The World Ends with You*, for example, the story centers around a deadly game that lasts for seven days. Against all odds, the heroes, Neku and Shiki, manage to survive until the last day, clear the final challenge, and defeat the ominous figure running the game. But just when it seems that their adventure is at an end, a new villain shows himself and reveals that the game is far from over. These fake or mini final dungeons and challenges, if done correctly, can throw players off balance and/or serve as good transition points between different sections of the story. Just as Luke had a different challenge to deal with at the end of every movie, and Harry a new villain to face and mystery to unravel at the end of every book, game stories can similarly be broken down into volumes or episodes of sorts. In some games, these points merely serve to break up a long story into easily identifiable sections; in others they actually do mark the end of a volume or episode and try to leave the players with a partial sense of closure and a lot of anticipation for the sequel.

Stage 8: The Great Ordeal

This is it: the big moment, the event that the entire journey has been building toward, and the last stage of the second act. At long last, the hero has made it through the final dungeon, and only a single challenge remains. In most video games, and many books and movies for that matter, the great ordeal will take the form of a final boss battle, with the hero facing off against the ultimate enemy. Sometimes it's a physical battle fought with swords, guns, or magic, like Luke's battle with the Emperor or Harry's battle with Voldemort. But in some games, such as *Sam & Max: The Devil's Playhouse*, it can take the form of a battle of wits that plays out more like a puzzle than an actual fight. Then there are games such as *Braid* in which there's no boss at all and the great ordeal is a final test of the hero and player's skills.

During the ordeal, the hero often has to face not only the physical villain or challenge but his or her own inner demons as well, and can be victorious only in the physical ordeal by completing the inner ordeal, almost as if the hero is dying and being reborn, a metaphor that in some cases is handled in a very literal fashion. The completion of this ordeal serves as the culmination to much of what the hero has worked for throughout the story and often (though not always) serves as the hero's last great trial. But the story isn't over quite yet – there's still the third act.

Stage 9: The Prize

With a few exceptions, heroes don't hunt down evil villains or complete difficult and dangerous challenges for fun (or at least not only for fun), they're doing it to rescue the princess, claim the treasure, save the world, or fulfill some other personal goal or desire. Sometimes they legitimately claim their prize and other times they steal it or just get lucky, but either way it represents the reward for all their hard work and effort up to this point.

Depending on the hero and story, the prize and how the hero reacts after acquiring it will vary greatly. Many heroes celebrate after obtaining the prize or pause to think back on all the things they've been through to reach this point, perhaps achieving some form of understanding or enlightenment. But in some stories it turns out that the prize isn't what they expected at all, which can lead to anger, grief, or disappointment.

However you choose to present it, this stage should be fairly short, and regardless of whether everything turns out the way the hero had hoped, it should provide the player with at least some measure of success and accomplishment.

Stage 10: The Road Home

With the prize in hand (whether literally or metaphorically, depending on what the prize actually is), it's time for the hero to return home, either to the ordinary world where he or she started out or to a new home discovered during the journey. Some heroes choose to never return home, but the majority do, for one reason or another. Luke and Harry, for example, just wanted to live out peaceful lives free from the threats posed by their enemies. In other stories, the hero's home may be in desperate need of the prize. Then there are some heroes like Zack, in *CRISIS CORE – FINAL FANTASY VII*, who merely want to see their friends and loved ones again.

In many stories, especially in video games, this stage is often quickly glossed over or even skipped entirely. Dragging it out too long can create an anticlimax, causing the story to end with a drawn-out whimper rather than a big bang. However, you can make good use of this stage as well. With the villain defeated and the prize in hand, returning home might seem to be an easy task, but that's not always the case. In *CRISIS CORE – FINAL FANTASY VII*, Zack finds himself hunted by his former allies, leading to a very epic and emotional ending (which we'll discuss in depth in Chapter 5). In this stage, it's fairly common to see a new villain (who was, of course, secretly manipulating everything behind the scenes) emerge or a previously defeated foe make an unexpected return to cause one last bit of trouble for the hero. This can also be the place to work in a final plot twist or surprise, as in *Shadow of the Colossus* (which we'll talk about in Chapter 4). Or, if you prefer a more clichéd event, the fortress, cave, space station, or other structure that the hero is in could start to collapse, because everyone knows that all evil lairs self-destruct shortly after their owner is defeated.

There really are a lot of things you can do with this stage; it all depends on what direction you want the story to go. It's an opportunity to throw a final challenge in the hero's path, give the hero one last chance to correct a mistake or realize an important truth, wrap up any remaining loose plot threads, or provide a shocking revelation that makes the hero and the player reexamine the events of the journey in a new light. These things don't always have to happen on the road, though – they can also take place in the hero's home itself as a final obstacle preventing him or her from returning to ordinary life.

Stage 11: The Return

At last the final stage of the story has been reached. The hero has returned, any last threats have been dealt with (unless you decided to save them as a sequel), and it's time to bring the story to a close. For many, endings are the hardest part of any story to write. A good ending needs to tie up at least most of the major issues present in the story (with the exception of a cliff-hanger ending, which can best be thought of as a break in the middle of the journey rather than a true ending), show the hero's ultimate fate, and provide a certain degree of closure and satisfaction to the player. There's a fine degree of balance needed here. You want to tie up loose ends to avoid annoying the player with dropped plot threads and unanswered questions, but if you wrap everything up too neatly, the ending may seem cheesy or contrived. You also don't want an ending that's too short or abrupt, in which case players may feel cheated or disappointed because they weren't able to really see things through to their full conclusion. Yet if you make an ending too long, it'll drag and players will lose interest.

Some endings also contain an epilogue, giving the players a glimpse at what happens to the world and characters long after the ending proper. If done right, an epilogue can satisfy the player's curiosity about the hero's life after the adventure, help with the all-important sense of completion and closure, and/or help set things up for an eventual sequel. But if done poorly, an epilogue can drag or feel tacked on and unimportant.

Writing a good ending is something that can't really be taught and is a challenge that even many of the most experienced writers struggle with. Ultimately, it's less a skill to be acquired than it is an art form, something beautiful and complex that in the end you'll have to discover for yourself. We'll be talking about endings quite a lot over the course of this book and will examine the endings of many different games as well, so pay close attention to how those games handle their ending scenes and what did and didn't work for them. If you can avoid the more common mistakes, you'll at least be off to a good start.

I'll Give It a Try Myself

I'll relate my own personal experience with the structure. I had been hired by THQ to design an N64 role-playing game. *Zelda* had not come out yet, and Nintendo players were hungry for role-playing titles. I had recently come across Vogler's explanation of the journey, and I devoured it. The assignment arrived, and I wanted to experiment with the structure (even though I, like many others, had written stories using the structure without truly knowing what it was). I copied out the main points of the story, used Campbell's archetypes to populate the game, and cobbled together the structure and some basic thematic fantasy material from my own brain. I wrote a couple drafts and presented it to my assistant designer.

He liked it, and as he was a great writer, we riffed on the details a bit, especially the characters. The formal presentation at THQ was coming up in a couple of weeks, and we talked to their external producer on the phone. "I'm a big fan of RPGs," he said. "I'd like the game to have as good a story as *FINAL FANTASY VII*." I gulped.

"Great," I replied. "I do too. We're working on the story right now, and we'll pitch it to you when we come to visit."

The weeks passed, and we went to visit THQ. The development team sat around in a room and pitched the story to the two external producers and the VP of development. There were, in all, about fifteen people in the room. I got up in front of them and started into the story of Alaron and his journey to discover his magical self. I wove together all the beats from the journey, Meeting to Mentor to Crossing the Threshold to the Refusal of the Call, all told in very specific events in the story but (obviously) not making overt connections to the Hero's Journey or Joseph Campbell in any way.

Twenty minutes later, when I got to the part about Alaron needing to die so as to be reborn, I became aware that no one in the room was making a sound. No one had coughed, or was checking their email, or was looking at their fingernails. They were listening to the story.

I got to the end, when Alaron ascends to the throne after defeating the lords of chaos after his rebirth, and the fourteen other people in the room stood up and gave me a standing ovation. My own dev team, THQ's VP of production, my agent – everyone.

And at that moment I knew it wasn't just my weeks of effort paying off so much as the power of the journey at work.

—Chris

Modifying the Structure

It's important to realize that you don't have to follow the hero's journey to the letter – nor should you. The hero's journey is a set of guidelines, nothing more and nothing less. At times, it's best to step outside those guides and go with what you think is best for your story. Feel free to add or subtract stages as needed or modify the existing stages and order to suit your story. If you think your story should start out in the middle of Stage 6, for example, with the events of the previous stages revealed via flashbacks, that's fine. Although many good stories follow the hero's journey pretty closely, many others veer wildly off course and still produce excellent results. Furthermore, the hero's journey isn't the only structure out there. If your story doesn't seem to fit well within its confines, feel free to find another more appropriate structure or even create one of your own. After all, writing isn't just about knowing the rules – it's about knowing when to break them.

Case Study: *Lunar Silver Star Harmony*

Developer: Game Arts
Publisher: XSeed Games
Writer: Kei Shigema

System:	Sony PSP
Release Date:	March 2, 2010 (US)
Genre:	RPG
Previous Versions:	*Lunar: The Silver Star* (Sega CD, 1993), *Lunar Silver Star Story Complete* (PlayStation, 1999), *Lunar Legend* (Game Boy Advance, 2001)

Lunar Silver Star Harmony is the latest in a long line of ports and remakes of the Game Arts classic RPG *Lunar: The Silver Star.* It tells the story of a young boy named Alex who dreams of becoming a Dragonmaster and his friends as they journey across the land to save both the world and Alex's childhood friend Luna from the clutches of the former hero turned villain, Ghaleon. Aside from its charming story, endearing characters, and frequently hilarious dialog, *Lunar* is also known for its challenging strategic battles (though the exact battle system changes a bit in each release). Both the Sega CD and PlayStation versions of Lunar have often been listed among best RPGs of their respective generations and have become popular collector's items.

The story of *Lunar* follows the hero's journey structure very closely. The following sections provide a breakdown of the plot, formatted to show how it fits within the structure.

Stage 1: The Ordinary World

Alex lives in the small, peaceful village of Burg with his talking pet Nall and his friends Luna and Remus. Though happy with his life, Alex often dreams of having adventures as did his hero, the legendary Dragonmaster Dyne, who is buried in Burg.

FIGURE
3.2

Alex, Nall, and Luna live a peaceful life. *Lunar: Silver Star Harmony PSP* **©1992 Game Arts/Toshiyuki Kubooka/Kei Shigema, © 1996 Kadokawa Shoten Publishing Co., Ltd./ Game Arts/Jam, © 2009 Game Arts.**

Stage 2: The Call to Adventure

While searching for treasure in a nearby cave, Alex and his friends encounter the dragon Quark. He senses potential in Alex and urges him to travel and seek out the other dragons so that he can complete their trials and become the new Dragonmaster.

Stage 3: Refusing the Call

Alex jumps at the chance to live out his dreams, as does Remus (who hopes to find his fortune in the city of Meribia), but Luna is unsure. Worried about Alex's parents (who have raised her since she was a baby) and afraid to leave the place she's lived all her life, she plans to return to Burg before reaching the city.

Stage 4: The Mentor

As they journey to the city, Alex's group finds themselves surrounded by a large number of monsters when a powerful swordsman named Laike comes to their rescue. Although he doesn't join the party, he and Alex have numerous run-ins throughout the game. Aside from his skills with a sword, Laike seems to know quite a lot about the dragons and acts as a mentor to Alex, preparing him to better face the challenges ahead.

FIGURE
3.3

Alex's group runs into trouble and is saved by a passing swordsman. *Lunar: Silver Star Harmony PSP* ©1992 Game Arts /Toshiyuki Kubooka/Kei Shigema, © 1996 Kadokawa Shoten Publishing Co., Ltd./Game Arts/Jam, © 2009 Game Arts.

Stage 5: The First Threshold

The first threshold comes at the port town of Saith, where the group prepares to board a ship and leave their home island far behind. This is the point where Luna fully refuses the call and attempts to turn back (as mentioned in Stage 3).

FIGURE
3.4

Luna is reluctant to leave the island where she grew up. *Lunar: Silver Star Harmony PSP*
©1992 Game Arts /Toshiyuki Kubooka/Kei Shigema, © 1996 Kadokawa Shoten
Publishing Co., Ltd./Game Arts/Jam, © 2009 Game Arts.

However, she's stopped and reassured by Alex. Though still nervous, she follows
him onto the boat and they set off, leaving everything they know behind and
taking their first steps into the new world that awaits them.

Stage 6: The Journey

This stage constitutes the vast majority of the game and is when many important
events take place. As Alex continues his quest to become a Dragonmaster, he parts
ways with old friends when Remus decides to stay behind in Meribia, but meets
many new friends and companions including the magicians Nash and Mia,
the cleric Jessica, and the bandit Kyle. He makes enemies as well, in the form of
the evil Magic Emperor and his top henchmen, a trio of powerful witches. Alex also

FIGURE
3.5

Alex and his new friends on their journey. *Lunar: Silver Star Harmony PSP* ©1992 Game
Arts/Toshiyuki Kubooka/Kei Shigema, © 1996 Kadokawa Shoten Publishing Co., Ltd./
Game Arts/Jam, © 2009 Game Arts.

suffers betrayal and loss when Ghaleon, the friend of his hero Dragonmaster Dyne, reveals himself to be the Magic Emperor, kills Quark, and kidnaps Luna. These events and several other big revelations make Alex's quest much more personal as he begins seeking the power of the remaining dragons – not for fame and adventure, but to gain the strength he needs to stand up to Ghaleon and save Luna.

Stage 7: The Final Dungeon

After gaining the power of the dragons and failing in their first attempt to infiltrate Ghaleon's fortress, Alex and his friends regroup with the help of Laike and prepare for an all-out assault. Pressing on, they manage to fight their way to Ghaleon's inner sanctum and defeat the last and strongest leader of his forces.

Stage 8: The Great Ordeal

Alex's team faces Ghaleon, who tells them of his intentions to use Luna (who was previously revealed to be the reincarnation of the goddess Althena) to revive the goddess and gain her powers, becoming a god himself. With his plans nearly complete, he brings his full power to bear on Alex's party, but after a long hard battle, he is defeated.

Stage 9: The Prize

With Ghaleon dead, the world is safe and Luna is free. At long last, Alex has achieved the things he fought so hard for.

Stage 10: The Road Home

Alex and his friends are ready to take Luna and return home, but it turns out that they were too late. The Luna that Alex knew and loved is gone, replaced by the

FIGURE
3.6

Alex's ocarina playing awakens Luna's memories. *Lunar: Silver Star Harmony PSP* ©1992 Game Arts /Toshiyuki Kubooka/Kei Shigema, © 1996 Kadokawa Shoten Publishing Co., Ltd./Game Arts/Jam, © 2009 Game Arts.

reborn Althena. Unwilling to leave without her, Alex faces the angry goddess and – after barely escaping death at her hands – manages to awaken Luna's memories and return her to her normal form.

Stage 11: The Return

Now that everything has been set right, Alex, Luna, and their friends return to their peaceful life at home.

As you can see, *Lunar*'s story is a near-perfect fit for the hero's journey, making full use of every stage. The only particularly notable deviation is in Stage 3, in which it's the hero's companion (Luna) and not the hero himself (Alex) who resists the call. But despite its strict adherence to the structure, *Lunar* avoids many of the clichés that often plague hero's journey stories. The mentor (Laike), for example, doesn't sacrifice himself and manages to survive the entire adventure. And Alex's near death (or actual death, if the player isn't careful) at the hands of Althena after Ghaleon has been defeated comes as quite the surprise to most first-time players. Twists like these and the enduring popularity of the story (as evidenced by *Lunar*'s many ports and remakes) go to show that even though it's been around since the earliest myths and legends, the hero's journey can still be used to create interesting and enjoyable stories even in new mediums like video games.

FIGURE
3.7

Alex and Luna together again in Burg. *Lunar: Silver Star Harmony PSP* **©1992 Game Arts/ Toshiyuki Kubooka/Kei Shigema, © 1996 Kadokawa Shoten Publishing Co., Ltd./Game Arts/Jam, © 2009 Game Arts.**

Common Themes and Clichés in Game Storytelling

As any gamer can tell you, there are certain themes and clichés that have a tendency to pop up in what can seem like at least every other game. But this is by no means a phenomenon unique to video games. Fantasy novels, sitcoms, Hollywood action movies, and just about every other story type or genre you can think of comes complete with its own set of clichés. Whether such clichés are good or bad is a matter of debate (and something we'll discuss further a little later on), but either way, they're a firmly ingrained part of storytelling and one that's unlikely to ever disappear, so it's important to be familiar with them.

Common Clichés and Themes

Like all forms of storytelling, video games have a laundry list of common, clichéd characters and scenarios. Some are glaringly obvious and others are more subtle, but it's hard to find a game that doesn't make use of at least one or two of them. A complete list of game clichés would be extremely long (a quick Google search can easily turn up hundreds of them) and many are related to the gameplay, not the story (like how everyone leaves exploding barrels lying around and then decides that they'd make excellent cover during a gun fight), and are therefore something for designers, not writers, to worry about, but the following list covers a few of the most prevalent story-based clichés in gaming.

The Amnesiac Hero

Soap opera heroines aren't the only fictional characters who seem to develop amnesia at the drop of a hat; it's quite common for a game's main character and/or the occasional party member to start out with a bad case of amnesia. This cliché seems to be especially popular in RPGs, a fad most likely caused by the Square Enix's tendency to feature amnesiac heroes in their genre-leading *FINAL FANTASY* series.

So what's the point? Well, when it comes to video games, amnesia makes for a very convenient plot device. Most newer games, for example, and many older ones as well, start out with a tutorial section designed to help players (especially those who haven't read the instruction manual) get used to the controls and gameplay. On the surface, this sounds like an excellent idea (which is made even more excellent when said tutorials can be skipped by more experienced players). But from a story perspective, there's a problem. Although it makes sense that a fresh-faced kid from a farming village could use some serious training before heading out to battle, it's difficult to explain why your veteran adventurer or hardened space marine suddenly needs to be told how to move and fight ... unless he or she has amnesia. It also provides a good excuse for the hero's friends to constantly point out details about the world and/or the hero's past, all things that the player needs to know but the hero him- or herself, without amnesia, wouldn't need to be reminded of. Then, of course, it can also set the stage for a big reveal when the hero regains his memories and discovers that he's really not Bill the Legendary Space Marine but a fruit vendor who just happens to look like him.

Of course, amnesia has many legitimate and noncliché uses in storytelling as well. It can make for some interesting character development, especially if the hero, after regaining his or her memories, realizes that his or her past beliefs and allegiances were far different than they are now. It also helps if the amnesia fits well with the rest of the plot and wasn't just caused by a random bump on the head so that the hero would need to learn how to swing a sword all over again.

FINAL FANTASY VII, though probably partly responsible for the amnesia fad, uses an extremely interesting and unconventional take on the amnesiac hero. In fact, for the first two-thirds of the game, you don't even realize that the hero, Cloud, has amnesia at all. Therefore, it comes as quite a shock when it's revealed that many of his memories are, in fact, a twisted mixture of fact and fiction created by his mind when his original memories were lost. Many fans, myself included, consider the point where he at last pieces together his real memories and discovers the truth about certain past events to be one of the highlights of the story.

A Powerful Tool in Your Belt

One of the most powerful tools in dramatic storytelling is the Major Dramatic Question, or MDQ. This question is created in the mind of the audience the moment the hero accepts the journey, and is a form of the question "Will the hero succeed?" Will Luke avenge his aunt and uncle? Will Frodo throw the ring into Mount Doom? Will Indiana Jones find the Ark? It is the nature of our storytelling curiosity that we, the audience, stick around until the end of a story in order to see how it all comes out. The instant we get the answer to the dramatic question, all the energy drains out of the story for us and we want to move on, head to the parking lot to find our car, check our cell phone, and so on. It is a saying in theater that as soon as the question is answered, you've got maybe five minutes, max, until the audience gets so antsy that they stop paying attention. The clearer you can state the MDQ of a story for yourself and the more clearly you can implant that question in the mind of the audience, the better chance you have of keeping their interest until the very end. We've all been to movies where we said, "When will this end?" Often, when you deconstruct those stories, you will find that either the MDQ is unclear or that the MDQ stated at the beginning of the film was answered ten minutes ago and we're still hanging around watching something else unfold.

—Chris

The Evil Vizier/Minister/Aide/Lackey

It's no secret that betrayal makes for a great plot twist (and a convenient way to bring all the hero's plans crashing to the ground halfway through the game), and if the betrayer is a person in a position of power, he or she can really do some damage when finally revealing his or her true allegiances. Unfortunately, after being betrayed by just about every vizier, general's aide, and king's minister, the usual player reaction to such a "shocking" plot twist isn't so much "I can't believe it!"

as "Duh – they should have figured that out ten hours ago." On that note, after the vizier, the hero's best friend is the second most clichéd person to betray him.

Betrayal can still make for a very good plot twist, but it's best to make the betrayer a less obvious choice, or at the very least, not give the vizier an evil hair-cut and script full of suspicious one-liners. Even better, take advantage of the cliché and make the seemingly evil vizier a good guy to draw the player's attention away from the real enemy agent.

No One Noticing the Evil Vizier/Minister/Aide/Lackey

Of course, the goal of being a spy or traitor is to play your role so well that no one realizes your true allegiances. In many video games, however, the evil vizier or other character who is plotting to betray the heroes usually does such a poor job of hiding his or her intentions that it seems ridiculous that none of the heroes have figured out that he or she really isn't on their side. As noted earlier, the future betrayer really shouldn't look, act, or talk like a villain. If most players realize the vizier is evil long before the heroes do (and the players aren't privy to any extra information unknown to the heroes), you have a problem.

The Last of His Race

Having a hero who is the last survivor of his clan, race, family, village, or so on gives the hero a good excuse to go after the villain (someone had to have killed off everyone else, of course) and is also a convenient way to explain why the hero has special powers that nobody else does and is the only person who can possibly save the world. Though overused, this cliché usually doesn't seem to bother people as much as some of the others do.

I Am Your Father

Whether or not the hero is the last of a dying race, it's quite common for the hero's father or other close relation (brother being the second-most clichéd) to be either the main villain, a high-ranking follower of the main villain, or, in some cases, a legendary hero who once opposed the main villain (and probably isn't as dead as everyone thinks). Like most clichéd plot twists, it can actually be done very well if handled correctly, but it's hard to avoid either giving away the surprise too early or having too little foreshadowing, making the eventual "I am your father" moment seem sudden and random.

A Party of Clichés

The hero's friends, allies, and/or party members often include several of the following characters: a beautiful mysterious girl (often the last of her race) who holds the key to either saving or destroying the world and will eventually get kidnapped;

a rebellious princess (sometimes combined with the mysterious girl); a gruff, tough-as-nails warrior girl (who will eventually soften up and fall in love with the hero); a grizzled, battle-hardened warrior who is actually (or eventually becomes) a really nice, friendly guy; an unemotional or emo character who slowly learns to open his heart and trust others; and a cute creature (often the last of its race) who is pretty useless in battle but hangs around for comic relief. Although these basic character setups work quite well in humorous stories, in a more serious tale they should ideally be avoided or have a lot more depth to them than is first apparent. We'll talk more about creating good characters in Chapters 4 and 5 – for now, just keep these clichés in mind.

Saving the World from Evil

Regardless of the original goals and accomplishments on the game's journey, the hero and his or her friends will almost always end up having to save the world. Quite often, the threat to the world comes from an ancient evil that was either recently revived (often by a misguided villain or hero) as in *Arc the Lad* or that just likes to stop by and destroy everyone every thousand years or so like in *Mass Effect*.

Of course, saving the world or universe is far more impressive and epic than just about any other possible goal and brings a definite sense of accomplishment to the player. But it's important to remember that it's still perfectly possible to tell a good story in which the heroes have far less lofty goals, such as in *THE WORLD ENDS WITH YOU*, *Shadow of the Colossus*, and *FRONT MISSION 3* (all of which are covered in detail in other chapters).

The Ancient Civilization

One last common game cliché is the ancient civilization. Said civilization was usually made up of beings with highly advanced technology or magic (far more so than anyone in the modern day world) and was mysteriously wiped out long ago, leaving nothing but ruins and artifacts. Such a setup adds a bit of mystery to a story and allows you to toss in otherwise inappropriate technology wherever it's convenient.

Unfortunately, what happens next has become very predictable. Either the hero or the mysterious girl is usually the last of the ancient race and the villain is either the one who destroyed said race in the first place or is foolishly trying to resurrect the monster or technology that did. This cliché has formed the basic backstory for many excellent games, but is still one that you should try to avoid when possible.

Why Clichés Are Used

If you've played a lot of games, you probably found yourself nodding your head and maybe even chuckling a bit as you read over the previous list. They're all elements that are used in many games – even ones that are known for their excellent stories. So why are these clichés used and reused so often? First off, they're popular. Nearly every big cliché got its start in a very popular game, book, or movie and, since it worked so well before, other writers decided that it would probably work well again, and again, and again, and again, until it eventually became overused enough to be deemed a cliché. Second, clichés provide something familiar for the players to identify with. Sure, all gamers know that the grizzled warrior and mysterious girl are clichéd characters, but they're also familiar with (and quite likely fond of) incarnations of those characters in other games and have a basic idea of what to expect from them, which can actually help raise many players' interest in the story (at least early on). And, finally, clichés simply work well. They may be overused and predictable, but they got that way for a reason. In the hands of a good writer, clichés can be used to create excellent characters and plot elements. However, if mishandled, they'll make a plot feel generic, corny, and generally uninspired.

When to Use and When to Avoid Story Clichés

When using clichés, keep in mind the following rules.

Rule 1

Try to limit how many clichés you use in a single game. Most players probably won't mind if you make use of one or two clichés from the previous list, but if you use all of them, you're probably asking for trouble (unless you're either a really amazing writer or making fun of those clichés in a humorous story).

Rule 2

Make the clichés feel different and new. With a bit of clever writing, you can twist clichés around to make them more interesting. For example, maybe the mysterious girl is really just an ordinary orphan and the ancient civilization was destroyed in a natural disaster instead of by an evil force or super weapon. There's no reason you can't take part of a cliché and change the rest to something different and new.

Rule 3

Use clichés to mislead the player. Because clichés are so overused, most players can quickly pick them out and predict what's going to happen next, so why not use this against them? You could have an evil-looking but actually good vizier draw the player's attention away from the true spy or really play up the mysterious girl only to reveal that the key to saving the world actually lies in a much more ordinary character instead. With a bit of imagination and a good setup, you can use clichés to keep players guessing for the entire story.

Rule 4

Don't use clichés for the sake of using clichés. Because clichés are based on popular story elements, it's not uncommon for novice writers to smash as many of them as possible into their stories, using them almost like a checklist. This is, of course, a very bad idea. If you truly feel that the story you're writing has need of a cliché element, go ahead and use it. If you do it right, the players won't mind. But, if you start adding in unnecessary amnesia, clichéd character types, and ancient civilizations, the story will seem forced and, of course, cliché.

Case Study: *Arc the Lad*

Developer:	Sony
Publisher:	Working Designs
Writer:	Kou Satou
System:	Sony PlayStation
Release Date:	April 18, 2002 (US), November 23, 2010 (Playstation Network rerelease)
Genre:	Strategy RPG

Arc the Lad is the first in a series of strategy RPGs created by Sony. Although the first game was released in 1995 in Japan, it wasn't until 2002 that it came to the United States as part of a collection containing the first three games in the series, along with a large number of extras and bonus items. The first two games, *Arc the Lad* and *Arc the Lad II* (which we'll talk about more in Chapter 7), act as a set, with the first game serving as more of a prologue than a full story and the sequel picking up shortly after it ends. Although the first portion of *Arc the Lad II* focuses on a different set of characters, they eventually join Arc with the others from the first game to continue the original quest. Players are even given the option to import their saved data from the first *Arc the Lad*, which allows the original heroes to transfer their levels, equipment, and items into the second game.

The plot revolves around a boy named Arc and his companions as they struggle to stop the leader of Romalia from using the power of an ancient evil known as the Dark One to command armies of monsters and further the expansion of his empire.

Although Arc's story does get pretty interesting – especially in the second game, in which nearly every character in his large party (which eventually grows to include a mysterious girl, rebellious princess, grizzled warrior, unemotional character, and cute thing, among others) has his or her own detailed backstory and set of side-quests – the first game (and, to a lesser extent, the second) makes heavy use of clichés.

To start, Arc's father was a hero who fought against the Dark One (a vaguely defined evil force that destroyed an ancient civilization) only to go missing and is, as it turns out, not dead like everyone thought he was. Arc's first companion in his quest is Kukuru, a beautiful girl who is the last of her clan of shrine guardians who protect the Dark One's seal (or at least the last person in her clan who is still doing her job). And that's just the beginning. It turns out that the king of their country, whom Arc and Kukuru meet shortly after (and who later reveals that he is Arc's uncle), is being served by an evil minister no one realizes is evil and later betrays them all. To top it off, he's only the first of several high-ranking figures who also turn out to be monsters in disguise and to betray the party over the course of their adventure.

In the end, despite its reliance on clichés, *Arc the Lad* still managed to tell a fairly good story (particularly when combined with *Arc the Lad II*) and proved to be a fairly popular title, especially in Japan. In fact, most complaints about *Arc the Lad's* storyline are centered around the second game's ending, rather than the overabundant clichés.

Summary

Storytelling is a complex art, and the parts of a story that come naturally to one writer may be extremely difficult for another. Games provide many advantages for storytellers, including their audiovisual presentation, length, and interactivity, but also come with their own set of challenges and problems. Sticking with types of stories that support large amounts of fighting, puzzle solving, or other common gameplay elements can make writing for games much easier, as can following tried-and-true narrative structures such as the hero's journey. But that doesn't mean you have to do either one. With the right idea and careful planning, there's no limit to the types of stories that can be told in games.

Another issue to be aware of is clichéd story elements that have been heavily overused, such as the evil vizier and highly advanced ancient civilization. Though these clichés can still be used, and can in fact make for some excellent plot twists and character development opportunities if done correctly, you need to be careful about the way you use them if you want to avoid having your story come across as generic and predictable.

Things to Consider

1. When writing a story, what parts do you have the easiest time with? What parts are the most difficult?

2. List some video games you've played which used nonideal story types. Did the writers and designers succeed in turning the stories into enjoyable games? Why or why not?

3. Take a look at the story from one of your favorite games, break it into stages, and see how well it fits within the hero's journey structure.

4. Choose a game you've played recently and make a list of all its clichés. Feel free to list clichés that weren't discussed in this chapter.

5. Think of a game that used a cliché in a very different and unexpected way. How did the writer change the cliché to accomplish this?

Four

The Story and the Characters

Story Flow and Progression

Having your story idea and structure all planned out is a great start, but when it comes to good storytelling in games or any other medium, what really makes a story great isn't the basic idea or the structure – it's the details. With smooth pacing and an interesting cast of believable characters, even a generic or seemingly dull idea can make for a great story. Unfortunately, the opposite is true as well. Characters that are boring or that the players can't relate to can quickly suck the life out of even the best story idea, and poor pacing will turn large sections of a game into a tedious slog, no matter how good the story itself is. Neither of these issues alone will completely ruin a story, as long as the rest of the elements are done well, but failing in just one of them can mean the difference between creating a good story and a great story. Just as pacing and characters are individual elements of the whole story, the story itself is a single element of the game, and failing in even one element can be the difference between making a good game and making a true masterpiece. If you want to be a great writer, you need to make sure that every element is in place, even the small ones.

The Importance of Proper Flow and Pacing

A story's pacing can be compared to the flow of a river. Big twists and exciting events are like rapids or fast-moving sections; parts of the story in which the characters relax or engage in unimportant activities can be thought of as slow, calm sections. For proper pacing, you need both fast areas to excite players and keep them interested and slower sections in which you can focus on character development and give the player a chance to unwind. Game designers know that gameplay pacing works in much the same way. If your pacing is constantly fast and furious,

71

players will get worn out by the endless barrage of information and won't have time to take it in or calm down; you also won't have the time to adequately develop your characters and their worlds. But if your slow sections stretch out too far, players will grow bored and wonder when things will get interesting again. A fine level of balance is needed to ensure that the pacing never becomes too slow or too fast. Though perfect pacing is very difficult to achieve, adequate pacing is a must if you want players to stay interested in your story.

The Interest Curve

Writers kick around terminology like "act break," "increasing tension," and "climax," but the thing that is sometimes tough to remember is that the story runs by the audience in a continuous stream of emotional response (that is, hopefully the audience is responding, eh?) and that you are architecting that response moment by moment, beat by beat, scene by scene, sequence by sequence, and act by act. There's a whole universe of moments, all of which need to contribute to generating the emotional response. The "pace" that Josiah is talking about is that back-and-forth of the contrasts inherent in these moments. In Jesse Schell's book *The Art of Game Design*, he talks about a phrase in game design (well, actually, entertainment design) called the "Interest Curve." This phrase is used to describe (wait for it …) the moment-by-moment design of the game wherein the player gets whip-sawed back and forth through contrasting loud and quiet, exciting and reflective, and angry and loving moments (for example). The point is that, indeed, those wonderfully exquisite game moments are created through the identical method that writers use to architect our classic stories. At other points in this book, you'll hear me say that writing great stories uses the same skills as game design, and it is mainly due to this singular fact.

I was trained as a playwright by a great teacher, Milan Stitt. He would talk about classic story structure as a five-act emotional journey. Act I is what you'd expect, the send-off into the story and the implantation of the Major Dramatic Question (MDQ) into the mind of the audience. In fact, the moment when the audience could articulate what that question is would be described as the end of Act I. The ends of Acts II, III, and IV occur when the story becomes much more difficult for the hero through a series of increasingly difficult complications, and indeed the hero must alter his or her plan (example: in *Raiders of the Lost Ark*, think of the end of Act II as when Indiana *discovers* the Ark [the MDQ being, until that point, "Will Indiana find the Ark before the Nazis do?"] only to lose it to Belloq. Act II transitions into Act III, with the MDQ being, "How will he get it back?").

Those complication points in a five-act structure add tension and make it more difficult for our hero to get to his or her goal.

A diagram of the five-act structure is shown in Figure 4.1.

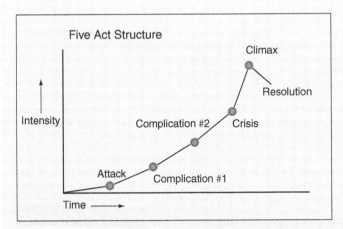

FIGURE
4.1

Five-act story structure.

This diagram depicts the "interest curve" for the story. One of the most telling aspects of storytelling is the idea that not only do overall stories follow this structure, but *so does every scene, every act, and every sequence.* This point is so crucial to understand that I cannot emphasize it enough. When you write a scene, it must have an attack, a complication, a crisis, and a resolution. This all comes from the way you have set up the scene, and the conflict you have built into that setup.

One last comment on this note: a great visual depiction of the way interest curves work in cinematography can be found in Bruce Block's book *Visual Story*.

—Chris

As with endings, creating good pacing is something of an art form that can't entirely be taught. If you still have trouble grasping the concept after reading the rest of this chapter, try looking at the stories in some of your favorite books, movies, or games and think about how they flow between big events and smaller, more subdued moments. If there are any parts that seem to drag on for too long, make note of them as well. Before long, you should have at least a general idea of how to pace your own stories.

To Learn Story, Deconstruct It

If this idea of structure confuses you (and, at first, it probably will, because we're so trained to look at the actors and listen to what they say that we perceive story as happening through and about the characters), here's the best way to learn: pick a writer whose work you really admire. Choose someone who's not just a one-hit wonder, but someone who has repeatedly proven that he or she can write more than a little bit. Sit down with that writer's work (if it's a TV writer, for instance, get his or her shows' DVDs) and get to know your remote control intimately by working your way through at least three of his or her episodes. Be certain that this writer wrote the episode you're watching. Watch each episode once through, so that you get familiar with the storyline. Then start the episode over again, and describe each scene as it goes by, stopping the DVD as each scene ends to summarize the events. You should also note the length of each scene, because in a time-bound medium such as TV, the length of a scene is as crafted in the final cut as the dialog. If you're watching carefully, you should also note the conflict in each scene, and also how the conflict is resolved. By the end of the episode, you'll have a roadmap to the story. Then draw yourself a little graph like the previous one, noting the high points and low points. Perform this exercise for three episodes. You'll learn so much about the way that writer thinks about story, how he or she sets up reversals, and so forth. In effect, you begin to assemble a list of all the "bullets" that writer carries around in his or her gun. When you do that, you'll begin to understand how you react as an audience member, and how that writer has pushed your buttons so successfully.

—Chris

Don't Neglect the Little Things

When you're writing a story, it's tempting to want to jump from big moment to big moment without putting much of anything in between. When you're a writer, it's quite common for certain parts of a story to excite and interest you more than others, but it's something you need to be wary of.

To give a simple example, let's say you're working on the story for a modern-day crime game. You've already got the structure laid out and you're ready to go. You're going to open the story big, with an epic car chase when a routine heist goes wrong, and you've got an exciting ending planned around a complex robbery in a Las Vegas casino. Between those two events, you also want to feature a clever museum heist, another car chase (because, as Hollywood has taught us, you can never have too many car chases), and a tense game of cat-and-mouse between your hero and some federal agents set in a large office building. These are your key scenes and the things you're building the entire story around. You've got great plans for them and are sure that the players will love them as well. Nothing wrong with that. But because all those heists are so big and fantastic, you don't want to slow things down and write about all the planning, reconnaissance, team recruitment, and the like that takes place between those scenes. This is where you can run into problems.

Sure, the heists may be cool and exciting, but if you want the story to be something that players care about rather than just a vague backdrop for the action, you need more than that. You need to show the players who your characters are, what their personalities are like, and why they're so set on robbing these places. Maybe the thief is a cop who lived an honest life but is being forced to commit these crimes by a shadowy cartel that kidnapped his daughter. You could sum that up in a line or two of text, like I just did, but that's not going to make players feel much sympathy for the guy. If you want the story to hit home, you need to get into the details. For example, you could put in some flashbacks of the guy and his daughter before the kidnapping.

The Problem with Flashbacks

Flashbacks are tricky, because one thing you need to do in drama is keep the story moving forward. If the flashback contains only setup information (information that might be better served by integrating it into the story), you will find that after you've returned to the drama, it can feel as if that was a waste of a few minutes. However, artfully done flashbacks can work, as long as they contain information that is crucial to the successful resolution of this story (Frodo needs to bring the Ring to Mount Doom to be destroyed because that is where it was created, so telling the story of the Ring's creation isn't just fluff – it's a crucial piece of information). Following is an example of the best way to handle backstory (dialog is approximate).

In the pilot episode of *The West Wing*, there is a scene in Act I in which we find out why Josh's job is in jeopardy. It turns out that on national TV, he made a cheap joke to a member of a conservative Christian organization. The scene opens with Josh watching a tape of the quote playing over and over. His assistant, Donna Moss, enters his office with a cup of coffee. Remember, this is the pilot episode, so the writer, Aaron Sorkin, needs to not only tell the story, but also introduce all the main characters to give you a little sense of their history.

So Donna enters with the cup of coffee, Ordinary, right? Not so much.

Donna enters with the coffee, and Josh says, "What's that?" Donna says "I brought you a cup of coffee?" Josh says "What?" Donna says "Coffee." Josh replies "Donnatella Moss, how long have you worked for me?" "Four years." "And in that time, how often have you brought me a cup of coffee?" She looks down at the coffee. "Why do you ask?" she says. Josh persists: "How many times?" She stammers a bit, "Well ..." Josh pushes further: "I'll tell you how many times. None." She is caught red-handed. "Never," he continues. "You've never brought me a cup of coffee. Donna, if I get fired, I get fired."

So what Sorkin masterfully does is use a prop to do multiple things. First, it allows him to show that Donna is really worried about Josh. Second, it allows Sorkin to tell a little of the backstory about their relationship in an organic way without either character launching into a dreary sort of "back when we were working on the campaign" speech. And third, the revelation moves the story forward because now we know Josh is aware of how dire his situation is.

—Chris

Perhaps the girl was rebellious and the two really didn't get along, even though he loved her and tried his best. Maybe she was kidnapped right after they had a big fight and never having apologized is tearing him up. The way he goes about planning and preparing for the heists can also show a lot about his personality and that of the people he works with. Because he's a good cop, having to commit crimes could very well be destroying him on the inside, causing him to question his entire life and beliefs, and changing the way he relates to others. These are the kinds of things you need to show if you want to really draw players in. Similarly, if your story takes places in a really interesting world or location, players are never going to have the chance to explore or learn about its culture and history if you're just jumping from big scene to big scene. Sure, the key scenes are important, but in the end, it's the details that really make a story special.

Keeping the Player Engaged

As previously mentioned, it's important to maintain player interest throughout the game by using good pacing. Part of the way to do that is by making sure to spend time on the details to help players get to know and care about your world and characters. But you also need to make sure that the really interesting stuff – plot twists, big reveals, and story scenes in general – is placed regularly throughout the game. Though you don't necessarily need a big epic scene taking placing every hour, you probably don't want the player to go for an hour or two without any story elements, either (keep in mind that we're assuming the player is playing through the game normally and not stopping to kill extra monsters, play cards, or do other optional activities). To keep players interested in the story, you need to keep the story moving. Moreover, although every story scene doesn't need to drive the main plot forward, it should still be interesting and/or entertaining, even if you're just bringing up a bit of trivia about the world or showing how the characters relate to each other.

Same Question, Different Day

One traditional method to keep the story moving is to morph the MDQ as you go along. When it is done artfully, audiences will view this as an organic evolution of the story rather than an abrupt change. Example: Act I of *Raiders of the Lost Ark* ends when Indiana takes off after the Ark and launches Act II. The MDQ at that point is: will Indiana find the Ark before the Nazis do? Note how each bit of tension in the story during Act II relates to this question: do the Nazis know more than Indy does? How could they? Indy has the medallion! Oh, wait, they're digging in the wrong spot! And so on. Then Indiana finds the Ark, but Belloq takes it away. Complication! The MDQ morphs to "How will Indy get it back?" Chases ensue. Indiana gets it back? Oh, wait, the Germans board the boat, and they take it again. End of Act III (another complication) and beginning of Act IV. Indy is on the sub! Yeah! How will he do it this time? The Nazis have gotten the Ark to the island, where they are going to do the ceremony. Holy crap! What will he do now? He ambushes the Nazis as they head to the spot for the ceremony. How's he gonna get it? Oh, I see, a bazooka. He'll force them to give it up. What? He surrenders. Oh no! End of Act IV (crises) and beginning of Act V, during which the final answer is given: Indy doesn't find the Ark before they do, but it doesn't matter because the Ark kills the Nazis (reversal). Each morphing of the MDQ alters the story in an organic way and moves the story forward.

—Chris

The PlayStation 2 game *Magna Carta: Tears of Blood* provides an excellent example of how not to spread out your story scenes. Despite some problematic gameplay issues, *Magna Carta* contains a very interesting tale about a mercenary unit embroiled in the midst of a massive war between humans and a race of beings called the Yason. The story starts out strongly enough, with information about the war, some hints at the hero Calintz's mysterious past, and a run-in with an amnesiac girl named Reith. Unfortunately, a few hours into the game, the story falters as Calintz's group is sent on a long series of fetch quests that have them running all around the country to collect items needed for the war effort.

During this stretch (which can easily take players fifteen to twenty hours), the main plot all but grinds to a halt with no new information revealed about the war, Calintz's past, Reith's identity, or any of the other questions brought up during the first part of the game. Though a definite problem, the interesting cast of characters could have helped keep players engaged and entertained during that part of the game, making up somewhat for the lack of plot developments. Unfortunately, that wasn't the case, either as most interactions between the heroes and other characters during that portion of the game were very short and simple, showing off none of the characters' personalities or charm. In one particularly memorable (or perhaps unmemorable) exchange, Calintz calls a big meeting with his team just to say that the volcanic cave where they'll be heading on their next mission will probably be hot. *Magna Carta*'s story managed to somewhat redeem itself in the final few hours, which feature a long series of revelations, plot twists, and interesting character interactions leading up to a very strong finish. But, as good as the last part of the game is, only the players with the perseverance to press on through the long and boring middle section are able to see it.

On the other hand, *FINAL FANTASY XIII* (which we'll discuss more later in this chapter) rarely lets players go more than twenty minutes between story scenes. And although not all of those scenes contain big events or important plot points, they go a long way toward exploring the feelings and personalities of the characters and teaching the player about the world where the game takes place, making for a very strong contrast with *Magna Carta*'s poor pacing.

General Pacing Do's and Don'ts

- DO space plot twists, character development, action sequences, and other big scenes fairly evenly throughout the story. This ensures that the player will never have to go too long between interesting sections.

- DO ensure that there's time for slower sections between the big scenes. Use this time to focus on things like character development, the setting, and the backstory.

- DO analyze the pacing in popular stories and use it as a guide for your own. This is not to say that all popular stories have perfect or near-perfect pacing, but it's important to learn from others' mistakes as well as their triumphs.

- DON'T make your story all action all the time. Players need a break now and then and even big, high-energy scenes can get dull if that's all there is.

- DON'T let slower sections last for too long without a big event or story revelation to spice things up.

- DON'T fill sections with pointless chatter or busywork. Even in the slower parts of the story, you should do your best to keep things interesting and/or entertaining.

- DON'T save all your big reveals and answers for a single part of the story; work them in here and there as the story progresses to keep players interested.

- DON'T add in unnecessary action scenes or slow scenes just to try and even out the pacing. If a part of the story feels tacked on or unneeded, it's likely to hurt more than it will help.

Case Study: *Xenosaga Episode II: Jenseits von Gut und Böse*

Developer: Monolith Soft
Publisher: Namco
Writers: Tetsuya Takahashi, Saga Soraya
System: Sony PlayStation 2
Release Date: February 15, 2005 (US)
Genre: RPG

The heroes of *Xenosaga*.

FIGURE
4.2

The *Xenosaga* series is a trilogy of sci-fi RPGs on the PlayStation 2. Supervised by Tetsuya Takahashi, one of creators of the PlayStation cult classic *XENOGEARS* (considered by many to have one of the best stories of any video game), the *Xenosaga* trilogy takes place in a far future when humanity has spread across the universe. Recently, human planets and colonies have come under attack from an alien race known as the Gnosis. As Gnosis are invulnerable to most conventional weapons, a group of scientists including Shion Uzuki have created KOS-MOS, an anti-Gnosis battle android with a revolutionary, near-human AI. However, the Gnosis threat is only one of several problems facing the universe, as various cults, religions, and powerful organizations work to gain power and pursue dangerous plans of their own. Meanwhile, behind the scenes, a mysterious group of seemingly immortal figures seems to be manipulating all the different angles for reasons of their own. Thrown into the middle of this conflict, Shion, KOS-MOS, and several unlikely companions join together to fight for survival and slowly uncover the truth. *Xenosaga*'s deep, twisting plot earned it many fans, and though it can be a little hard to follow at times, it remains one of the best and most unique game stories to be found.

FIGURE
4.3

In the world of *Xenosaga*, giant robots are commonplace.

Although *Episodes I* and *III* were occasionally criticized for their long cut-scenes, they received very positive reviews overall, thanks to their enjoyable mix of on-foot and giant robot combat, memorable characters, and, of course, their amazing story. *Episode II* received generally positive reviews but is frequently regarded as the weakest entry in the series. Though the story was still excellent, various graphical and gameplay changes met with very mixed responses from fans. Unfortunately, the pacing was rather problematic as well. *Episode II* did a good job making use of both fast, action-packed scenes and slower, story-focused ones and spaced them out well throughout the game. However, many of them tended to drag on a bit too long. At many points, the player has to spend several hours fighting through dungeons with little to no plot development; in others, he or she is faced with hours of dialog and cut-scenes with no battles and very little interaction on his or her part. The cut-scenes and dialog were very well done, featuring excellent voice acting and contributing a lot to the overall plot, but much of the information revealed (particularly in the early portions of the game) – though interesting – wasn't crucial to the main story and might have worked better if it had instead been incorporated into optional conversations and quests, thus allowing the player to get back into the action a bit sooner. Another problem – one that was probably unavoidable – is that *Episode II* was the middle game in the trilogy. As such, there were far fewer characters and mysteries to introduce than there had been in *Episode I* and, with the story far from over, many of the big revelations had to be saved for *Episode III*.

Fortunately, Monolith learned from its mistakes and *Episode III*, in addition to a host of gameplay improvements, contained excellent pacing. Story scenes were frequent, even during long dungeon crawls, and most of the technical details and less-critical information was placed in optional conversations and the in-game information database, allowing players to review it at will over the course of the game. The superb mix of action, important story scenes, and slower sections keeps players engaged throughout the game as the answers to the series' many mysteries are revealed, finishing with a satisfying ending that succeeds in wrapping up the complex story while leaving players still hoping for more. Despite *Episode II*'s pacing problems, the *Xenosaga* trilogy is one that everyone interested in game stories should play, both for its amazing storyline and to watch the way the series progressed and evolved with each installment, as Monolith constantly strove to improve both their gameplay and storytelling.

Character Development

If you look at a lot of game stories, or just stories in general, you'll notice that many different characters have similar personality traits and roles in their respective stories. We touched on this when discussing clichéd characters in the previous chapter. Clichéd character types like the mentor, amnesiac hero, and mysterious girl are all examples – albeit rather extreme ones – of character archetypes. Simply put, an archetype is a sort of general character template that can then be customized and personalized to fit into nearly any story. To put it in game terms, an archetype is like a character class. Choosing to make your character a rogue instead of a knight or monk, for example, automatically assigns certain traits to that character. A typical rogue may be fast and agile, but he probably won't have the defensive skills of a knight or the barehanded prowess of a monk. However, that doesn't mean that every rogue is the same. Your rogue could specialize in bows or knives, traps or lock picking. He could be a jolly and helpful Robin Hood–like figure or a cruel, uncaring murderer. The choices are endless. Like story structures, choosing an archetype merely gives you a place to start.

Common Character Archetypes

There are hundreds of different archetypes used in storytelling, though some are far more common than others and many can be combined into a single broader archetype, depending on your preferences. A full discussion of the many different archetypes and their variations and uses could easily fill an entire book of its own, so here I'll just introduce you to ten of the more commonly used archetypes in video games. Keep in mind that although I refer to each of the following archetypes as either he or she, they can all be applied to characters of either gender.

The Young Hero

The archetypical young hero is often between twelve and twenty-five years old and is eager to go out and prove his worth by having adventures, succeeding in business, successfully performing a difficult task, or something similar. He tends to be cheerful, enthusiastic, and optimistic, and is often eager to help those in need.

Examples include Tidus (*FINAL FANTASY X*), Sora (*KINGDOM HEARTS*), and Guybrush (*The Secret of Monkey Island*).

The Reluctant Hero

In many ways the opposite of the young hero, he never had any interest in the task or adventure at hand. Forced into it by circumstances beyond his control, his only goal is to find a way out of it or, failing at that, to get it over and done with as soon as possible. On that note, he often tries to avoid helping others or engaging in anything that will add to his workload unless it greatly benefits him. Though initially not the most likable guy, he often matures and changes his attitude over the course of his journey.

Example include Kain (*Blood Omen*), Neku (*THE WORLD ENDS WITH YOU*), and Laharl (*Disgaea*).

The Best Friend

The hero's best friend or sibling, she never leaves the hero's side. Sometimes enthusiastic, sometimes reluctant, she provides a balance for the hero, either pushing him to action or urging him to slow down and carefully consider his actions. If the best friend and hero are not related and of opposite genders, they often grow to love each other.

Examples include Max (*Sam & Max: The Devil's Playhouse*), Lucca (*CHRONO TRIGGER*), and Ryogo (*FRONT MISSION 3*).

The Special Person

Sometimes a hero, sometimes a villain, sometimes neither, she tends to be fairly young (rarely older than the hero) and somewhat mysterious. Alone in the world, she possesses a special power or ability that others seek to exploit, forcing her to act cautiously and often live life on the run. Having had a difficult life, she either maintains a bright and cheerful personality, always certain that things will improve, or withdraws within herself, becoming aloof and difficult to approach.

Examples include Reith (*Magna Carta*), Aeris (*FINAL FANTASY VII*), and Luna (*Lunar Silver Star Harmony*).

The Mentor

Wiser and more experienced than the hero (and usually far older), he takes the hero under his wing in an attempt to teach him and prepare him for the things to come. Often a former hero himself, he hopes the new hero will be able to complete an important task that he cannot. Believing firmly in the hero, he is willing to sacrifice anything, even his life, to ensure the hero's success.

Examples include: Angeal (*CRISIS CORE – FINAL FANTASY VII*), Auron (*FINAL FANTASY X*), and the Boss (*Metal Gear Solid 3*).

The Veteran

A battle-hardened warrior who has lived through many battles: tough and practical, he focuses on completing his mission and getting out alive. If he himself isn't the hero, he'll lend the hero his aid and experience, often acting as a pseudo-mentor. Because of his difficult and dangerous life, in which any day could be his last, he tends to be either gruff and solitary or laid back and eager to enjoy the time he has.

Examples include Snake (*Metal Gear Solid*), Shepard (*Mass Effect*), and Ziggy (*Xenosaga*).

The Gambler

For her, everything is a game, with life being the biggest and most high-stakes game of all. She takes on jobs for the thrill and challenge, siding with whatever person or persons strikes her as the most interesting. Skill is important, but in the end, it all comes down to chance – and Lady Luck hasn't failed her yet. Depending on her mood, she may side with the hero, the villain, or neither, and occasionally switches alliances to ensure that she ends up on the winning side.

Examples include Mion (*Higurashi*), Setzer (*FINAL FANTASY VI*), and Joshua (*THE WORLD ENDS WITH YOU*).

The Seductress

Beautiful and confident, the seductress is also greedy and opportunistic, always ready to use her looks and charms to get what she wants. Fiercely jealous, she's merciless toward anyone she considers a threat to her ambitions. Because she sees love and compassion as just parts of the act, their true meanings are often lost on her. Her façade is difficult to penetrate, but deep down hides the heart of either a cruel villain or an insecure girl who wants desperately to be loved – not for her looks, but for who she is.

Examples include Eva (*Metal Gear Solid 3*), Caster (*Fate/Stay Night*), and Echidna (*THE BOUNCER*).

The Hardened Criminal

At home in the city's seedy underbelly, he can obtain any item and perform any job for the right price. He may enjoy his work, reveling in the challenge and wealth it brings; he may just need the money; or he may simply know of no other way to live. Sometimes beneath his gruff exterior lurks a heart of gold, but he could just as easily be a scheming opportunist, ready to turn on his companions the moment it suits him.

Examples include Kyle (*Lunar Silver Star Harmony*), Niko (*Grand Theft Auto IV*), and Jack (*Mass Effect 2*).

The Cold, Calculating Villain

Driven, intelligent, and utterly ruthless, he's working toward a certain goal and won't hesitate to destroy anything or anyone that gets in his way. His plans are often big and complex, requiring years of planning and preparation, but he doesn't mind being patient as long as his ends are eventually achieved. Whether he seeks power, wealth, revenge, or some other prize, all that matters is success. He may not even see himself as a villain, but instead as a hero, working toward the greater good, and may even lament the many innocents sacrificed along the way. But to him, their deaths were necessary. In fact, they should be grateful that they were able to give their lives in pursuit of his vision.

Examples include Wilhelm (*Xenosaga*), Primarch Dysley (*FINAL FANTASY XIII*), and Liquid Ocelot (*Metal Gear Solid IV*).

Advantages of Using Archetypes

Basing your characters around an existing archetype helps you ensure that their thoughts, personalities, and actions remain consistent with what they're supposed to be, which is an important part of making characters seem real and believable (as we'll talk more about shortly). As with story structure, archetypes can also give you a good place to start if you're unsure of how a specific character fits into the story. And, much as with clichés, players are familiar and comfortable with common character archetypes. If a character stays true to his or her archetypical role, players can quickly gain a sense of the character's personality and goals without the need for lots of dialog or backstory.

That said, unlike clichés, archetypes are endlessly customizable and by no means have to fit perfectly within the cookie-cutter descriptions I've provided. Furthermore, characters don't need to be locked into a single archetype throughout the entire story. In *FINAL FANTASY XIII* (which we'll discuss in depth later), Hope starts out as an extremely reluctant hero, cursing his fate, refusing to fight, and following the rest of the heroes only because he has no other choice. But as the game progresses, he learns and grows, first becoming possessed by a desire to become stronger and extract revenge on the people he blames for his predicament, and eventually embracing his role and becoming one of the most positive and heroic members of the group. Mixing multiple archetypes like this can make for very deep and nuanced characters, which goes a long way toward turning an average story into an amazing story.

Disadvantages of Using Archetypes

Because common archetypes are familiar and often fairly easy to recognize, characters run a serious risk of becoming predictable and even cliché if they stick too closely to their base archetype. That doesn't necessarily mean that they won't still be good characters, but it can certainly reduce their overall appeal.

More practically, trying to shoehorn every character you create into a predefined archetype or flipping through a list of archetypes for ideas every time you create a character is not only time-consuming but very restrictive as well. Archetypes aren't meant to be used as a checklist. Some stories may need all ten of the archetypes I listed; others could be fine with two or three or maybe even none at all. Although you may occasionally want to think about what archetypes your characters fit into to try and ensure that they act appropriately, even that can be problematic. Sure, it might seem strange when a cold, calculating villain acts in a way more befitting a hero, but depending on that villain's personality, mindset, and backstory, it might be perfectly within her character to do so. A certain character in *Heavy Rain*, for example (see the Heavy Rain case study in Chapter 9), spends much of the game acting like a hero only to eventually be revealed as a cold, calculating villain. However, when taken in context with his past and personality, the complete archetype reversal is believable and makes sense.

Though every writer has his or her own way of doing things, unless you're trying to appeal to a specific market segment that really likes a particular archetype, I usually find it best when designing characters to forget about archetypes and just think about the type of character you want to create. What do you want him to act like? Why does he act that way? How was he raised? What important events took place in his past and how did they affect him? What will he add to the story? It's questions like these that you should be asking yourself – not "Which archetype haven't I used yet?"

Using Archetypes

The choice of archetype needs to be done artfully. Campbell's archetypes are organically related to his story type, which is a journey from darkness to enlightenment. In Campbell's Journey, for the hero to successfully navigate his or her path, he or she needs a mentor who has gone there before. If you're writing *Othello*, in which that journey is not navigated successfully but instead ends in the tragic death of Desdemona, what you need instead is a bigger role for the Trickster, who is Iago.

—Chris

Case Study: *KINGDOM HEARTS II*

Developer: Square Enix Co., Ltd.
Publisher: Square Enix, Inc.
Writers: Tetsuya Nomura, Kazushige Nojima
System: Sony PlayStation 2
Release Date: March 28, 2006 (US)
Genre: Action RPG

FIGURE
4.4

Square Enix and Disney characters combine to battle the Heartless in *KINGDOM HEARTS II*. © Square Enix, Co., Ltd. All rights reserved.

The extremely unlikely pairing of Square, known for bestselling RPGs such as *FINAL FANTASY* and *CHRONO TRIGGER*, and Walt Disney caused a stir among fans when it was announced. At first, most were sure that nothing good could come from a collaboration between such seemingly mismatched companies, but they would soon realize just how wrong they were. The original *KINGDOM HEARTS*, an action-packed world-hopping adventure featuring a wide range of characters from both Disney movies and *FINAL FANTASY* games, won over fans of both and went on to win critical acclaim and commercial success, launching one of Square's most popular series. *KINGDOM HEARTS II* is actually the third game in the series, being released after *KINGDOM HEARTS: CHAIN OF MEMORIES* (a side story meant to fill in the gap between the end of *KINGDOM HEARTS* and the start of *KINGDOM HEARTS II*), but was the true successor to the first game, taking the original formula and gameplay and improving on them in every way.

The story of *KINGDOM HEARTS* follows Sora, a young boy who awakens one night to find his best friends missing and his home overrun by shadowy beings called Heartless. Unable to stop the destruction of his world, even with the help of the mysterious Keyblade, Sora finds himself in a strange town, where he meets Donald Duck and Goofy. As it turns out, Sora's world was only one of many (most of which are based on various Disney movies) and all are under threat from the Heartless. As the Keyblade wielder, he joins Donald and Goofy in their search for King Mickey in order to find his friends and stop the Heartless. *KINGDOM HEARTS II* picks up around a year after the first game (and a bit less time after *KINGDOM HEARTS: CHAIN OF MEMORIES*) as Sora and his friends find themselves facing a new threat in the form of the Nobodies and the deadly Organization XIII.

FIGURE
4.5

So don't be sad, and always know, we'll come back soon to say hello!

A number of famous Disney characters make appearances throughout the game. © Square Enix, Co., Ltd. All rights reserved.

With most of their movies based around fairy tales and other classic stories, Disney has a long history of creating their characters around common archetypes such as the princess, the hero, and the cold, calculating villain. When looking over their large collection of films, you'll quickly notice that it's rare for Disney's characters to deviate too far from their standard archetype. However, the fact that their characters still retain their charm and popularity after so many years is a testament to the strength and creativity that goes into them. Even though they generally behave in predictable ways that are fully appropriate for their archetype, Disney characters have very well-established and entertaining personalities, be it Ariel's driving curiosity or Aladdin's wit and confidence. They also exhibit strong, believable emotions and react to situations in ways that perfectly fit their personalities. Just because they're characters in a children's cartoon doesn't prevent them from showing love, anger, and even despair as the situation warrants it. Standard archetypes or not, Disney characters are all surprisingly human (even the nonhuman ones).

KINGDOM HEARTS II follows this trend, not only by accurately portraying the Disney characters, but by imbuing the series' cast of original characters with the same style and charm. Cheerful, adventurous, and always eager to push forward, Sora easily fits the standard hero archetype, but even he becomes overcome with loneliness and depression at times when worrying about the unknown fate of his friends.

FIGURE
4.6

Despite following the standard hero archetype, Sora is a strong and believable character. © Square Enix, Co., Ltd. All rights reserved.

Xemnas, *KINGDOM HEARTS II*'s main villain, is a similarly interesting character. Despite being a perfect example of the cold, calculating villain with a complex master plan, careful manipulation of those around him, and a focus on his ultimate goal over all else, he still comes across as a deep and even pitiable character when his true purpose is revealed.

Although I do think that archetypes should be at most a secondary consideration when creating characters, if you want to see the many different ways in which even the most common and clichéd archetypes can be used to create an endless variety of interesting and entertaining characters, look no further than *KINGDOM HEARTS II*.

Making Characters Believable

Creating cool designs and interesting backstories and personalities for your characters is all very important. But no matter how good a character is, if he or she acts in an unrealistic way players will have trouble connecting with and growing attached to the character. Of course, video game characters do unrealistic things all the time, like hurling fireballs, jumping twenty feet into the air, and destroying armies of demons with nothing but a sword. But when I say "realistic," I'm not talking about the characters' special powers or superhuman strength and agility – I'm talking about how they speak and the ways they act and react to various situations. After all, in other worlds things like magic, superhuman powers, and demon armies could all be perfectly normal parts of everyday life, but human behavior doesn't change much with time or place. Although there's plenty of variation to be found based on the specific character's beliefs and personality, once you know a bit about someone, it should be fairly easy to predict how he or she will speak and react in different situations (barring a few extremely unpredictable situations and character types). When your characters don't react in those predictable ways, then you might have a problem.

Grand Argument Theory

One way in which theater plays (dramas, mainly) have been described is as a Grand Argument. That is, the entire play is written in order to examine a particular point of view. Example: *A Midsummer Night's Dream* discusses at length the nature of love. It uses multiple characters and situations, all designed to look at different points of view regarding love. These types of stories don't use the Hero's Journey, but instead have characters created to articulate different attitudes and points of view about the topic. Only at the end of the story do we discover what the author's point of view about the topic might be, and this is done as the resolution of the story is revealed.

In those structures in particular, characters are created to function as diametrically opposed points on the circle so the arguments can evolve out of the drama.

The Hero's Journey doesn't work for every type of story.

—Chris

Character Actions and Decisions

The decisions characters make and the ways in which they react to different situations say a lot about them. Though simple decisions such as deciding whether to go out for pizza may generate a quick off-the-cuff response, when facing a more serious choice, many factors come into play. In the PlayStation 3 hit *Heavy Rain*, one of the characters is Ethan Mars, a father on a desperate and dangerous mission to find his kidnapped son Shaun before it's too late. Forced to complete a series of challenges given him by Shaun's kidnapper, Ethan is eventually tasked with murdering a certain man. Sensing danger, the man attacks Ethan with a shotgun, resulting in a tense chase sequence, but in the end, the man finds himself at Ethan's mercy with a gun pointed at his head.

Heavy Rain leaves it up to the player to decide whether Ethan pulls the trigger, but let's think about what would be going through Ethan's mind at the time. Even though it might take only a few seconds to make the decision, there's a lot going on behind the scenes. First and foremost, of course, is Ethan's desire to save his son. If he fails the test set by the kidnapper, he has no idea whether he'll have another chance or whether Shaun will be lost forever. In addition, the man is someone Ethan has never met before, admits to dealing drugs, and was gleefully chasing Ethan with a shotgun only moments before. Those can all be taken as good reasons to go ahead and shoot the guy. But there's more at work. Although *Heavy Rain* doesn't delve into Ethan's religious and moral beliefs, he may have very strongly formed opinions about murder and whether it's permissible. There are also repercussions to consider. If the police find out about the murder, Ethan could spend the rest of his life in jail. He may even be arrested before he gets a chance to save Shaun, rendering the murder and everything else he's done worthless. And finally, on an emotional level, the man holds up a picture of his daughter and pleads with Ethan to let him go so that he can see her again, something Ethan can clearly relate to. Although *Heavy Rain* doesn't bring up every issue I just mentioned, they're all things that would be going through Ethan's mind as he stands there with the gun. In the end, it's a rather hard choice to make and it's a credit to the writing and Ethan's previous development that either decision fits very well with his character.

Other actions and decisions, however, are clearer cut. For example, earlier in *Heavy Rain*, before Shaun is kidnapped, Ethan is given a couple chances to spend some time with him. Depending on the player's actions, Ethan could act as a concerned and loving parent or ignore Shaun entirely and do his own thing. However, if the player chooses to portray Ethan as a selfish, uncaring father, it won't fit with the desperation and determination to save Shaun that he displays in later scenes, reducing his believability.

To give another example, though I won't mention any names, I've seen far too many games in which the hero returns home to find his family murdered only to react in a rather emotionless and completely unbelievable manner. Usually something along the lines of, "Well, that's too bad. Guess I'd better go avenge them now." (Note that this is a general summation of the hero's attitude and actions, not an actual quote.) Unless the hero really hated his family, their murder would be an extremely traumatic event. Sure, if he has a certain type of personality, he might seek revenge, but he'd also be an emotional wreck, most likely shifting between extreme cases of anger and despair. He may even find himself completely paralyzed by grief or contemplating suicide. Having him react in a calm and off-handed manner completely destroys the hero's believability.

In a less extreme example, if your hero is portrayed as an honest, law-abiding person and is later given the option to rob a bank, he shouldn't do it. Or, at the very least, it should be a very difficult thing for him to do. It makes no sense for an honest hero to commit a crime just because it's convenient for the plot or the player feels like doing so. It would take a really serious situation (such as his girlfriend being held hostage) to make the hero do something that goes so clearly against his beliefs. Because of this, many games that give the player frequent choices between two or more opposing actions either offer strong incentives to encourage the player to stay firmly on a single path (therefore keeping the character's actions fairly consistent) like in *Mass Effect*, or make the hero a generic blank slate so he or she has no predetermined beliefs, personality, or backstory, making consistency far less of an issue (though losing the chance to develop an interesting and memorable hero in the process).

Characters can change, but only gradually and over time. Similarly, they may occasionally make decisions that don't fit the way they normally react, but only for specific reasons or if they're under extreme duress. Any time a character, either as part of the predetermined story or due to player choice, performs an action that doesn't fit his or her personality, the character loses a bit of believability, making it harder and harder for players to really identify with him or her.

Character Dialog

It's also important to ensure that characters are consistent in the way they speak. People's manner of speech can be affected by many things, including their personality, upbringing, social status, gender, and where they were raised. Even if they're both speaking English, an orphan who grew up on the streets of New York and a Japanese businessman will have vastly different styles of speech. The orphan will probably talk in a fast and rough manner, with lots of contractions, slang, and broken grammar. By contrast, the Japanese businessman will likely speak slowly and politely in a very formal manner while avoiding slang and American expressions (which he may not fully understand).

If a character's speech is too formal or too casual for his or her background and personality, the character is going to be less believable. Similarly, if a character uses terms, expressions, and idioms that he or she likely wouldn't have learned, believability will suffer as well. For example, it would be strange for most Japanese people to use the expression "a penny saved is a penny earned," both because it's an American phrase and because Japan doesn't have pennies. Naturally, a character in a fantasy world who says that would seem even more out of place.

Finally, when writing, be sure to remember that not every character is going to speak the exact same way you do. In fact, most of them probably won't. That said, it can be a good idea to read your characters' dialog out loud and think about how well it flows and how you'd phrase it if you were the one speaking. Doing so can help ensure that, if nothing else, your dialog at least flows naturally and doesn't sound strange or stilted.

Case Study: *FINAL FANTASY XIII*

Developer: Square Enix Co., Ltd.
Publisher: Square Enix, Inc.
Writers: Yoshinori Kitase, Daisuke Watanabe, Kazushige Nojima,
             Sachie Hirano, Harunori Sakemi

System: Sony PlayStation 3 and Xbox 360
Release Date: March 9, 2010 (US)
Genre: RPG

FIGURE
4.7

Lightning, Snow, and Vanille are all very different and believable characters.

Launched after a very lengthy development period, *FINAL FANTASY XIII* maintained the series' history of top-quality graphics, music, and storytelling while continuing to experiment with different types of RPG gameplay. Some of these changes were better received than others. Though *FINAL FANTASY XIII*'s unique, fast-paced battle system was met with near-universal acclaim, Square Enix's decision not to include the sprawling towns and complex mini-games that have been present in most past *FINAL FANTASY* titles (and, for that matter, most RPGs in general) was faced with very mixed reactions. Whether those were wise moves will likely be debated for years by fans, but we're here to talk about *FINAL FANTASY XIII*'s story – and surprisingly enough, the lack of towns and limited exploration options actually served it quite well.

FINAL FANTASY XIII starts out in Cocoon, a planetoid of sorts floating high above the world of Pulse. For centuries, the two worlds have been at war, and even though it's been hundreds of years since the last great battle, the people of Cocoon still maintain a deep fear of Pulse. In addition to humans, Cocoon and Pulse are also home to beings known as fal'Cie, who serve as rulers, protectors, and aides to the humans. If they desire, fal'Cie can also take human servants. Known as l'Cie, these humans are tasked with a single objective (called a Focus) and given great powers and magic in order to complete it. If they succeed, l'Cie are said to be rewarded with eternal life, but if they fail, they become Cie'th, mindless monsters who can do nothing but blindly destroy everything around them. Early in the game, five of the heroes – Lightning (a former member of Cocoon's military), Sazh (a middle aged pilot), Hope (a young boy), Vanille (a cheerful, carefree girl), and Snow (a self-proclaimed hero and the fiancé of Lightning's sister, Serah) – come into contact with a Pulse fal'Cie and are branded with the mark of l'Cie. Given a Focus they don't understand, and on the run from virtually everyone in Cocoon (who consider the Pulse l'Cie to be a grave danger to their world, which is why the heroes can't go strolling around towns and shops), this unlikely group struggles to find a way to escape their cursed fate.

FIGURE
4.8

The l'Cie mark grants great power but at a terrible price. © Square Enix, Co., Ltd. **All rights reserved.**

Though *FINAL FANTASY XIII*'s tale of Cocoon, Pulse, and fal'Cie is interesting enough on its own, what really sets the game apart is the characters. Lightning, Sazh, Hope, Vanille, Snow, and their later companion Fang make for some of the most emotionally complex and believable characters in gaming history. They all seem to start out as fairly predictable archetypes, but watching them grow and change over the course of the adventure is one of the highlights of the game. Lightning begins as a no-nonsense military type, unemotional and always focused on finding and destroying the enemy. However, as time goes on, you discover that her tough exterior is a façade created to help her deal with the challenges of working and raising her young sister after their parents' death. Beneath her shell, she's just as scared and confused as the others and isn't sure whom or what she should be fighting.

Hope, who starts out doing nothing but blaming others and bemoaning his fate, eventually becomes obsessed with the desire to grow stronger and get revenge on Snow, whom he blames for the death of his mother, but slowly learns to take responsibility for his own actions and to stand up to protect the people who are important to him, becoming one of the most optimistic and committed members of the party.

Even the characters who start out seeming extremely one dimensional, like the perpetually cheerful Vanille and the confidently heroic Snow, turn out to be wrestling with many deep and troubling issues and are nowhere near as certain of their goals and actions as they want the others to believe. The major villains are very interesting as well. Some could easily be considered heroes in their own right, struggling to protect Cocoon against the l'Cie and other perceived threats – and even the true villain, who is willing to enact large-scale genocide to see his plans fulfilled, truly believes that what he's doing is necessary to save the world from decay and destruction.

The way the heroes relate to each other and the world around them is also well done. Unlike most RPG heroes, who are perfectly willing to join together to fight evil the moment they meet, the cast members of *FINAL FANTASY XIII* start out with very different goals and motivations and spend much of the game trying to get away from both their fate as l'Cie and each other before events finally convince them to band together. They also have to deal with the fear and hatred of the citizens of Cocoon and the horrifying realization that, in order to save themselves, they may have to destroy the home they know and love.

Above all else, their problems, dilemmas, and uncertainty make the characters in *FINAL FANTASY XIII* feel extremely real and believable, making it easy for players to get drawn into the quest and share the characters' confusion, sorrows, and triumphs. We hope that other game developers will look to *FINAL FANTASY XIII*, like they've looked to the series in the past, and use its example to create deep, complex, and believable characters of their own.

How Much to Tell and Not Tell Players

When you're writing a story, there's a lot more to it than just the events that take place in the game itself. Chances are good that your characters didn't all magically spring into existence the moment the story starts. They have lives, histories, families, and years or decades of events and experiences that took place before the main story began. And then there's the setting. Sure, a character might have a history spanning several decades or even a century or two, but the world in which your story takes place is probably far older, with a history stretching back thousands of years. Some of that information may be important to the main story and some might not, but it's there ready for you to create, reference, and use whenever and however you please.

But how do you know how much of that information to use? Writing out the complete political history of your main characters' homeland could be fun and would doubtless interest some players, but is it really the best way to be spending your time? Perhaps you should instead be writing detailed biographies for the important characters. Or maybe you should just ignore all of it and focus on nothing but the main plot. Deciding what information to spend your time creating, what to tell players, and how to tell them is yet another challenge you'll face when writing for games.

Backstory or Not

Although this method may not work for everyone, Aaron Sorkin (*The West Wing*, *Sports Night*, *A Few Good Men*, *Charlie Wilson's War*) is famous (or infamous, depending on your point of view) for not working on extensive backstory for his characters. He invents background about the characters on demand, as he needs it. When asked about this process, he stated that he'd rather keep his options open, that as he watched the actors grow into their roles, storylines would grow out of their performance and he didn't want his hands tied.

One story that illustrates this method: early in The West Wing the president (Martin Sheen) and his wife (played by Stockard Channing) were in a scene at an official government ball, and they were to enter together down a staircase. This was their first scene they played together. At the top of the stairs, as they awaited their cue, Martin and Stockard began to compare notes about their characters. Martin had been in the pilot, but Stockard was cast only after the show had gone into production.

"How many children do we have?" Stockard asked.

"Well, the pilot mentioned one, so we have at least one," replied Martin.

"You don't know?" Stockard was surprised.

Martin laughed. "No, I actually have no idea."

Stockard said "Well, I'll ask Aaron."

"Don't bother," Martin replied, "he doesn't know either."

When you look back on the series, and the crucial role that another Bartlett daughter came into play (indeed, not the one actually mentioned in the pilot), it is astonishing that Sorkin made this stuff up as he went along.

—Chris

The Importance of Backstory

Backstory, or the events that took place before your main story began, serves two main uses. First and foremost, it can help set up and expand upon the main story. Perhaps your hero has a strange aversion to fire. If that's the case, at some point in the game you should probably spend a bit of time explaining the character's backstory to show how he or she became that way. Similarly, if two countries in your world are at war because of an event that happened fifty years ago, you should consider having a story scene or in-game book that explains how the war began.

Of course, the more important these elements are to the main plot, the more vital it is that you explain them. If your hero's fear of fire is a minor thing that's only brought up once or twice, you might not need to bother explaining it. But if it plays a major role in the story, you can be certain that players are going to want an explanation. In some cases, backstory can play such a large role in current events that without it, the story really wouldn't make much sense. For example, in *Lunar Silver Star Harmony*, many key plot points – including Ghaleon's change from hero to villain and Luna's true identity – are all related to the actions of the four heroes who saved the world long before the game began. If *Lunar* didn't take time to explain the heroes' quest and what became of them afterward, it would be very difficult (if not impossible) to fully understand the story.

Second, even if certain parts of the backstory have little to no bearing on the main plot, if your story is a good one, there are always going to be some fans who want more information about a particular character, place, or historic event just to satisfy their curiosity and learn more about the world and characters they've come to love. Adding in a lot of extra backstory elements will be sure to please those fans – though it should be noted that they're usually in the minority, so the main plot should always be your primary focus and you should not force a whole lot of extra information on uninterested players.

How to Tell the Backstory

Thanks to their interactive nature, games offer a myriad of ways to reveal backstory without having to worry about bogging people down with details or boring uninterested players. Elements that are very important to the main plot should be revealed throughout the game in conversations, cut-scenes, flashbacks, and the like, but there are many optional and subtler ways to convey the rest of your backstory.

The first is through in-game books (or scrolls, data discs, or similar means of transmission, depending on your setting). If the hero will be visiting various towns throughout the game, you can place libraries in one or more of them and fill the books with notes and trivia about the world and its history. Or, if the hero won't have the chance to visit any libraries, he or she can get such books in treasure chests or from enemies. Backstory can also be revealed as part of optional side-quests or during conversations with various NPCs scattered throughout the world. Even important NPCs can give players the option to ask for more details about a particular person or event or just skip to the critical information.

If you want to make all the backstory and supplemental information very easily accessible to players, you can follow the current trend and place a database or log of some sort in the main menu. These databases generally contain anything from a brief summary to highly detailed information about the vast majority of characters, locations, and items in the game, among other things. Like libraries and optional conversations, they provide players with a wealth of extra information that they can choose to read or ignore. However, as all the information is contained in the menu, it makes it easy for players to read and reference it at their leisure at nearly any time during the game, which is far more convenient than hunting down books or NPCs. However, if you still want to give players some incentive to explore or at the very least want to avoid giving them too much information at the very start, you can set up the database so that certain entries become available only after the player has progressed far enough in the game or completed other specific requirements.

Earth and Beyond: *The MMO*

We worked in the backstory for *Earth and Beyond* in a method that illustrates one unique way to handle this issue. This was wholly the invention of our great lead writer, Angela Ferriaolo. *Earth and Beyond* was an MMO published by Electronic Arts in 2002 that told the story of humans originating from Earth as they colonized the solar system hundreds of years in the future. The game's setup was that our part of space was invaded by aliens. But the puzzling thing for the players was that when the aliens first arrived, their ships would ply the human trade lanes and not *do* anything – instead just flying back and forth. They didn't attack, they didn't communicate in any way the players could understand – nothing. Players didn't know what to make of them. The alien ships would fly up to the player ships and broadcast a message, which appeared to be gibberish.

Separately from those ships, the players would be killing mobs (enemy groups). Some of those mobs would drop loot, called "fragments," from their inventory. These fragments seemed to be inventory lists, pieces of some bigger document, but with no apparent worth. None of the NPCs in the game mentioned these fragments, so most players sold them as vendor trash. Then one player started to collect them (each fragment was numbered). The number of fragments exceeded the amount of space in any single players' bank, so that player enlisted another in order to begin to collect all the different fragments.

Back to the aliens. One player began to play around, trying to translate the gibberish they were broadcasting. It turns out that they were speaking in a simple offset substitution cipher, and he began to translate the broadcasts. The aliens were broadcasting about two dozen different coded messages, so the players began to band together to assemble the translations.

As the different fragments were being assembled, players working on both sides of this mystery realized that the fragmentary messages were related to the alien messages, so websites sprung up within the player community outside the game to work on putting together the two sets of communications. Both the fragments and the alien messages were sending information about the ancient history of the galaxy, which in turn explained what the aliens were doing here. This all began to be unraveled as the story advanced with the next content push, at which time all the old messages were erased, along with all the old fragments, and both were replaced with new messages (with a new code) and additional fragments. At the same time, the aliens turned aggressive and the invasion began in earnest.

—Chris

Deciding What to Tell

As I mentioned earlier, in most stories there are at least some parts of the backstory that tie heavily into the main plot. As a general rule of thumb, if a certain piece of information is important to fully understanding the main story, be sure to include it. If information isn't vital to the main story but explains a lot more about important characters, events, or locals, it's good to include it (though perhaps in an optional form) and it should be fairly easy for players to find and access. Finally, if the information has little to no bearing on the story and is just there to further flesh out the setting, it's nice to include in an optional form, but you shouldn't put much time or effort into it until after you've finished creating the more important story elements.

As always, keep in mind that there are situations where these rules are best broken. In certain types of games – MMOs, for example – players often expect and want a large amount of backstory and supplemental material. In other games, some of which we'll discuss shortly, it may be in your best interest to not reveal even certain parts of the main plot, no matter how important they are.

Case Study: *FINAL FANTASY TACTICS: THE WAR OF THE LIONS*

Developer: Square Enix Co., Ltd.
Publisher: Square Enix, Inc.
Writer: Yasumi Matsuna
System: Sony PSP
Release Date: October 9, 2007 (US)
Genre: Tactical RPG

Original Version: *FINAL FANTASY TACTICS* (PlayStation, 1998; PlayStation Network, 2009)

FIGURE
4.9

History has branded Ramza and Agrais as heretics, but their true story is long forgotten.

In addition to the main numbered entries, the *FINAL FANTASY* series has seen numerous spin-off titles. While some are direct sequels or prequels to other *FINAL FANTASY* games, most focus on new worlds and stories of their own. One of the most popular spin-offs, *FINAL FANTASY TACTICS*, was originally released on the PlayStation (and later rereleased as a downloadable title on the PlayStation Network) where it became a cult classic and went on to inspire a spin-off series of its own (*FINAL FANTASY TACTICS ADVANCE*). *FINAL FANTASY TACTICS: THE WAR OF THE LIONS* is a greatly improved PSP port of the original *FINAL FANTASY TACTICS* that contains new cut-scenes, quests, and game and multiplayer elements, along with an entirely new and vastly superior translation. What sets *FINAL FANTASY TACTICS* apart from the main *FINAL FANTASY* series is its battle system. Best thought of as a combination of a real-time-strategy game and a traditional *FINAL FANTASY* game, battles play out on large grid-based maps and focus heavily on careful strategy and planning in order to succeed. In this game, unlike most normal RPGs, players need to consider terrain, movement and attack ranges, charge time for spells and special attacks, and various other factors in order to be victorious. *FINAL FANTASY TACTICS* also features excellent character and party development in the form of a deep and highly customizable job system. Even now, more than ten years since its original release, *FINAL FANTASY TACTICS* is still considered by many tactical RPG fans to feature some of the best gameplay and character development in the entire genre.

Aside from its excellent gameplay, *FINAL FANTASY TACTICS* is also known for its deep and complex story. The opening starts out with Arazlam Durai, a historian in the country of Ivalice, who is seeking to discover the truth about the War of the Lions, which took place several hundred years before. Though history is quite clear on the events of the war, its heroes, and its villains, there are certain forbidden writings that paint the war and its key players in a much different light. Using his texts, Durai attempts to reconstruct the actual events, and it's within this flashback or re-creation that the majority of the game takes place. The tale is long and complex, focusing on Ramza Beoulve, a young man condemned as a heretic whom Durai believes may have actually been the true hero of the war. The entire story covers several years of time, from the events leading up to the war to its sudden and shocking conclusion, and contains numerous important characters and locations.

FIGURE
4.10

A complex political tale weaves its way throughout the game. © Square Enix, Co., Ltd. All rights reserved.

Between the sheer complexity of the plot and Durai's role as a historian, there's a large amount of backstory and other information available, which is presented in several different ways. The first is optional conversations. Though *FINAL FANTASY TACTICS* doesn't provide fully explorable towns, each town features a tavern where the player can, among other things, choose to listen to the current batch of rumors. Aside from providing information about occasional side-quests, these rumors contain information on local events and history and help explain how the common people are reacting to the war and other important events taking place around them. The player is also given access to an extensive database containing detailed biographies of every character in the game and summaries of important events, all written by Durai. As the story progresses, these writings are updated to reflect the latest information available, providing both a convenient reference and a large amount of supplemental material to better explain the characters' histories, motivations, and roles in the war. Throughout the game, Ramza can also dispatch his party members on various optional quests, some of which result in the discovery of ancient ruins or treasures. These items are given their own database entries as well and serve to further explore Ivalice's rich history while also referencing past *FINAL FANTASY* games. Finally, the player is able to obtain several books about the lives of various key figures in Ivalice's past. Reading these books allows the player to play visual novel games to learn more about these ancient heroes (for an explanation of visual novel games, see Chapter 9). Unfortunately, for unknown reasons, the visual novels were removed from all English releases of *FINAL FANTASY TACTICS*, leaving only one of the books readable. Nevertheless, they were a very unique and clever way to explore Ivalice's history.

Despite the disappointing removal of the visual novels in its English releases, *FINAL FANTASY TACTICS* provides an excellent example of the many different ways in which backstory and other noncritical information can be conveyed to the player in interesting and unobtrusive ways. The extreme popularity of the world of Ivalice, which led it to be used as the setting in several later Square Enix games, also goes to show how delving into the history of your worlds and characters can help them come alive and excite players.

Sometimes a Mystery Is Best

Explaining most of the key story elements in your game is usually the best way to go, but at times you can create a much greater impact and more memorable experience by leaving out a few critical pieces and letting players form their own conclusions. However, leaving out important information while still keeping players happy is a difficult task. First, you need to include enough of the story that players have some idea of what's going on and can form a reasonable guess as to the rest. That guess doesn't have to be correct, and it's perfectly fine if several different players come to several different conclusions, but making sure they have enough information to work with is vital. Without it, they'll likely feel cheated or suppose that you don't know the answers either and were just making things up as you went along. Second, you must ensure that despite any lingering mysteries, the ending still provides the player with a sense of accomplishment and closure. Without those two elements, the story will seem decidedly incomplete and will leave players discontented. Finally, you need to learn which parts of the story are okay to leave hidden and which aren't. Though different people have different opinions on this matter, if you look at enough stories, you'll discover that there are some things you simply can't leave out without angering a large portion of players. For example, you wouldn't want to end a murder mystery without revealing the identity of the killer. However, you could consider leaving the killer's motives or methods a mystery and letting the player piece together the solution.

Unfortunately, deciding what to explain and what to leave out is a very complex subject, so I can't simply give you a list of acceptable mysteries and leave it at that. You should also realize that anything you don't explain in the story is bound to annoy and possibly anger some players. It's really impossible to please everyone. However, if you examine other stories featuring mysterious elements and put a lot of thought into your story structure and what should and shouldn't be left out, you may be able to craft a tale that will keep fans guessing and theorizing for months or even years after its release.

Case Study: *Shadow of the Colossus*

Developer:	Team Ico
Publisher:	Sony Computer Entertainment
Writer:	Fumito Ueda
System:	Sony PlayStation 2
Release Date:	August 6, 2008 (US)
Genre:	Platformer / Puzzle

Shadow of the Colossus is the second title from Team Ico, the creators of the PlayStation 2 cult classic *Ico*. Despite their short track record, Team Ico's games have become well known for their hauntingly beautiful worlds, rousing musical scores, brilliant puzzles, and subtle yet deep storytelling.

In *Shadow of the Colossus*, players take on the role of an unnamed young man who is often referred to as Wanderer. The game opens with Wanderer traveling to a lost valley, where an ancient temple sits. Entering the temple, he lays the body of a girl on the alter and begs Dormin (a mysterious supernatural entity) to bring her back to life. It is for this purpose that he broke the laws of his people and traveled to the forbidden land. Dormin agrees, but only if Wanderer can find and slay the sixteen colossi that roam the land. Wanderer's quest is a mostly solitary affair and focuses entirely on exploring the world and finding and then defeating the colossi. There are no battles or puzzles on the way, putting the primary focus entirely on the colossi battles. The beasts themselves are unique and enormous – many towering several stories into the sky, making Wanderer seem like a mouse or ant in comparison. Finding ways to scale and kill such enormous and powerful creatures provides for what many consider to be some of the best boss battles in the history of video games.

The story is subtle, yet well told. Aside from the opening, ending, and a few brief scenes in between, things are rarely clearly stated. Instead, it's left to the player to see the worry in Wanderer's eyes as he looks at the girl and to watch as his body grows darker and more corrupted as each successive colossus is slain. Without even asking the question, it also forces the players to wonder if what they're doing is really right. The colossi each have their own grace and personality and many seem to be perfectly gentle giants, not even trying to fight back until Wanderer plunges his sword into their bodies. We are told that land itself and Wanderer's attempts to revive the dead are forbidden, and that he is being pursued because of it, but Wanderer's relationship with the girl and the reasons for her death are shrouded in mystery. The months after *Shadow of the Colossus*'s release were filled with talk and speculation among fans about these very questions. Many thought the girl to be Wanderer's sister or lover; others surmised that she was someone he had unjustly killed and the entire quest was an effort to atone for his sins. Dormin's origins and intentions and even the ending itself are also vague and mysterious, leaving many unanswered questions and unsolved mysteries.

However, despite the lack of backstory and context, the story of Wanderer's quest and ultimate fate is fully told. Even though questions were left unanswered, the ending does reveal the ultimate outcome of Wanderer's actions and the consequences for him, Dormin, and the girl. In this way, it completes the story arc that began when Wanderer laid her body on the altar and provides the sense of closure necessary to keep players satisfied, while still leaving enough mysteries to keep them talking and thinking about the story longer after they've seen the credits roll.

Case Study: *Braid*

Developer: Number None, Inc.
Publisher: Number None, Inc.
Writer: Jonathan Blow
System: Microsoft Xbox 360, Sony PlayStation 3, PC
Release Date: October 18, 2005 (US)
Genre: Action Adventure

FIGURE
4.11

A deceptively simple journey.

Jonathan Blow's *Braid* is an independent game created almost solely by Blow himself and artist David Hellman. It was released on the Xbox 360 to surprising critical acclaim and commercial success and later ported to both the PC and PlayStation 3. Since then, it has become a showcase title for both the independent game industry and the argument for video games to be recognized as a legitimate art form.

Braid's story is told primarily in small bits of text contained in books that can be found at the beginning of each world. Though sparse, they hint at a rich tale filled with allusions and metaphors. On the surface, the story is about Tim, a man with the ability to rewind time, who is on a journey to rescue the princess he loves. Unsure of how to find her, he pauses to organize his thoughts and memories in hope of uncovering a previously overlooked clue. Thus begins Tim's journey through a series of beautiful landscapes filled with devilishly clever puzzles that make full use of Tim's time manipulating powers. To further tie the gameplay to the story, each world introduces a different element such as shadowy clones that mimic Tim's actions and a ring he can use to slow time, all of which are related to the part of Tim's story told at the start of that world. In the end, you can never be sure whether the places, creatures, and challenges Tim encounters throughout his adventure are actual memories or metaphorical representations of past events.

As the game progresses, it's slowly revealed that things aren't as simple as they first seemed. Tim isn't merely a heroic friend and his relationship with the princess was far more complex than players are first led to believe. It all leads up to a brilliant final level that really can't be done justice by a few lines of text and must be experienced firsthand.

FIGURE
4.12

What will be revealed when Tim and the Princess finally meet?

The epilogue provides further details about Tim's life and his search, but once again raises far more questions than it answers. However, just as Tim feels that he's made progress by finally sorting through his conflicting thoughts and emotions, the player is also left with a sense of accomplishment. Tim may not have found the princess – and in fact, you can question whether the princess even existed in the first place – but like Tim, the player has completed a difficult journey and come away with something, even if that something is not completely clear. Depending on whom you ask and how you interpret the text and gameplay, *Braid* could be the story of man in a fairy tale trying to rescue a princess, the narrative of a modern man grappling with the course of his life and the decisions he's made, a haunting tale of the dangers of obsession, an allegory about the creation of the atomic bomb, or a clever metaphor on the relationship between the game and the player himself. Perhaps it's all of them or none. With Jonathan Blow refusing to provide a definitive answer, we may never know for sure – but does it really matter? *Braid* weaves its plot threads together into a complex braid of its own, leaving all players to untangle the pattern and decide what Tim's journey means. Regardless of whether the conclusion they come to is "right" or "wrong," it's the correct answer for them, showing what they learned and gained from the experience, and that's far more important than any single meaning or solution that Jonathan Blow could give.

Summary

Games have the power to convey feelings and emotions as well – if not better than – any other form of media. But to tell a story of that caliber, many elements need to be done correctly. The story's flow and pacing need to be adjusted to ensure that sections don't drag on for too long while still providing time for little scenes to help develop the world and characters. The characters themselves also need a considerable amount of attention. Regardless of whether they're based on popular archetypes, they need to speak and act in realistic and believable ways in order for the player to form a close bond with them. The use of backstory to explain the history of your characters and world is also an important element that can add considerable depth to a story. Whether your story is an emotionally charged epic or simply a lighthearted romp, mastering these elements will ensure that players get the most out of your world and characters.

Things to Consider

1. Think of a game you've played that had poor pacing and identify the problem sections.

2. Pick a game you've played recently and try to figure out which archetype each main character belongs to. Do the characters follow that archetype for the entire story or do they change partway through?

3. Think of a game character that behaves in an unbelievable way. What does he or she do or not do that makes the character seem unbelievable or unrealistic?

4. Of all the games you've played, which had the most creative or interesting way of telling its backstory? What made it stand out?

5. Do you prefer games that answer every question or ones that leave some mysteries for you to think about? Why do you prefer that style?

Five

Making Stories Emotional

One of the hallmarks of a good story is the way it makes the player (or reader or viewer) feel. You want the player to feel fear when the heroes are in danger, triumph when they succeed, and sadness when they fall. Naturally, some people are more easily affected than others. I'm sure you all know someone (whether a friend, family member, or even yourself) who is easily swept up in the moment when playing games, reading books, or watching movies and often screams, laughs, and cries as the story plays out. I'm sure you also know people who can sit through those same stories stone faced with little to no hint of outward emotion, though that doesn't necessarily mean they aren't feeling the emotions – just that they're better at suppressing them. In the end, a good writer can reasonably expect the majority of the audience to feel specific emotions at specific points in the story.

Connecting with the Characters

So why are emotions so important? It's just a story, right? Yes, but the entire point of stories is to let us experience other places and other lives. When we feel sympathy for a tragic heroine or deep hatred for a villain, it proves just how much a part of the story we've become. We're no longer just observing a fictional event; to us, the place and characters have become alive and real. They're not strangers on a page – they're our friends, companions, and enemies, and as such, we truly care what happens to them.

Not all stories achieve this level of involvement. Some never even try and instead strive to be merely enjoyable without forming any sort of complex emotional attachment. And there's nothing wrong with that. As I've said before, there's room in the world for all types of stories. Heavy emotional tales are good, but at times people just want to sit back and be entertained.

Case Study: *Metal Gear Solid 3: Snake Eater*

Developer: Konami
Publisher: Konami
Writers: Hideo Kojima, Tomokazu Fukushima, Shuyo Murata
System: Sony PlayStation 2
Release Date: November 17, 2004 (US)
Genre: Stealth Action
Other Version: *Metal Gear Solid 3: Subsistence* (PlayStation 2, 2006)

FIGURE
5.1

Snake's mission requires him to remain alone and unseen.

Metal Gear Solid 3: Snake Eater is the fifth game in the *Metal Gear* series, but acts as a prequel, trading the near-future setting of the other titles for the Cold War era of 1964. At the start, an American covert agent code-named Naked Snake (a father of sorts to Solid Snake, the hero of most of the other games) is sent into a remote part of the Russian wilderness to help evacuate a Soviet scientist who wants to defect to the United States. However, the mission quickly falls apart when Snake's mentor, The Boss (a woman revered as the mother of the American special forces), defects, takes two small nuclear warheads with her, and joins Colonel Volgin, leader of a rogue faction within the USSR. In order to prove the innocence of the United States in the resulting nuclear strike and prevent an all-out war, Snake is tasked with stopping Volgin's plans and eliminating The Boss.

With the exception of the superhuman powers used by a handful of villains and a few instances of technology that seems a little ahead of its time, *Snake Eater*'s plot remains realistic and historically accurate. But the intricacies of the Cold War, nuclear deterrents, and secret weapon development take backstage to the goals and emotions of the characters themselves.

Snake is strongly conflicted about his mission. Though he understands that killing The Boss is necessary to prevent an all-out nuclear war, he's naturally upset at the thought of murdering his longtime friend and mentor. He also finds himself consumed with the question of why a woman who had dedicated her entire life to the service of her country has chosen to defect. From the mysterious double agent Eva to the members of The Boss's Cobra Unit (each of which has named himself after the single emotion that consumes him when in battle), and Snake's helpful yet eccentric radio support team, each character is interesting and memorable. The characters have a goal that drives them and a backstory explaining how those goals came about. In the end, even the more outlandish characters like the electricity-shooting Volgin feel quite real and believable.

FIGURE
5.2

The Boss's betrayal deeply affects Snake.

In the center of it all lies the relationship between Snake and The Boss, leading to an emotionally charged debate about the importance of loyalty and to whom or what that loyalty should be given before the two engage in their final battle. When the game pauses, waiting for the player to pull the trigger one final time to end her life, the player can feel the conflict and sorrow filling Snake's mind. Over the course of the game, it has become clear just how close he and The Boss were, and that whatever her reason for defecting, killing her is a mistake – but unavoidable. The shocking revelation that follows, explaining the true goal and purpose of The Boss's final mission, adds even more to Snake's and the player's conflicted feelings, leading up to a highly emotional ending as Snake ignores the honor and accolades given to him by the government to instead stand before The Boss's grave, saluting the woman who was, above all else, a true patriot.

Players have often cited *Snake Eater*'s ending as one of the most emotional moments in gaming, yet the ending has such a strong impact only because the rest of the story spent so much time building up the characters and their relationships. Without knowledge of Snake's feelings, The Boss's dedication, and the heavy stakes riding on their missions, all of which are carefully explained and developed over the course of the game, the ending would lose much of its impact and nearly all of its emotion. As *Snake Eater* shows, it's only by taking significant time and effort to make players care about the characters that any serious emotional connection and impact can be made.

The Fine Line Between Drama and Melodrama

Many of you are likely wondering exactly what melodrama is. Essentially, a melodrama is a story that features clearly defined and highly stereotypical good and evil roles (often so much so that they're rather ridiculous). For example, a classic melodramatic hero will dress all in white and be the perfect saint and gentleman, kind and compassionate to everyone he meets, without any selfish thoughts or vices. His enemy, the classic melodramatic villain, will dress in black with a monocle and curly mustache and be completely mean, rotten, and dishonest in everything he does. A true melodrama rarely – if ever – contains moral shades of gray, and the villain always loses. Classic examples of melodrama include the 1965 film *The Great Race* and many old cartoons such as *Wacky Races* (itself inspired by *The Great Race*).

Nowadays, however, full melodramas are extremely rare and the term is more often used to describe plot twists and overacting that are taken to the point of near absurdity. Soap operas, for example, are often called melodramatic. In the realm of games, *FINAL FANTASY IV* can be considered somewhat melodramatic as well. The most blatant examples of melodrama in the game are the way the hero's party members frequently sacrifice themselves in heroic ways in order to save their friends, only to turn up later in the game alive and well (with one notable exception). The revelation that hero Cecil's former best friend turned enemy, Kain, is being controlled by a villain named Golbez, who (it is later revealed) is actually Cecil's brother, is not evil, and is being controlled by the real villain Zemus (who, depending on how you interpret the ending, can be considered to be merely a pawn of the dark spirit Zeromus) is rather melodramatic as well.

Though melodrama is often looked down upon, there's nothing necessarily wrong with using it. Soap operas maintain loyal followings despite their over reliance on clichés and melodrama and some *FINAL FANTASY* fans still consider *IV* to be the best entry in the series. Melodrama can also be put to great use in comedies, where overacting and ridiculous plot twists can make for a lot of hilarious situations. If you're trying to tell a particularly deep and moving story, however, too much melodrama is almost certain to cause a negative impact.

To avoid melodrama, it's important to make your characters act and speak in believable ways. I previously explained how it's important that characters don't underreact to events; it's just as important that they don't overreact, either. For example, though the death of a loved one could potentially lead to an angry, tearful lament, something less traumatic such as a stolen wallet or broken arm probably shouldn't. Also, try to avoid reusing the same plot twist multiple times in a story, especially if it's a clichéd one. Every villain doesn't need to be related to the hero or be mind controlled by someone else. Once is usually enough!

Making the Player Cry

Of all the emotional reactions people can have to stories, being moved to tears is often seen as the most intense and hardest to achieve. As discussed earlier, some people react to stories more easily than others and cry often, but creating a story that can actually make most of its audience cry is a very difficult thing. Not only does the event have to be particularly sad and moving, but the audience also needs to have formed a very strong bond with the characters for them to feel that sadness strongly enough that they themselves start crying. Though very hard to achieve, creating a story that can make the majority of its audience cry is a mark of good writing and character design.

Always Be Specific

One common mistake young writers make when they design characters is to make them general instead of specific. They fear that if the character is too specific, it will feel to the audience as if this is someone so unique that they couldn't possibly relate to them which will alienate the character from the audience. Nothing could be further from the truth.

One very unique character in recent film history is Forrest Gump. He is perhaps one of the most unique and quirky characters to inhabit modern cinema, yet the film was a big hit and the character was universally hailed as a great hero and extremely likeable. To a large part, that was due to the portrayal of the character by Tom Hanks, as he delivered the performance truthfully and honestly. But the biggest success of the character was his humanity, expressing his emotions through his actions, his inability to be brave except when put to the test, and his emotional honesty (again when forced). I'd bet that when his character was described in early meetings, there was great concern people wouldn't like him or be able to relate to him. But his unique, specific character was perhaps the greatest charm of the film.

—Chris

Before we go any further I should probably point out that although good stories can make their audience cry, a story doesn't have to make people cry in order to be good. There are many excellent stories that simply don't have the type of extremely sad and emotionally charged scenes that could bring someone to tears. These scenes aren't missing because the writer wasn't good enough to create them, but simply because they aren't necessary for the story. For example, though many people consider the original *Star Wars* trilogy and *Harry Potter and the Sorcerer's Stone* to have excellent stories, no one would say that they're the types of stories that should make you cry (some of the later *Harry Potter* books and *Star Wars* movies, perhaps, but not these titles in particular). However, I've yet to hear anyone deride or criticize them for not trying to make their audience cry. Such tearful scenes don't fit within those stories, so they aren't there – nothing strange or unusual about it.

In the end, though, making people cry is often considered the hallmark or pinnacle of good storytelling. So if you ask people who are critical of video game storytelling (whether inside or outside the game industry) why game stories aren't just as good as those in books or films, you'll probably hear the response, "Because they don't make you cry." But is this really a valid criticism? As I just explained, it's perfectly possible to tell an excellent story without making people cry. Furthermore, why is it so easy to believe that games can't move people to tears just like books or movies? If games don't make you cry, that doesn't mean game storytelling is poorly done or immature – it just means that you're playing the wrong games.

Sure, you're unlikely to see anyone burst into tears while playing *Counter Strike* or *Super Mario Bros.*, but as well made and popular as those games are, they aren't in any way known for their deep, emotional storylines. Similarly, most books and movies don't make people cry either – it's all about looking at the right titles. A bit of time spent on game message boards or talking to gamers will reveal that many games have in fact made people cry. The aforementioned *Metal Gear Solid 3: Snake Eater* is frequently mentioned, as is its sequel *Metal Gear Solid 4: Guns of the Patriots* (which we'll talk about in Chapter 7). *Shadow of the Colossus* and various *FINAL FANTASY* games (especially *VII*, *X*, and *CRISIS CORE*) have also brought many players to tears. And those are just a few of the most popular examples.

For a more personal example, and to avoid embarrassing anyone I know, here are my own experiences on the matter. As I said in the first chapter, I love stories. At pretty much any given time, I'm in the middle of at least one book, one game, and one television show – the vast majority of which I pick up primarily for their stories. And as my friends and family can attest, I really get into the stories I read, watch, and play and can easily spend hours discussing them and mulling over their characters, twists, and implications. Despite that, I don't tend to show much emotion when reading, watching, or playing. I feel the emotions – I just tend to keep my feelings inside. There are plenty of stories that have left me happy and elated and lots of others that tied my stomach in knots and cast a cloud of depression over the rest of my day, but it's extremely rare for a story to hit me so hard that I actually cheer, shout, or cry because of it. In fact, over the last ten years, I can only think of four stories that have made me cry (though several others came very close). One was a book, one was a movie, and two were video games (*Metal Gear Solid 4* and *CRISIS CORE*, if you're curious). Because of both my own experiences and the things I've heard from so many other gamers, I simply can't believe that game storytelling isn't good enough to make people cry. Anyone who thinks that way clearly needs to play more games.

Case Study: *CRISIS CORE – FINAL FANTASY VII*

Developer:	Square Enix Co., Ltd.
Publisher:	Square Enix, Inc.
Writers:	Hideki Imaizumi, Kazushige Nojima
System:	Sony PSP
Release Date:	March 25, 2008 (US)
Genre:	Action RPG

FIGURE
5.3

Sephiroth! Have you completely lost your mind?

CRISIS CORE: **Prior to Sephiroth's betrayal, he and Zack often worked together.**
© **Square Enix, Co., Ltd. All rights reserved.**

Even after thirteen years, *FINAL FANTASY VII* (which we'll discuss in Chapter 6) remains one of the most popular and beloved entries in the series. This continued popularity eventually led to a collection of spin-offs, prequels, and sequels dubbed *COMPILATION OF FINAL FANTASY VII*, which included the CG movie *FINAL FANTASY VII: ADVENT CHILDREN* and the PlayStation 2 game *DIRGE OF CERBERUS: FINAL FANTASY VII*. Though some parts of the compilation met with mixed reviews, *CRISIS CORE – FINAL FANTASY VII* received near-universal acclaim and is generally considered to be the best entry in the entire compilation. In addition to featuring impressive graphics and music, *CRISIS CORE's* fast gameplay and moving story were also the subject of considerable praise.

Set several years before the beginning of *FINAL FANTASY VII*, *Crisis Core – FINAL FANTASY VII* tells the story of Shinra soldier Zack Fair. Zack was first introduced in *FINAL FANTASY VII* though relatively little information about him was revealed. Going into *CRISIS CORE*, fans knew that Zack was a Soldier First Class (the highest rank of Shinra's elite Soldier division and the same one held by *FINAL FANTASY VII's* villain Sephiroth) and that he was present during the destruction of the town of Nibelheim. After leaving Soldier, Zack was latter gunned down by three Shinra troopers when returning to Midgar.

One of the most powerful aspects of *CRISIS CORE – FINAL FANTASY VII's* story is that many players enter into it fully knowing Zack's eventual fate. However, over the course of the game Zack is revealed to be not just another soldier, but a caring young man determined to help others and be a hero, as he feels every Soldier should be. As Zack completes missions and rises through the ranks, growing closer to attaining his dream, he makes friends and enemies, faces a shocking betrayal, and is even faced with the dark sides of Soldier and the Shinra Company. Zack's reactions to each of these life-changing events shake his faith in others and himself, but despite it all, he still manages to cling to his beliefs and push on, determined to be the kind of hero his family, friends, and former mentor Angeal can be proud of. Because of his determination, friendly attitude, dedication to his duty and his friends, and the way he handles his many trials and disappointments, Zack is a very likable character, making the knowledge of his eventual fate all the harder to accept.

FIGURE
5.4

Zack passes on his sword and dreams to Cloud, the hero of *FINAL FANTASY VII*.

As the game nears its close with the traitorous Genesis defeated, Zack and Cloud, now on the run from Shinra forces who wish to completely bury the truth about what happened in Nibelheim, make their way toward Midgar. The experiments performed on them have left Cloud in a near vegetative state, but Zack refuses to abandon him and even spends the ride to Midgar describing how he plans to earn enough money to support them both until Cloud recovers. Unfortunately, it's not to be, as Zack is thrust into an impossible final battle in a desperate attempt to win freedom for himself and Cloud (a tense and epic event, only the smallest part of which was shown in *FINAL FANTASY VII*). In a very nice touch, the player is allowed to control Zack during this last hopeless fight, significantly increasing his immersion and personal investment in the event. The combination of Zack's inevitable fate, his desperate will to survive and the player's will to keep him alive (as demonstrated in the final battle), the haunting music, and Zack's final words make for one of the most emotional moments I've encountered in any story – and prove that games do indeed hold the power to make people cry.

Summary

A good story works on the player's emotions, causing him or her to feel joy and sadness along with the heroes. However, for players to become emotionally invested in a story, they have to connect with the characters, which is why it's so important to create deep and believable heroes and villains. As important as it is to create an emotional experience, you need to ensure that you don't go overboard with the big emotional moments and turn your story into a melodrama.

When a player has a deep emotional investment in a story, certain events can even move that person to tears. Making people cry is a mark, but not a requirement, of good writing. Though powerful, not every story needs a tearjerker scene. Though some people argue that game storytelling hasn't reached the point where it can make people cry, many gamers will be quick to refute such claims. Games, just like every other form of storytelling, can make you cry – you just need to play the right ones.

Things to Consider

1. List three games in which you felt a particularly deep connection with one or more characters. What was it about those characters that appealed to you?

2. What do you have in common with those characters (upbringing, personality, beliefs, etc.)? In what ways are you different?

3. Can you think of any games you've played that were especially melodramatic? Briefly describe the three most melodramatic stories and discuss how you would improve them.

4. List some stories (video games or otherwise) that have made you cry. What parts of them did you find particularly moving and why?

Six

Defining Interactive and Player-Driven Storytelling

What Makes a Story Interactive?

If you were to ask a room full of writers, game designers, and English professors for the definition of "interactive storytelling," you'd get quite a lot of different answers. Video games would be a popular one, but I've also heard people classify things like pop-up books and novels with upside-down text as interactive. The more you research notable opinions on the subject, the more you'll realize that there is no official consensus as to what is or is not an interactive story. By some definitions, nothing short of *Star Trek*'s holodeck would qualify; by others, virtually everything is interactive storytelling as long as you have to turn a page or push a button from time to time.

Is It Interactive?

One of the illusions of the "interactive" age is that great art is not interactive. Okay, so indeed not all art has buttons to click or hyperlinks to follow, but all deep and long-lasting art is participatory in some fashion. Whether it simply evokes an emotion in the viewer or alternatively invites analysis to truly understand the work itself, any art that lasts is multilayered and reveals more upon each repeated examination. To me, this is the very essence of interactivity: the invitation to probe deeper. The technique of the MDQ is not limited to storytelling. Visual arts, such as painting, use the same technique. Is Mona Lisa smiling? What is she smiling about? Who is she? Is Shelley's poem *Ozymandias* about Ramses the Great or about the shifting nature of time and power? Or both? We can debate these things at length, and we can each have our own opinion, and that is what makes art participatory. Art evokes reaction in the audience, which is in part what makes gaming a wonderful medium for artists. The invitation to participate is evident and needed for enjoyment of the art. Games are just more up front about the process than most historical forms have been.

—Chris

Finding the true meaning of interactive storytelling among all the arguments and conflicting definitions can be confusing, so let's think about it logically. First, the terms "interactive storytelling" and "interactive stories" imply that you can in some way interact with the story. That seems obvious enough. But what does it mean to interact with a story? Mark Z. Danielewski's rather unusual novel *House of Leaves*, for example, is frequently cited by English professors as an example of interactive storytelling, but is that really the case? *House of Leaves* features many strange aspects, including its "story within a story" structure; a plethora of footnotes (referencing a variety of real and fictitious sources); coded messages; and text that's written upside down, sideways, and in twisting spiral patterns. But does reading footnotes and turning the book from side to side mean you're interacting with the story? Of course not. You're not interacting with the story – you're interacting with the book itself. Just like turning the pages in a regular novel or pausing a DVD, your actions have no bearing whatsoever on the story. No matter how you read *House of Leaves*, you can never have any sort of effect on or interaction with the characters or the setting, so it really can't be called an interactive story. Pop-up books are the same. Although they offer additional ways for readers to interact with the book itself, the story remains firmly noninteractive.

On the opposite end, to be interactive, a story doesn't need to give the player complete and total control over how everything plays out. Players just need to be able to directly interact with the story in some way, shape, or form, regardless of whether their interactions have a significant effect on the story. For example, *CRISIS CORE – FINAL FANTASY VII* (which we discussed in Chapter 5) is an interactive story. On the one hand, no matter what actions the player takes, he or she is unable to change the way the main story plays out. Zack will still meet the same characters, make the same friends and enemies, experience the same triumphs and failures, and suffer the same fate – no matter what the player does. But that doesn't mean that the story isn't interactive. Between those important unchangeable scenes, Zack is free to explore the city; talk to other characters to learn more about them, the world, and current events; and engage in a variety of optional missions, many of which contain additional information about the story and the world where it takes place. Furthermore, without the player's help fighting battles, creating new equipment, and so on, Zack would never be able to complete his adventure. So even though the player can't significantly alter the story, he or she can still interact with it and its characters in many different ways. It's this interaction with the world and characters that makes a story interactive, regardless of whether those interactions have any real effect on the main plot.

What Makes a Story Player-Driven?

Player-driven storytelling is a term I coined (though I wouldn't be surprised if others were using it before me) to differentiate stories that are merely interactive from ones in which the player is given a more significant role in their progression and outcome. To state it simply, if an interactive story is one in which the players can in some way interact with the story, a player-driven story is one in which, through their interactions, players can alter the story in significant ways. By definition, all player-driven stories are interactive, but not all interactive stories are player-driven.

Of course, there are many different types of player-driven stories, all of which offer different levels and types of interaction. In some, the player's impact on the story may be fairly minimal or limited to a single important decision; in others, the player may be given an enormous amount of control over the story's progression and outcome. Knowing about the different types of player-driven stories will help you better understand the structure of current game stories and decide which type or types fit best with the stories you want to create.

Interactive Storytelling as a Spectrum

Because there are many types of interactive and player-driven storytelling, it helps to have a way to classify them for easy analysis and discussion. However, every single story can't be neatly fit into a box. All the styles overlap in many ways, and often a particular story will skirt the line between different styles, making it difficult to classify. To better understand the many types of player-driven storytelling, it's best not to think of the different styles as separate entities, but rather points on a larger storytelling spectrum.

My storytelling spectrum begins with the most traditional, unchanging, and noninteractive form of storytelling on the left. As we move toward the right, stories become more open and player-driven until we get to the very end, at which point the player is in complete and total control over the story. Along the way, I've marked key types of storytelling. All of these except fully traditional storytelling (at the far left end) are used frequently in video games and can be roughly defined as the five main forms of game storytelling. We'll cover each of these storytelling styles in depth in later chapters, but for now, here's a brief overview of all of them.

FIGURE
6.1

The Interactive Storytelling Spectrum

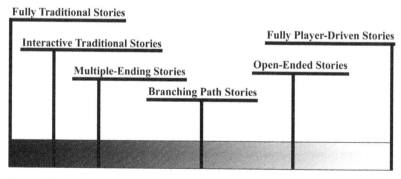

Storytelling as a spectrum.

A Camel Is a Horse Designed by Committee

The idea that stories can be created by multiple people all at once is a controversial subject. One of the aspects audiences have historically enjoyed the most about stories is surprise. Surprise is also one of the most delicious aspects of game playing. Randomness is a tool that can deliver surprise to a game audience. In fact, our storytelling brain will try and connect disparate events and make "sense" of them. Artful use of this tendency within interactive stories can be a real challenge, as writers often want to be in total control, so as to make the most of the audience's attention span. If multiple people tell a story, the whole can be greater than the sum of the parts, if each author in turn writes, for example, one chapter in succession after the others. Everyone gets to be author and audience at once. In "open worlds," even if the players have total control, I believe there has to be some author who has the big picture in mind (remember the way we architected the meta puzzle in *Earth & Beyond*). Then the players can explore and discover, but at the end of the day there is *something* to be uncovered that was created by the writer. I do not believe "random" content creation is capable of anything deep and interesting.

—Chris

Fully Traditional Stories

As the most traditional form of storytelling, fully traditional stories (see Chapter 7) are entirely noninteractive. No matter how many times they're read or watched, they remain exactly the same without any changes. Though most books and movies make use of fully traditional storytelling, its nature makes it wholly unsuited to video games. There have been some attempts at creating games using fully traditional stories, but it's debatable whether the results can truly be called games due to their complete lack of interactivity.

Examples include *Harry Potter and the Sorcerer's Stone*, the *Star Wars* movies, and the visual novel *Higurashi When They Cry*.

Interactive Traditional Stories

As the most traditional type of interactive storytelling, interactive traditional stories (see Chapter 7) allow players some degree of freedom to interact with the world and characters. However, no matter how much control the player has over other aspects of the game and story, the main plot can't be changed in any significant way.

Examples include *FINAL FANTASY XIII*, *Metal Gear Solid 3: Snake Eater*, and *Lunar Silver Star Harmony*.

Multiple-Ending Stories

Multiple-ending stories (see Chapter 8), despite being nearly identical to interactive traditional stories, are the first truly player-driven form of storytelling on the spectrum. What sets them apart is that the player is allowed to choose between two or more different endings. Depending on the game, this choice might be a conscious decision or one made automatically based on the player's actions.

Examples include *CHRONO TRIGGER*, *Castlevania: Dawn of Sorrow*, and *Bioshock*.

Branching Path Stories

Multiple-ending stories only allow the player to change the main plot in a single (though important) way; branching path stories (see Chapter 9) provide the player with a series of choices to make throughout the course of the story. Some choices may change the story only slightly; others can have an enormous impact, sending the main plot off in entirely different directions.

Examples include *Choose Your Own Adventure* books, *Fate/Stay Night*, and *Heavy Rain*.

Open-Ended Stories

Open-ended stories (see Chapter 10) can best be thought of as highly complex branching path stories. They feature far more decision points, and those decision points tend to be much less obvious than in branching path stories, with the story's direction chosen more by the player's actions than his or her response to specific prompts.

Examples include *Fable II*, *The Elder Scrolls III: Morrowind*, and *Fallout 3*.

Fully Player-Driven Stories

Set on the far right of the spectrum, fully player-driven stories (see Chapter 11) offer the players total or near total control of their actions. They are allowed, for the most part, to do whatever they want whenever they want. Because of this, there is usually only a very basic main plot, if any. Instead, the player is provided with a setting and his or her actions within that setting form a story of their own.

Examples include *The Sims*, *Animal Crossing*, and tabletop RPGs (such as *Dungeons & Dragons*).

These storytelling styles are all used in games, some far more frequently than others. We'll discuss the specific reasons behind why some styles are used much more or less than others in future chapters; for now, just keep in mind that interactive traditional stories are the most common by far, with multiple-ending stories second, then branching path stories, and fully player-driven stories and open-ended stories occupying the next two slots (though it's rather hard to say which is the more common of the two). Finally, fully traditional stories are extremely rare (almost nonexistent) in games due to their noninteractive nature.

How Stories Are Classified

As you can probably see from the previous descriptions, I classify games based primarily on how much the player can affect the main plot. But because storytelling is a spectrum, some games naturally sit between the more clearly defined points, making them hard to categorize definitively as a specific storytelling style. *Grand Theft Auto IV*, for example, has many of the characteristics of an open-ended story, with its wide open city and plethora of optional mission chains, activities, and characters to try and befriend. However, in other ways it's closer to a branching path or even multiple-ending story, with only a handful of points where the main plot can be changed – especially because all of those changes except the last (which determines the ending) are fairly minor with few (if any) lasting effects. Similarly, games such as *Heavy Rain* and *Mass Effect* seem to offer the player a large amount of freedom and a variety of ways to change the story, making them look like open-ended stories. But upon further examination, it becomes apparent that most of the choices given to the player are far less important than they initially appear and have little to no real effect on the main plot, making the stories far less player-driven than it would first appear.

Classifying player-driven stories is far from an exact science; there were a few games that could have easily ended up in either of two categories. But I've done my best to study each game mentioned in this book and place them in the proper storytelling categories.

Games Without Stories

Games that lack stories entirely are far less common today than they were in the early days of arcade machines and the Atari 2600, but there are still many modern games – some of which are extremely popular – that don't have stories. Sports games, for example, rarely have stories, and neither do puzzle, music, fitness, and brain-training games. It could be argued that the addition of stories would improve these games, and in fact several very successful story-based games have been released in each of those genres. However, history has shown quite clearly that some types of games simply don't need stories in order to appeal to their fans. We'll probably continue to see more story-based games released in these genres over time, but it's unlikely that stories will ever become a key feature the way they have in other genres.

Summary

There's a lot of debate in the professional world about what makes a story interactive. However, it's necessary to differentiate between actually interacting with the story (the world, characters, etc.) and merely interacting with the medium (reading upside-down text in a book, skipping chapters on a DVD, etc.). Also, just because a story is interactive doesn't mean that it's truly player-driven. A story is player-driven only if the player is given some degree of control over the story itself. The amount and type of influence the player has on the main plot determine just how player-driven a story really is.

The best way to think of interactive and player-driven storytelling is as a spectrum containing six primary types of storytelling: fully traditional storytelling, interactive traditional storytelling, multiple-ending storytelling, branching path storytelling, open-ended storytelling, and fully player-driven storytelling. However, because storytelling is a spectrum, some stories don't fit perfectly within any single style.

Finally, it's important to remember that as much as a good story can add to a game of any type, many games – particularly those in certain genres – are fully capable of providing a fun and entertaining experience without any story at all.

Things to Consider

1. Other than video games, what are some things that you consider to be interactive stories?

2. List one game you've played (other than the examples listed in this chapter) for every major type of storytelling on the spectrum. (It's okay if you can't think of any games with a fully traditional story.)

3. Why do you think some types of storytelling are used much more often than others? Make a note of your answer and see how it compares with the reasons discussed later in this book.

4. List several games you've played that don't have any stories. Do you think the addition of stories would significantly improve them? Why or why not?

Seven

Fully Traditional and Interactive Traditional Stories

For the next several chapters, we'll discuss the different types of storytelling shown on the spectrum in detail, along with their uses in games, including the advantages, disadvantages, and specific challenges involved in their creation. In this chapter, we'll cover fully traditional and interactive traditional stories, as they share a similar structure, with interactive traditional stories building on the foundations set by fully traditional stories.

Fully Traditional Stories

FIGURE
7.1

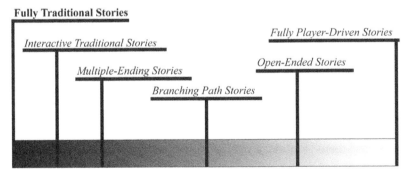

Fully traditional storytelling.

Fully traditional stories are the classic form of storytelling, which has been used for centuries. Films, books, plays, and cave paintings are all examples of fully traditional storytelling. The defining characteristic that sets them apart from the other

125

types of storytelling covered in this book is that fully traditional stories are entirely noninteractive. The "player" isn't a player at all, but rather a viewer who can only watch as scenes unfold. No matter how many times the story is watched or read, it remains unchanged.

Keep in Mind the Nature of Drama

One aspect of storytelling, as mentioned elsewhere, is that dramatic stories (film, plays, and – dare I say – games) all differ fundamentally from fiction in two very important ways. First, in a dramatic story, the story takes place in front of the audience member; the audience member watches the story. This setup has a huge effect, because the audience member's imagination as to what characters look like, how they gesture, and what the environments in which the story take place look like are all decided by the creative team for the piece. You've probably heard people say, after they've left the theater having seen a film that was based upon a book, "It looked better in my head." When the audience experiences this effect, it can jolt them out of the story in an unfortunate way. With an original dramatic work, elements like the way it looks and which actor was cast to play which part either work or don't on their own merits. Thus, one aspect of traditional interactivity in "words on paper" fiction is taken away in drama. This aspect also has the secondary effect of not allowing the audience to hear characters think, which is often done in fiction. There is no way in drama for the audience to perceive hidden motivation (for example, whether a character is lying) unless they see it through the character's actions.

The second aspect that makes dramatic stories different is that they are time-bound. The story unfolds at a specific rate (determined by the authors) and the audience must keep up. This aspect is a serious writing challenge that is not present in fiction, because when the author must, for comprehension reasons, make sure that the audience *sees* and *understands* something, he or she uses very specific techniques to maximize the chances of understanding. Dramatic writers often talk about something "landing," which translates to "did the audience get the point?" Also, one of the writing techniques used in drama is keeping one step ahead of the audience, so they don't figure out the story ahead of the writer. In fiction, readers have total control over the method they use to consume the story. They can go and read the last page if they wish, spoiling the surprise, because there is so much richness in the language of the story that it is often enjoyable to read even if you know the ending. Not so with drama.

This time-bound nature also changes the dynamics of the audience. Dramatic writers must keep the audience engaged; if they grow bored, they do things like change the channel. If readers of a book get bored, they can put the book down and resume later (as long as the book isn't *too* boring) or they can skip to the end of the chapter. The dramatic writer is constantly striving to set up the audience with a question, answer the question, set up another, and so on in order to keep tension high and release it all at the end of the story. These are very different writing challenges.

—Chris

Although the viewer of a fully traditional story may have the ability to flip to the back of a book or skip through chapters on a DVD, thereby experiencing the story out of order, this can't be considered truly interactive. First and foremost, doing so does not actually change the story, but merely the order in which the viewer sees it. Second, as discussed in Chapter 6, when a person turns pages or fast-forwards through movies, that person is not actually interacting with the story's world or characters but instead with the medium containing the story (the book or DVD). Nothing the viewer does can change the story itself.

Fully traditional storytelling has a rich history and is the style used to tell the world's most-loved and well-known stories. *Harry Potter and the Sorcerer's Stone* and the *Star Wars* movies, for example, are both fully traditional stories, as are ancient tales such as the *Iliad*, *Romeo and Juliet*, and the legend of Hercules. Story-tellers have spent thousands of years creating and refining the techniques used in fully traditional storytelling, creating a very mature and perfected style that is suitable for telling stories of any length and genre. The strength and beauty of fully traditional stories is that the writer is always in full control of the experience. Because of this, the author can shape the scenes in order to convey exactly the events and emotions he or she wants at exactly the right time. Ensuring proper pacing and keeping characters consistent and believable is far easier in fully traditional storytelling than in any of the other styles we'll discuss. The only problem is that in their pure form, fully traditional stories can't be used in video games.

Fully Traditional Stories, Video Games, and Why They Don't Mix

Video games are, by nature, a medium dedicated to interaction. Whether it's shooting aliens, pushing crates, talking to townspeople, or rearranging colored gems, all true video games are designed around letting the player interact with their world, characters, and story. The types of interactions allowed and the effect they have on the rest of the game vary significantly, but some level of interactivity is always there.

As such, the concept of fully traditional storytelling and that of video games are innately opposed. There have been some attempts at creating games that use fully traditional stories, but without interaction, is a video game really a video game? In the end, it would probably be more proper to call these "games" movies or digital novels. But that doesn't mean that they don't have good stories in and of themselves, with their own unique advantages – they just aren't true games.

Case Study: *Higurashi When They Cry*

Developer: 07th Expansion
Publisher: 07th Expansion
Writer: Ryukishi07
System: PC
Release Date: August 10, 2002 (Japan)
Genre: Visual Novel

FIGURE
7.2

At first glance, the village of Hinamizawa seems like a peaceful place.

Despite being one of Japan's most popular visual novel games, *Higurashi When They Cry* has a very important difference that sets it apart from the rest of the genre. Unlike normal visual novels, which feature complex branching path stories, *Higurashi* is one of the rare games that uses fully traditional storytelling (for a more detailed look at the visual novel genre and its storytelling methods, see Chapter 9).

As a visual novel, *Higurashi*'s story is told primarily via pages of text, like a book written in the first person. However, the text is displayed atop background images of the main character's current location and also features illustrations of the other characters, along with sound effects and a full musical score, making the story far more of an audiovisual experience than an ordinary novel. The player's only form of interaction is clicking the mouse to advance the text, clearly separating it from other visual novels in which the player takes a much more active role in the story.

Higurashi spans eight separate games (or story arcs), which were released individually over the course of four years. It went on to become a major hit in Japan, spawning novels, comics, an animated TV series, multiple live-action movies, and several ports and spin-off games, along with a wide assortment of merchandise. However, like almost all visual novels, *Higurashi* wasn't released outside Japan, though both the anime (cartoon) and manga (comic) were translated and released in the United States. Recently, however, the original *Higurashi* games were finally made available in English by the European company MangaGamer, allowing the English-speaking world to experience the story the way it was meant to be told.

Set in Japan in the mid 1980s, *Higurashi* follows teenager Keiichi Maebara, whose family recently left behind the hustle and bustle of Tokyo to move to the quiet mountain village of Hinamizawa. Keiichi quickly finds himself growing fond of his new life and becomes good friends with four of the girls in his school: the highly competitive Mion, the friendly and helpful Rena, the crafty Satoko, and the cute and resourceful Rika. The five of them make up the school's "unbeatable" club and are constantly challenging each other in all manner of crazy games and activities. *Higurashi*'s first arc, Onikakushi (which can be translated as Spirited Away by Demons), begins innocently enough, with Keiichi and his friends engaging in a series of enjoyable activities as the village's annual Watanagashi festival draws near. These early chapters serve as an introduction to Keiichi, the girls, and the village itself, and are a lot of fun to read due to the likable characters and amusing situations they find themselves in. However, Hinamizawa isn't quite the tranquil place that it seems. Things begin to go wrong when Keiichi learns that for the past four years, on the night of Watanagashi, one person has turned up dead and another has mysteriously disappeared shortly thereafter. Supposedly, all the crimes have been solved and the timing was just a coincidence. However, when visiting photographer Tomitake is discovered the night of the festival with his throat scratched out, the series of murders and rumors about the mysterious curse of Oyashiro are suddenly much harder to ignore. Determined to learn more about Tomitake's death, Keiichi ends up in over his head when his friends start acting strangely and he finds himself being shadowed by an unknown presence. To make matters worse, he becomes the victim of several near-fatal attacks, all designed to seem like simple accidents but hinting at a much darker intent.

FIGURE
7.3

The village and its inhabitants harbor many dark secrets.

I won't say what happens next, but Keiichi's story doesn't end well and leaves a lot of unanswered questions. In a very interesting twist, rather than continue the story where it left off, the second and third arc cover the exact same period of time – immediately before and after the Watanagashi festival. However, events play out differently each time, leading to new but just as tragic outcomes, with the fourth arc acting as both a prequel and epilogue to the others. Throughout this portion of the story, the player is faced with a myriad of mysteries, few of which are answered, and begins to learn of Hinamizawa's dark past. Because of this, the first four arcs are known as question arcs and the remaining four (referred to as *Higurashi Kai*) are answer arcs. The answer arcs continue to retell the story but break away from Keiichi, getting into the heads of the other characters in order to slowly explain the truth behind the murders and strange events of the first four chapters, eventually tying them together into a final epic conclusion to the bloody cycle that shrouds Hinamizawa.

Featuring likable characters that are far more than they first appear, a chilling series of murders, and a complex web of dark secrets and mysteries designed to keep players guessing right up until the end, *Higurashi* contains one of the most interesting and engaging mystery/ suspense stories I've ever read, with the art, sound, and music adding quite a lot to the experience. But, despite that, I have a problem calling it a game. With no interaction beyond advancing the text, *Higurashi* is entirely lacking in both interactive and game-like elements. Even the writer admits it, saying the "game" lies in trying to figure out the answers to the story's many mysteries before they're revealed in the later arcs. Although puzzling over the events in each subsequent arc is fun, and something I myself spent many hours doing, the same can be done with any book and in no way allows the player to interact directly with Hinamizawa or its inhabitants. So although *Higurashi* may be an excellent visual novel, it's mostly certainly not a visual novel game.

Interactive Traditional Stories

Interactive traditional stories combine the tightly controlled narratives of fully traditional stories with a degree of interactivity. They're the most common type of video game story, due to a combination of familiarity, structure, and creation process (for more details, see the rest of this chapter and Chapter 13). They're also extremely popular among players, as shown by the research data in Chapter 14. In an interactive traditional story, the main plot itself can't be changed, or at the very least can't be changed in any significant way. As with fully traditional stories, it will be the same no matter how many times the player experiences it. However, outside important story scenes, the player is given a degree of freedom to interact

FIGURE
7.4

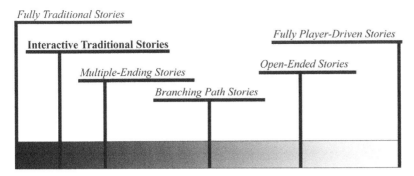

Fully Traditional Stories

Interactive Traditional Stories

Fully Player-Driven Stories

Multiple-Ending Stories

Open-Ended Stories

Branching Path Stories

Interactive traditional storytelling.

with the world and characters. In some games, the player's control is minimal and he or she is able to do little besides engage in battles and/or solve some puzzles. In others, however, the player is given a considerable amount of freedom to explore the world, talk to different characters, and engage in a variety of optional quests and activities if he or she so chooses. Although the player's actions may not have a significant effect on the main plot, they do allow the player to feel somewhat in control and responsible for the characters' actions and progression.

Emotional Architecture

One area of great potential artistic expression is in the area of evoking audience emotion. Regardless of the number of twists and turns a story possesses, the fundamental feature of a player-driven traditional story is what kinds of emotions are available to the writer. For example, in a traditional story, the audience experiences the emotional roller coaster of the story through empathy ("Oh, how sad for her that he left her to run off with the gang; I know someone that happened to, and it really stinks. I feel sad"). But not all emotions translate effectively through empathy. When a character in a drama makes a stupid decision, eliciting guilt from the character, the audience feels bad for him or her, certainly, but guilt is a first-person emotion. However, in interactive stories, emotions such as guilt can be much more powerful because the character is doing the action that the *player* determined. In the unreleased game *Stargate Worlds*, we had the players decide to kill an NPC they had interacted with, much akin to the scene in *2001: A Space Odyssey* in which the astronaut Dave must deactivate the computer HAL. The players felt the guilt of the decision they made to a degree impossible in standard drama.

—Chris

Case Study: *FINAL FANTASY X*

Developer:	Square Co., Ltd.
Publisher:	Square Electronics Arts LLC
Writers:	Yoshinori Kitase, Daisuke Watanabe
System:	Sony PlayStation 2
Release Date:	December 20, 2001 (US)
Genre:	RPG

FIGURE
7.5

FINAL FANTASY X's hero, Tidus, finds himself pulled into a new and dangerous world. © Square Enix, Co., Ltd. All rights reserved.

Square's famous *FINAL FANTASY* series is known for its complex storylines and well-developed characters – and its PlayStation 2 debut was no exception. As was expected of Square, *FINAL FANTASY X* featured some of the best graphics of its time, a memorable musical score, and many new gameplay innovations (including a more strategic battle system, the ability to switch out party members mid-battle, and the removal of traditional character levels in favor of the new Sphere Grid system). It was also the first *FINAL FANTASY* game to feature voice acting, with fully spoken dialog for all the major characters. Though die-hard fans of the series' earlier entries tend to prefer *FINAL FANTASY VI* or *FINAL FANTASY VII*, *FINAL FANTASY X* became the favorite of many of the newer generation of *FINAL FANTASY* fans and was also the first game in the series to receive a true sequel (*FINAL FANTASY X-2*).

FINAL FANTASY X starts in the futuristic city of Zanarkand. The main character, Tidus, is the young star player of the Zanarkand Abes blitzball team, but despite his fame, he can't seem to escape from the shadow of his father, who disappeared years before. However, when a giant monster destroys the city, Tidus awakens to find himself in Spira, a world far different from his own. People in Spira shun technology and instead rely on summoners (humans with the ability to summon and control magical beasts known as aeons) to protect them from attacks by Sin, the same monster that destroyed Tidus's home. Lost and unsure of how to return to his own world, Tidus falls in with Yuna, the daughter of the former high summoner, and her companions on a journey to gain the aid of the aeons and defeat Sin once more. Unsurprisingly, there's far more to the role of Sin and the summoners than they realize and the truth about Spira, Zanarkand, the aeons, and even Tidus's father rocks their beliefs and convictions to the core, causing a drastic shift in the nature and goals of their journey and culminating in one of the series' most emotional endings to date. In addition, Tidus's narration throughout much of the game adds an interesting perspective to the events, explaining his thoughts and motivations during each stage of the journey.

FIGURE
7.6

The bond between Tidus and Yuna grows gradually throughout the game. © Square Enix, Co., Ltd. All rights reserved.

Like all the main series *FINAL FANTASY* games (and most of the spin-offs), *FINAL FANTASY X* uses interactive traditional storytelling. The main story itself is fixed and the same events always happen in the same order, though the player's actions can cause some minor modifications to the plot. For example, in one scene, when they break off into pairs, Tidus will be put with the character he's been the friendliest with. However, these changes amount to, at most, some very slight changes in dialog and have no real bearing on the progression or outcome of the story as a whole. But that doesn't mean that the player is just an observer. Outside important story scenes, he or she is given a considerable amount of freedom. Naturally, the player is in complete control during battles and is free to fight and develop his party as he pleases, but that's only the beginning. Despite being one of the more linear *FINAL FANTASY* games, *FINAL FANTASY X* still allows the player to travel to and explore a variety of places (some of which make no appearance in the main story). As the player is doing this, he can power up the heroes and learn more about the world, characters, and backstory by talking to NPCs, finding lost video spheres recorded long ago by Tidus's father, and participating in a large variety of optional quests. Some of these activities have almost no bearing on the main plot and merely give a little more information about Spira and its inhabitants; others provide the answers to some lingering questions that are asked but never answered over the course of the main story.

Despite the player's lack of control over the story itself, the freedom the player has throughout the rest of the game clearly separates *FINAL FANTASY X*'s interactive traditional story from the fully traditional stories of books and movies. It also provides a strong illusion of control by giving the player an important role to play and the freedom to perform that role in many different ways. So although the plot itself remains the same, each player's experiences in the world of Spira are different and unique.

Creating Interactive Traditional Stories

In many ways, interactive traditional stories are the easiest type of video game story to create. As you'll see in the coming chapters, stories using more highly interactive styles such as branching path storytelling and open-ended storytelling require a considerable amount of extra work and planning to create. With interactive traditional stories, you don't need to worry about what would happen if the hero decides that he wants to become a villain or take up fishing instead of following the plot as it was originally planned. You don't need to write out complete scenarios for good, evil, and fisherman versions of the story or struggle to balance character consistency with player choice and freedom. As with a fully traditional story, you control the plot so that you always know how, when, and where all the key scenes are going to play out and can tweak and fine-tune them to produce exactly the type of impact and emotional response you want.

Because the player can't change the plot, writing an interactive traditional story is in many ways much like writing a novel or a movie script (in terms of formatting, it's closest to a script, though different developers prefer different layouts and organizational styles). You think of an idea; plan out your basic story, structure, and characters (or in some cases are given all of these by your boss); and then just write the story as you imagine it. Of course, there are some key differences. Unlike with a novel or movie script, you don't have to write out everything that happens. Though a fantasy novel may describe the hero's battle with the evil wizard's army or his journey across the treacherous mountains in detail, in a game the player will be the one actually doing the fighting and climbing, so you merely need to mention that those elements are there and let the designers and then the player handle the rest.

Tone Is Powerful

I have always believed that the most powerful tool a game writer has to tell story is the choice of what the character played by the player *does*. The more the writer can have influence over the activities the player can partake in, the more the writer can influence the tone, and tone is one aspect of the game many developers do not make as much use of as can a talented writer. One of the game aspects that Bioware does well is awareness of when to be funny, when to be dramatic, and when to mix the two.

—Chris

Of course, if you want to describe what types of creatures are in the army, what they look like, and how they fight, or explain what it is that makes the mountains so dangerous, you can do so in order to give the art and design teams more to work with, though it can vary a lot by where you're working. Some developers prefer that level of detail and like to try to ensure that everything fits well within the context of the story, but others would rather you leave the character and level creation entirely up to the art and design teams and just adjust the story to fit them.

When writing interactive traditional stories (or any type of story) for games, you also have to remember that you're not writing for a novel or a movie, but a game. Therefore, you need to ensure that your story provides plenty of places for the player to do his or her thing, whether that thing is fighting, exploring, puzzle solving, or some combination of the three. And that doesn't just mean leaving space between the story scenes for all those things to happen: you also need to consider how gameplay can be worked into the story scenes themselves. If the story calls for a tense showdown or a daring escape, think about the gameplay and whether it would lend itself to that scene. At times, you may decide that it's best to leave the scene entirely noninteractive (either for dramatic effect or because it simply wouldn't work within the confines of the game system), but at others you'll realize that there's no good reason not to give the player control. Just keep in mind that the gameplay has to fit. For example, though an interactive battle in a *FINAL FANTASY* or *Metal Gear Solid* game should be an actual battle with swords, guns, or fists, an interactive battle in a more puzzle-based game like *Sam & Max* or *Monkey Island* should be more of a duel of wits than a button-mashing fight. Even if you're given free rein over the story, knowing how the game will be played and tailoring your scenarios to fit that specific type of gameplay will make the final product feel far more natural and polished than if your puzzle-solving hero goes around beating down every villain with a kick to the head.

You may also need to think about how the player can interact with the world and characters. Even though the player can't change the main story, he or she may still be able to talk to NPCs, choose from multiple responses when speaking, and search out books or log entries containing additional information about the world and backstory. Naturally, you need to write all of those extra lines of dialog and information as well. Writing lines for NPCs or in-game books usually isn't too hard – just start with the subject and work from there. Each book and NPC doesn't need ten pages of writing or even have to convey anything important or profound. A book or log entry needs to be only long enough to adequately describe its subject; an NPC who makes a brief remark about the weather is just as realistic and believable as one who spews out long rants about the state of the kingdom. Both types of people exist in real life, so there's no reason why they shouldn't exist in your game.

Tell Story Every Way You Can

There are no throwaway items created by a writer in the game. Every chance you have to advance the story, you should take. Although it's true that NPCs the player meets on the street don't have much screen time, that makes their dialog even more crucial to get right. The cumulative effect of these "barks," as they are known, can absolutely inform the player as to the world's fabric in a very powerful way.

Disney's theme parks are filled with wonderful examples of storytelling that exemplify this ideal. They theme everything, from the costumes of the ride attendants to the coverings on the trash cans to the ride elements themselves. Their design staff preaches about both knowing the story inside and out and telling the story every way you can. Their success and the depth of storytelling at which they routinely succeed speaks for itself. It would behoove game storytellers to resist the urge to pander to the lowest possible inside jokes, and when they need to be funny, to find a way to be funny in a way that is organic to their game world.

—Chris

We'll talk a lot more about writing branching dialog in later chapters, but it's a bit easier in interactive traditional stories because the different branches always eventually end up in the same place without changing the story. So instead of thinking about how different dialog choices could change the story, think about how they can be used to provide additional information or show different ways the character could react to a certain request or situation. For example, when the hero is talking to a character about a dragon that needs to be killed, you could give the player the option to ask for more information about the dragon, ask about the damage it caused to the village, or just get right down to business and head out. None of these dialog choices will change what happens next, as the dragon still needs to be dealt with, but they give players the option of learning more if they want to and increase the interactivity and the illusion of control (an important concept that we'll discuss more in Chapter 13). If you prefer your branching dialog to be based around reactions rather than information, the hero could have the option to immediately agree to fight the dragon, to ask what's in it for him, or to try and weasel out of it. Once again, the story remains the same, with only a few lines of dialog changing, but the extra options increase the interaction and illusion of control.

Player's Characters Speaking Dialog

There are widely varying opinions about putting words in a player–character's mouth. Some players have said they don't *ever* want the game speaking for them, so the game should always speak generically for the player, as in "You ask the barkeeper about the best place to change money." Other people believe, as I do, that you must embrace your role as author and pick a tone for the player–character's voice, as many Bioware games do. "Hey, dude, where can I get some cash?" feels much different and delivers a totally different tone to the main character than "Um, sir, can you help me find the bank?" As the writer, you should make a choice. The power is always in a stronger choice rather than a weaker one.

—Chris

One very important thing to remember when creating branching dialog for an interactive traditional story is that even though the eventual outcome remains the same regardless of what is said, the choice the player makes should still change the conversation, with the other character reacting in an appropriate manner. When game writers add extra dialog choices merely for the sake of having something for the player to choose from or click on, without bothering to change the rest of the conversation to match, you end up with one of two highly undesirable scenarios. The first is when, after the player chooses his or her response, the other character continues talking without acknowledging the player's choice in any way. No matter which option the player chooses, the conversation remains exactly the same. While players might not notice this their first time through if the conversation is written well enough, those that do will probably be annoyed by it. A much worse version of this is when the player is given the choice between two or more lines of dialog that say pretty much the same thing. I won't name names, but I've played at least several games in which I was given the choice between saying "yes" and "yeah" (or two other more or less identical words). A choice like that is completely pointless and leaves the player wondering why he or she was even given a choice in the first place – there's nothing to choose between.

The second bad scenario takes place when the player is given the choice between two or more opposing options. Let's say that the player can accept or refuse a certain job. The problem is that the story requires the player to take (or maybe not take) that job, so only one option is actually valid. Choosing the wrong option will result in the NPC saying something like "Are you sure?" and giving the player the same choice over and over again until the right one is chosen. This type of conversation actually could be handled well if choosing the wrong option caused the NPC to reason with the hero and convince him to do the right thing, but just looping the choice endlessly until the player gets the hint and picks the right option is pointless and annoying. Although branching dialog options don't need to change the main story, they do at least need to have some purpose to them – otherwise, you're just making pointless busywork for the players.

Case Study: *Metal Gear Solid 4: Guns of the Patriots*

Developer:	Konami
Publisher:	Konami
Writers:	Hideo Kojima, Shuyo Murata
System:	Sony PlayStation 3
Release Date:	June 12, 2008 (US)
Genre:	Stealth Action

FIGURE
7.7

Solid Snake has aged significantly since his last outing.

Metal Gear Solid 4 didn't become the final game in the *Metal Gear* series as was originally intended (though all later releases have so far taken place earlier in the series' fictional timeline), but its release brought to a close the story that had stretched through the rest of the series (aside from *Metal Gear Solid Ghost Babel* and *Metal Gear Ac!d*, spin-off titles with their own continuities) from Naked Snake's defeat of The Boss in *MGS3*, through his own defeat in *MG* and *MG2*, and onward through Solid Snake and Raiden's adventures in *MGS* and *MGS2*. When it was released, *MGS4* impressed gamers not only with its highly detailed graphics and revamped control system, but also with the way it expertly tied up the myriads of mysteries and loose ends from past games in a way that both made sense and provided a satisfying and emotional conclusion to the story – something that many fans, myself included, had thought to be nearly impossible.

With the exception of the first *MGS*, which had a multiple-ending story, the series has always used interactive traditional storytelling to great effect. Though the series is occasionally derided for its long cut-scenes, it is frequently praised for its cinematic action scenes, long conversations between characters, and top-quality voice acting, which all serve an important purpose: causing the players to truly care about the characters, their goals, and their motivations. The graphics quality in *MGS4* further upped the ante, showing the characters' body language and subtle facial shifts far better than ever before, making for one of the most emotional stories in gaming and a frequently cited example of a game that can make people cry.

Set a few years after the events of *MGS2*, Snake is now an old man, due to a flaw in his genetics that has caused his body to suddenly and rapidly age. As Snake has changed, so has the world. Seemingly channeling the spirit of Snake's brother Liquid, Revolver Ocelot has created a series of private military corporations – armies for hire that are willing to serve whoever will pay. The use of emotion-suppressing nano machines has made these soldiers fearless and loyal: the perfect warriors. War has become a business, and business is good. Though still on the search for Ocelot and the shadowy group known as The Patriots, with Raiden missing and Snake's body rapidly deteriorating, he and Otacon have reached a dead end. However, when Ocelot resurfaces, Snake returns to the battlefield one last time to put an end to things once and for all. Snake's final mission features many interesting characters, both old and new, and reveals the shocking truth behind mysteries including Big Boss's defection, Ocelot's goals, and the identity of The Patriots.

FIGURE
7.8

Metal Gear Solid 4 **has a very diverse cast of characters, new and old.**

Like previous *MG* games, *MGS4* plays to the strengths of interactive traditional storytelling. Although the story scenes are scripted, unchangeable, and, with a couple of exceptions, noninteractive, this allows them to be done in a highly cinematic style that highlights the intense and breathtaking events. The story also features many shocking and emotional moments of the sort that are extremely hard to create when using more interactive and player-driven storytelling styles. (We'll discuss the reasons for that throughout the upcoming chapters.)

However, despite the unchanging and linear nature of the story, players have a significant amount of control and freedom available to them during the rest of the game, even more so than in the rest of the series. The story guides Snake through a series of war-torn battlefields but provides him with an endless variety of ways to pass through them. Stealth has always been Snake's specialty; he can choose to use his natural abilities and new camouflage technology to try to slip by unseen. But he can also take a more aggressive role, silently dispatching guards with a wide variety of weapons or distracting them through other means. Unlike the areas in previous *MG* games, which generally had only one path, the environments in *MGS4* are large and varied, providing many possible routes, each with its own advantages and disadvantages. Several areas also feature pitched battles between Liquid's soldiers and local freedom fighters. Although sneaking past them is always an option, players can also choose to aid the locals in their fight, allowing them to push forward, open new paths, and clear areas of enemy combatants. Or, if the player chooses, he or she can act as a lone wolf, dispatching soldiers on both sides of the conflict and taking their equipment to aid him in future battles.

This high degree of freedom in the gameplay makes each player's experience unique and allows for considerable experimentation and replay value while still providing the kind of deep, twisting, and tightly controlled narrative that fans of the series love. There are many games on the market that provide good examples of how to tell an interactive traditional story, but from its haunting opening to its tearful conclusion, *MGS4* is certainly one of the finest.

The Strengths of Interactive Traditional Stories

The strengths of interactive traditional stories lie in the fact that it's the writer who controls the flow, progression, and outcome of the main plot. Just as the writers of fully traditional stories have done for centuries, writers of interactive traditional stories can arrange and fine-tune every scene to ensure that it conveys the correct information and emotions in the best possible way. And, unlike in the more player-driven forms of storytelling, you don't need to worry about the player screwing up the story, missing some important piece of information, or losing track of the main plot. When well written, an interactive traditional story can carefully control the players' emotions, beliefs, and expectations and guide them toward a planned goal, whether that goal is a surprising twist or a satisfying conclusion. This no doubt contributes to their high popularity (see Chapter 14).

From a more practical standpoint, keeping the characters and story consistent and believable is far easier to do than in other more player-driven storytelling styles because there's no danger of the player mixing things up. You also don't need to think of suitable places for the story to branch, write multiple variations of the story scenes and conversations, or try to figure out how to make the plot interesting and engaging no matter which way it branches (issues that we'll discuss in depth in the upcoming chapters), all of which can take a considerable amount of time and money to plan and implement.

In the end, when done correctly, interactive traditional stories provide players with a well-structured, tightly woven experience that – like a good book or film – showcases the writer's imagination and creativity to the fullest. At the same time, they can provide players with a strong illusion of control, allowing players to feel that they have an important role to play in the story, even though they can't change the main plot itself.

Case Study: *FINAL FANTASY VII*

Developer:	Square Co., Ltd.
Publisher:	Sony Computer Entertainment, Inc.
Writers:	Tetsuya Nomura, Hironobu Sakaguchi
System:	Sony PlayStation
Release Date:	September 7, 1997 (US), June 2, 2009 (PlayStation Network rerelease)
Genre:	RPG

FIGURE
7.9

Cloud and Sephiroth are still famous figures among gamers. © Square Enix, Co., Ltd. All rights reserved.

As I mentioned in Chapter 2, *FINAL FANTASY VII* is a very important title in the history of games and game storytelling. Not only did it elevate console RPGs from a niche market in the United States to one of the most popular genres in existence, but it also showed both gamers and game developers outside Japan that a good story could both define a game and attract a significant audience. The explosion of RPGs and story-focused games of all types that followed brought stories – which were before often considered to be one of the less important elements of games – to the forefront in the eyes of many developers and gamers.

But what made *FINAL FANTASY VII* so popular that the industry as a whole had to stand up and take notice? Was it the state-of-the-art graphics and amazing FMVs, or perhaps Square's massive multimillion-dollar marketing campaign? Clearly not. Those factors no doubt helped to get it in the public eye and convinced gamers unfamiliar with the *FINAL FANTASY* series to give it a try, contributing to the strong sales during its first weeks; however, those elements can't account for the way it continued to dominate sales charts for months after its initial release, its enduring popularity, or the sheer amount of praise lavished upon it by the gaming press both back then and now. Its excellent musical score and solid gameplay were also only small parts of the puzzle. *FINAL FANTASY VII*'s greatest strengths, and the reasons for its immense popularity (which has led to multiple sequels and prequels, along with an endless stream of fan requests for a full remake), are its characters and story.

FINAL FANTASY VII starts in Midgar, a massive city run by the Shinra Corporation. From its beginnings as a simple power company, Shinra grew rapidly, taking over other industries and eventually the government itself. Though most people seem content with Shinra rule, rumors abound of a darker side to the company involving highly questionable experiments and power plants that suck the very life force from the planet. Cloud, a mercenary and former member of Shinra's elite Soldier division, has been hired by the guerilla group Avalanche to help destroy Shinra's mako energy plants and bring down the company. Despite his childhood friend Tifa being a member of Avalanche, Cloud is only in it for the money and has no interest in the group's ideals. But a series of events – including a chance encounter with the flower girl Aerith (spelled Aeris in the original release), the destruction of a large section of Midgar, and the sudden reappearance of the legendary soldier Sephiroth (who destroyed Cloud and Tifa's home town five years before) – give him a new purpose. The story is rife with surprising twists and revelations, including the extent of Shinra's twisted experiments, Sephiroth's plans, and the truth about Cloud's memories and the events of five years ago.

FIGURE
7.10

Aerith's death shocked and saddened millions of players. © Square Enix, Co., Ltd. **All rights reserved.**

I discussed a few of these elements in earlier chapters, such as the unique way *FINAL FANTASY VII* uses the old amnesia cliché to set up a series of fascinating twists late in the game, but there's more to the story than just the big reveals. What's most important is the characters. Each of Cloud's companions, from the sweet flower girl Aerith to the wolf-like creature known as Red XIII, has his or her own detailed backstory, well-developed personality, and reason for joining Cloud on his quest. The stories of their lives are interwoven throughout the main narrative, and their conversations – both serious and casual – clearly reflect their different beliefs and personalities. The steady and well-directed flow of events helps keep players engaged and wrapped up in the story, with every town and dungeon bringing about new information and developments. Even enemies such as the group of Turk agents who pursue Cloud's party feature well-defined personalities and relationships.

Sephiroth is exceptionally well done and has become both one of the most loved and hated villains in gaming history. Instantly recognizable, with his black cape, flowing silver hair, and impossibly long sword, the former Shinra Soldier First Class was once hailed as a hero but turned against not only Shinra but the world itself when he discovered the truth about his origins. This important event, shown as a playable flashback through Cloud's eyes, does an excellent job of demonstrating Sephiroth's power and his rapid descent into madness. At first he seems redeemable and even a possible ally against Shinra, but his focus on world destruction and his hand in Aerith's death (an event frequently called one of the most emotional moments in gaming) earned him the eternal hatred of not only the game's heroes but many of its players as well.

Like the rest of the series, *FINAL FANTASY VII* shows what is truly great about interactive traditional stories. Excellent pacing, a diverse cast of fully developed characters, emotional high-impact scenes, and a deep twisting plot revealed gradually over the course of a grand adventure – all elements that become increasingly difficult to create in the more highly interactive styles of storytelling – take center stage to create a game whose impact on its players and the industry as a whole can't be overestimated.

The Weaknesses of Interactive Traditional Stories

Some consider the lack of interactivity and player choice in interactive traditional stories to be a significant weakness, but that's a highly debatable point – and one that we'll discuss more in Chapters 12 through 14. The interactivity issue aside, it can actually be argued that the biggest weaknesses of interactive traditional storytelling aren't so much problems with the style itself, but with individual writers.

As I've said throughout this chapter, more than any other style, interactive traditional storytelling gives writers a chance to truly shine, putting them in control of every aspect of the main plot and giving them free rein to develop and present it the way they see fit (bosses and deadlines aside). The problem is that if the player doesn't like the way the story turns out, there's really nothing he or she can do about it. Of course, even the best and most well-loved stories have their critics. Like I said before, you can't please everyone. But, if a story angers, annoys, or disappoints a large number of players, it's reasonable to assume that there's something wrong with the story itself. There are a million different things that can go wrong with a story. We've already discussed issues like poor pacing and overreliance on clichés, melodrama, and overly generic or unbelievable characters, all of which are common missteps found not only in games but stories of all types. The other most "popular" place for a story to derail is the ending. As previously mentioned, endings can be tricky to write, and it's important to be sure that they provide a sense of accomplishment and closure. Although a poor ending can ruin a story in any medium, avoiding this problem is especially important in video games because the player feels partially responsible for the story's outcome (even if the player couldn't change the plot itself). You want players to finish a game feeling like what they did meant something, not like they just dedicated thirty hours of their lives to something only to fail. This is a very important part of writing for games, which we'll talk more about in later chapters.

Case Study: *Arc the Lad II*

Developer: Sony
Publisher: Working Designs
Writer: Kou Satou

System: Sony PlayStation
Release Date: April 18, 2002 (US), November 23, 2010 (Playstation Network
                 rerelease)
Genre: Strategy RPG

Though originally released in Japan in 1996, it wasn't until 2002 that *Arc the Lad II* was brought to the United States as part of Working Designs' *Arc the Lad Collection*. Picking up shortly after the ending of *Arc the Lad*, *Arc II* greatly expands on the first game's world, story, and gameplay and completes the storyline that it began. It's even one of the rare sequels that allows players to directly import their party from the first game, retaining all of their characters' levels and items.

The first part of the story focuses on Elc, a bounty hunter and warrior for hire. He and his friend and fellow hunter, Shu, end up on the wrong side of a dangerous group of people when trying to protect Lieza, a girl with the ability to talk to monsters, and end up on the run. As it turns out, Elc, Lieza, Shu, and the friends and companions they meet along the way all have reasons to fight against the evil empire of Romalia. This common ground leads them to eventually meet and join up with Arc and his allies from the first game as they set out to stop Romalia's ambitions and prevent its leader from releasing an ancient evil being known as The Dark One, which was sealed away long ago.

The vastly improved gameplay, long quest, and numerous optional missions available at the various hunter offices scattered throughout the world are all significant improvements over the first *Arc*. The story received a similar improvement. *Arc II* features a large cast of characters, all of whom have their own detailed backstory and optional quests, and the main plot itself is very long and detailed, featuring far fewer clichéd moments than in the first game. Arc and Elc's journey is a massive tale that has them traveling all over the world, freeing people from Romalia's rule, seeking out allies, and tracking down and defeating Romalia's top generals. There are many shockingly dark twists along the way, making for a very serious and mature story that would easily take several pages to adequately summarize.

The place where *Arc II* unfortunately stumbles is its ending. As I said before, Arc and Elc's goal is both to stop Romalia from taking over the world and prevent the release of The Dark One. As it turns out, however, Romalia's leader is surprisingly intelligent. Unlike most villains, who are certain that they can control whatever unstoppable evil force was sealed away long ago by people much more powerful than they are, he fully realizes that releasing The Dark One would be a very bad idea and is instead content to carefully siphon its power to strengthen his own forces. Unfortunately, when Arc's party breaks into his throne room (having penetrated his final stronghold and defeated his last and strongest followers), he understandably panics and decides that releasing The Dark One is his only hope. Upon release, The Dark One immediately kills Kukuru (Arc's girlfriend), and its very presence triggers a devastating series of natural disasters that go on to destroy a significant portion of the world, killing most of the people the player spent hours and hours helping and befriending throughout the course of the game. If that wasn't bad enough, upon defeating The Dark One, Arc and his friends discover that it can't be fully destroyed and will recover soon unless Arc sacrifices his own life to seal it away. A pretty tragic ending, right? Well, actually it's not quite over yet. Once the seal is restored, Romalia's fortress naturally starts to collapse, prompting the usual clichéd escape scene. But said escape doesn't go so well. Though the surviving heroes do manage to get out alive, one is seriously injured in the process, suffering permanent brain damage. In the end, though the heroes technically won, it certainly doesn't feel anything like a victory.

Now I'm not saying that games need to have happy endings. Several games we've already discussed (*CRISIS CORE – FINAL FANTASY VII*, *Metal Gear Solid 3 & 4*, and *FINAL FANTASY X*) feature endings that certainly can't be summed up by saying "and they all lived happily ever after." However, their endings all leave the player with a sense of accomplishment and the knowledge that although some terrible sacrifices were made, the heroes completed what they set out to do and made the world a better place because of it. *Arc II*'s ending, however, tends to leave players feeling like almost everything they did was a waste. Yes, they helped and freed a lot of people, but in the end most of those people were killed, rendering all the players' hard work pointless. Even worse, the destruction of the world and the deaths of Arc and Kukuru are entirely the heroes' (and by extension, the player's) fault. If they hadn't stormed in to stop Romalia's leader from releasing The Dark One, he never would have done so in the first place. Although life under a tyrannical ruler certainly isn't great, most people would probably agree that it would be preferable to destroying over half of the world. In the end, it's quite clear that things probably would have turned out much better if Arc and the others did things a bit differently or even decided to go home and forget about Romalia entirely. And the last thing you want players to feel after more than 50 hours of gameplay is that things would have been better off had they done nothing at all.

Arc II's ending could have worked as the bad ending in a multiple-ending story or even made for a workable (though rather depressing) ending to an interactive traditional story if the result felt inevitable, rather than being the heroes' and player's fault. And therein lies interactive traditional storytelling's biggest weakness. Without any branches or choices to be made, a single poorly written section can significantly detract from or even entirely ruin an otherwise good story.

Summary

Fully traditional stories are the oldest form of storytelling and have been used for centuries in fables, folklore, books, and movies. They give the writer complete and total control over the experience, allowing him or her to set the scenes perfectly to try and ensure that the correct information, impact, and emotions are conveyed. However, as fully traditional stories are unchangeable, they can't really be interactive and are therefore unsuitable for video games.

Interactive traditional stories are the most common type of story used in video games and seek to blend the best elements of fully traditional stories (such as the carefully controlled and fine-tuned pacing, scenes, and characters) with a measure of interactivity and player control. Though the main plot itself is unchangeable, players are given freedom to explore, interact with the world and its characters, and generally take their own approach to the rest of the game, giving them a strong illusion of control. Compared to other more player-driven forms of storytelling, interactive traditional stories are easier to create and give the writer more control over the finished product, giving them the best possible chance to create the type of story they want, whether it's an emotionally charged drama, an over-the-top comedy, or anything in between. This makes them very popular with both game developers and players. However, as the main plot is entirely under the writer's control, any mistakes or poor choices on the writer's part can seriously damage the story, disappointing and/or angering players.

Things to Consider

1. Do you consider "games" using fully traditional stories, such as *Higurashi*, to be true games? Why or why not?

2. List ten games you've played that use interactive traditional stories (if you haven't played that many, just list the ones you have).

3. Pick three of the games from your list. In what ways did they allow you to interact with their world and characters?

4. When you were playing those three games, were there any times that you really wanted to take control and change the story? Explain why and how you wanted to do so.

5. Do you think the changes you proposed in your last answer would have made the rest of the stories significantly better or worse? Why or why not? Do you think most other players would agree with you?

Eight

Multiple-Ending Stories

FIGURE
8.1

Fully Traditional Stories

Interactive Traditional Stories

Multiple-Ending Stories

Branching Path Stories

Fully Player-Driven Stories

Open-Ended Stories

Multiple-ending storytelling.

Multiple-ending stories represent the next step in interactivity after interactive traditional stories and are the first type of storytelling on the spectrum that allows the player to have a significant impact on the main plot. Therefore, they're the first type of story that can be called truly player-driven – although just barely. They're also quite popular with both game developers and players (as shown in Chapter 14).

For the most part, multiple-ending stories follow the same structure as interactive traditional stories. The only difference – and the style's defining feature – is that players are allowed to choose between two or more possible endings. Outside this single choice, the player can't seriously alter the main plot in any other way. Despite this limitation, there are many different methods for determining what types of endings a game should have and where to place them in the story (there's no reason why some endings can't take place sooner or later than others). Similarly, though players are often given a rather clear choice that determines which ending they see, there's no need to make the decision obvious or even to put it under the player's direct control. We'll discuss all these issues and more throughout this chapter.

Case Study: *Blood Omen: Legacy of Kain*

Developer:	Silicon Knights
Publisher:	Crystal Dynamics
Writers:	Jim Curry, Denis Dyack, Ken McCulloch, Sheatiel Sarao
System:	Sony PlayStation, PC
Release Date:	November 15, 1996 (US), September 10, 2009 (PlayStation Network rerelease)
Genre:	Action-Adventure

Blood Omen: Legacy of Kain and the rest of the *Legacy of Kain* series can best be thought of as cult classics. Known for their dark and brooding tone, excellent voice acting, and twisting story, the games were often called RPGs, even though the gameplay itself places them more squarely in the action or action-adventure genre. Although the dark, violent, and occasionally problematic gameplay kept the series from achieving widespread success, the *Legacy of Kain* games – particularly *Blood Omen* and *Soul Reaver* – still maintain a devoted fan following.

The story begins in the world of Nosgoth with the murder of Kain, a young nobleman. But Kain doesn't stay dead for long. He's brought back to life as a vampire by the necromancer Mortanius and immediately seeks revenge on those that ended his human life. Upon their defeat, however, Mortanius informs him that they were merely pawns and the real villains are the guardians of the Pillars of Nosgoth. Instead of protecting the pillars and the world they support, the guardians have become corrupted and must be destroyed if the world is to be saved. Unlike most game heroes of the time, Kain has little interest in what happens to the world and goes after the guardians in order to complete his revenge.

During the course of his search, Kain travels back in time to stop a tyrannical king before the king gains his full powers. But Kain later discovers that he was in fact being manipulated by one of the guardians and that his actions in the past triggered a bloody crusade that has left him as the only surviving vampire. He's later betrayed by Mortanius, who is revealed to be the true mastermind behind Kain's murder and the corruption of the guardians, all as part of a master plan to destroy the pillars. Upon learning this, Kain kills Mortanius and becomes the new guardian of the Pillar of Balance.

It's at this point that the game presents the player with an all-important choice. With the other guardians dead, Kain can choose to give up his own life in order to reset the pillars and restore the land, though doing so would also mean the end of the vampire race. Or he can refuse, keeping his own life and ruling over the world as the pillars collapse and the world falls into decay. Although the choice changes nothing but the ending movies, it allows the player to think about what he or she would choose to do if facing a similar dilemma, or perhaps how Kain himself would respond based on his character and personality. As neither choice leads to an "ideal" ending, it makes for an interesting decision between the noble and selfish. The later games in the series assume that Kain chose the latter option and doomed the world to save himself, though it's eventually revealed that his intentions weren't entirely self-serving and that there were deeper reasons behind his decision. But the choice itself made quite an impact on players at the time, leaving them to wonder just which option they would have chosen.

Creating Multiple-Ending Stories

For the most part, the creation process for multiple-ending stories is similar to that of interactive traditional stories, as they use a mostly non-player-driven structure that allows the writer a great degree of control over the story and its progression. There are, however, several additional things that need to be considered, each of which I'll explain in detail.

What Types of Endings Should a Game Have?

The first and most important question is what the endings are going to be and what purpose they serve. As in *Blood Omen*, multiple endings can be used to show the different outcomes of an important decision that the hero has to make (usually a choice between good and evil). However, they can also be used to represent good, bad, and/or neutral outcomes of an event, as in *Castlevania: Dawn of Sorrow* (discussed in the next case study), or just show different ways that the story could turn out if things had gone slightly differently, as in *Chrono Trigger* (discussed later in this chapter).

To start off, you need to ask yourself why you want to have multiple endings in the first place. If your only answer is "to have more endings," you may want to reconsider. As with any other story element, adding more endings simply for the sake of saying your story has a lot of endings is likely to result in a lot of writing that feels forced and unnecessary. But if you can think of two or more very interesting ways for the story to end or you want to challenge the players to think carefully about a certain decision or entice them to work harder to achieve the story's best possible outcome, then multiple endings may be the way to go. The important thing is to make sure that the endings fit naturally into your story and don't show up randomly or revolve around bizarre or unnecessary plot twists.

If He Dies, What Does That Mean?

One of the challenges in multiple endings is that of theme. In an ideal world, the way the story ends is exactly related to your theme – and not only "related": it *is* your theme. If the theme of *Macbeth* is that "greed for power corrupts even the best leaders and leads to destruction," it's difficult to write to that theme if in one possible ending Macbeth ends up as king of Scotland. It's best if you have multiple endings that the possible variations all lead to the same A-story climax, but get there through different pathways, and thus the theme then would shift to being carried by the B-story instead of the A-story.

Let's keep using *Macbeth* as an example. The story has to end with Macbeth and Lady Macbeth both dying. But if you've given the players a series of choices along the way, allowing them to avoid killing Macbeth's friends while Lady Macbeth still connives for power, the players can be pulled in a few directions related to his relationship to Lady Macbeth while the kingdom crumbles around him. Perhaps then the theme can be expressed through the *way* the kingdom collapses, how bloody it is, rather than simply that it *does*.

The desire to work in multiple endings can certainly make players happy and bolster their feeling of agency; the risk is that those kinds of stories will never feel very deep, emotionally, and may always tend to drift into melodrama. Writers need to guard against this kind of slippage at all costs if the medium is ever to be considered a serious storytelling venue.

—Chris

Case Study: *Castlevania: Dawn of Sorrow*

Developer: Konami
Publisher: Konami
Writer: Koji Igarashi
System: Nintendo DS
Release Date: October 4, 2005 (US)
Genre: Action-Adventure

FIGURE
8.2

Soma finds himself facing a wide variety of monsters over the course of his adventure.

Konami's long-running *Castlevania* series has gone through a lot of permutations over the years, from its beginnings as a humble platforming series, along with occasional forays into the 3D action and fighting genres, to the *Metroid*-inspired exploration-heavy action-adventure games that have come to define it. At the heart of each *Castlevania* game lies the simple story of a lone man (or in rare cases, a lone woman) venturing out to defeat Dracula (or occasionally another related villain) and restore peace to the land. According to series lore, both Dracula and his labyrinthine castle return to the world every hundred years as part of a never-ending cycle, and it's the job of the heroic Belmont clan (and/or a few other special individuals) to fight their way to the count and send him back into his grave for the next century.

Dawn of Sorrow, a direct follow-up to *Aria of Sorrow* on the Game Boy Advance, is one of the rare games in the series to change the traditional story. In 1999, Julius Belmont and his companions at long last managed to seal Dracula away for good, then in 2035, the dark lord's soul and power (castle) were separated from each other by a young man named Soma Cruz (who has the power to steal the souls and powers from monsters). One year later, Soma and his friend Mina are attacked by dark creatures that have been raised by a mysterious cult. Convinced that the world needs an ultimate evil if god is to be considered the ultimate good, Celia (the leader of the cult) has gathered people containing fragments of Dracula's power (of which Soma is one) to create an existence to replace the defeated count. Soma ventures into Celia's base, hoping to bring an end to her plans and protect his friends.

The *Castlevania* games have never been particularly known for their stories, as even in the most plot-heavy titles, the story takes a back seat to exploration, fighting, and some RPG-style character development. However, the plots of the entire series do tie together into a consistent, if rather convoluted, timeline and have featured some pretty interesting characters, such as Dracula's son (and general fan favorite hero) Alucard. The series has also used multiple-ending storytelling in many of its games, starting all the way back on the NES with *Castlevania II: Simon's Quest*. Instead of focusing on moral choices or "what if" scenarios, the endings in *Castlevania* games use the good and bad – or at times good, bad, and neutral – structure. Often, as is the case in *Dawn of Sorrow*, the endings are spaced throughout the game and the player needs to meet certain requirements in order to avoid the bad and neutral endings and reach the later parts of the game and receive the good ending.

FIGURE
8.3

Stealing the souls of defeated monsters gives Soma many different powers.

Dawn of Sorrow features three endings. One is clearly the good or best ending, and the others bad and neutral endings. The first ending can take place after Soma's second battle with the cult member Dario, who – like Soma himself – has some of Dracula's power inside him. If the player fights and defeats Dario normally, Soma will be victorious but will reach a dead end in his search and have little choice but to exit the castle and return home, leaving many issues unresolved. To avoid this ending, the player has to have acquired the power of the Paranoia Soul, which he can use to find and destroy the source of Dario's powers. This prompts Celia to open a previously blocked area and challenge Soma to meet her in the castle's central chamber. It's there that the second ending can take place. Soma arrives just in time to see Celia murder Mina, and his shock and anger causes him to lose control over his dark powers and transform into the new Dracula. That isn't the good ending, either! To avoid this one, the player needs to enter the room while wearing a talisman given to him by Mina. The talisman suppresses the dark energy long enough for Soma's friends to arrive and tell him that the real Mina is safe and the one murdered by Celia is a fake. The following events result in the last section of the castle opening up, which leads to the true final boss and the best possible conclusion to the game.

Although *Dawn of Sorrow's* bad endings don't do much to expand upon the story, they do show what would happen if Soma failed at certain points along the way and also set the stage for an unlockable bonus mode that follows the efforts of Soma's friends to defeat him after he becomes Dracula. Most importantly, as the bad endings are clearly not the proper conclusion to the story, they force the player to think about how they can be avoided and to thoroughly search the game for the items and/or skills necessary to do so. The other *Castlevania* games are much the same, with their bad endings encouraging players to further explore the world and figure out how to avoid them. Because of this, they do an excellent job of supporting the gameplay by further emphasizing the games' focus on exploration and experimentation.

Choosing Where to End the Game

Once you've decided on what types of endings you want and how they're going to fit into the story, the next step is deciding exactly where to place them in the game. Quite a lot of games such as *Blood Omen* and *STAR OCEAN: SECOND EVOLUTION* (which is another title we'll talk about later in this chapter) have all their endings at the end of the game, which seems like the natural place. And that's fine if all the endings focus on different ways that the final battle or decision could have played out, or just serve as different possible epilogues for the characters. But, just as *Dawn of Sorrow* demonstrated, there's no reason to limit endings to the end of the story. Different things the hero does or doesn't do could easily cause his journey to come to an early end (for better or worse). There's also no reason for the story to not have several important decision points instead of just one, with one decision leading to an early ending and the other allowing the game to continue.

When looking at the structure or outline of your story, consider the points at which the hero is going to face an important decision or a particularly difficult challenge. Then consider what would happen if the hero made a different choice or performed significantly worse (or better) than expected. What would happen next? Could it lead to an early ending? If so, would that ending add anything important, interesting, and/or enjoyable to the story? For example, an ending in which the hero decides to stay home and sleep in instead of going out on an adventure would probably be pretty boring and wouldn't be worth the time to write and program. But an ending in which the hero miraculously manages to defeat the main villain when they first meet early in the game could show an interesting "what-if" scenario and also reward the players who are able to win a battle that's skewed heavily against them.

When using this approach, be sure to keep in mind that every ending your game has requires extra writing and programming, and quite possibly art and sound as well. All of those processes take time and money, so think carefully about each ending and whether it will add enough to the game to be worth it.

Case Study: *CHRONO TRIGGER*

Developer:	Square Co., Ltd.
Publisher:	Square Electronic Arts, LLC
System:	Super Nintendo
Writers:	Yuji Horii, Masato Kato
Release Date:	August 22, 1995 (US)
Genre:	RPG
Other Versions:	PlayStation (included in *FINAL FANTASY CHRONICLES*, 1997), Nintendo DS (2008)

FIGURE
8.4

The accidental creation of a time portal sends Crono and his friends on an epic journey to save the future. © Square Enix, Co., Ltd. All Rights Reserved.

Frequently called one of the greatest games of all time, *CHRONO TRIGGER* was the result of a "dream team" collaboration between *FINAL FANTASY* creator Hironobu Sakaguchi, *DRAGON QUEST* designer and writer Yuji

Horii, and *Dragon Ball Z* creator Akira Toriyama. Though never quite achieving the popularity of any of those series, *CHRONO TRIGGER* did become a hit and went on to spawn a sequel (1999's excellent *CHRONO CROSS* on the PlayStation) and enhanced ports on both the PlayStation and DS. It's remembered fondly for many reasons, including its bright cartoon graphics, catchy musical score, fun and memorable characters, time travel mechanics, and numerous endings. It also introduced the New Game+ feature, which lets players who have finished the game restart from the beginning while keeping their characters' levels, spells, and items.

CHRONO TRIGGER begins with spiky-haired teenager Crono heading off to visit the kingdom of Guardia's Millennial Fair, where he meets a cheerful girl named Marle (who is actually the princess in disguise). While having fun at the fair, the pair eventually agree to try out an amazing new teleportation device created by Crono's friend Lucca, but the machine malfunctions, sending Marle through a strange portal. Crono dives in after her, with Lucca promising to follow as soon as she's figured out what went wrong. Crono finds himself transported 400 years in the past, where Marle has been confused for her own distant ancestor (the then queen of Guardia), creating a time paradox. Fortunately, Crono, Lucca, and a warrior named Frog manage to find the real queen and restore the timeline. Unfortunately, things aren't all well in the present and Crono is soon arrested on suspicion of kidnapping Princess Marle, despite her own protests to the contrary. She and Lucca help Crono escape, but the trio is forced to jump into another time portal in order to avoid the pursuing guards. They find themselves a thousand years in the future in a world that has been destroyed by Lavos, a powerful monster that had been slumbering beneath the planet's surface for millions of years prior to its awakening. The friends decide that it's their duty to prevent this sad fate and begin journeying through time to find a way to destroy Lavos.

Along the way, they visit six different time periods and recruit several additional allies, including Frog (a warrior from Guardia's history), Robo (a robot from the distant future), Ayla (a cavewoman from the distant past), and the mysterious magician Magus (who is also searching time for Lavos). Exploring the world across multiple time periods offers many opportunities for players to see how their actions in the past change future times, something that is made use of throughout the story and in many optional quests as well. In addition, the heroes themselves all have a set of optional quests that tie into their backstory and personal goals, and there are lots of other quests and hidden areas to discover as well – all of which serve to further expand on the story and setting.

FIGURE
8.5

***CHRONO TRIGGER* features one of the most unique and eccentric casts to be found in any game. © Square Enix, Co., Ltd. All rights reserved.**

Shortly after escaping from the post-apocalyptic future, the heroes find a portal that will allow them to travel to the day of Lavos's awakening at any time to challenge him. However, trying to fight the final boss early in the game is sure to end in failure, as the heroes don't have the levels or equipment needed to survive. It's not until the end, or near the end, of the main plot that they'll be strong enough to have a chance against Lavos. But that's where New Game+ comes in. After beating the game, players can restart from the beginning, keeping all their levels and abilities and nearly all of their items. New Game+ also allows the players to reach Lavos at an even earlier point in the game. Although breezing through enemies with powered-up characters is fun, the real purpose of New Game+ is to obtain the rest of the game's 12 endings (13 in the DS version), some of which also contain several variations. Fighting and defeating Lavos at different points in the game results in different endings. Four of the endings are joke endings, with two consisting of various characters running around during the credits, one allowing players to talk to members of the development team, and one featuring a hilarious slide show narrated by Marle and Lucca. Of the remaining eight, one is the normal ending and the others constitute a series of what-if scenarios, showing how things would have changed had the heroes defeated Lavos and ended their quest early before meeting certain characters or altering various events. Some of these endings are fun, some are interesting; they all serve to further expand the world of *CHRONO TRIGGER* and provide the player with fascinating glimpses of what could have been.

CHRONO TRIGGER's large number of endings and the unique way in which the players choose between them are among its defining features and served as many players' introduction to multiple-ending storytelling. What's most impressive is that they manage to both expand on the story and provide significant replay value without cheapening the main ending or hiding the best ending behind a series of complex or frustrating requirements, two problems that plague many multiple-ending games. *CHRONO TRIGGER* was far from the first game to use a multiple-ending story, but even after all these years, it's still one of the best.

How Many Endings Does a Game Need?

Blood Omen has two endings; *Dawn of Sorrows,* three; and *CHRONO TRIGGER,* twelve or thirteen. So how many endings should your game have? First off, remember the amount of work that each ending takes to create and make sure you keep this in mind throughout the planning process. Next, remember that you want every ending to be interesting and/or enjoyable and add something to the story. Finally, consider where your endings are placed. With all these things taken into account, you should have a fairly good idea of how many endings you'll need. If your goal is to show what becomes of your hero if he or she becomes good or evil having two endings is probably fine; if you want to explore the different outcomes of an important decision or have endings that are better or worse based on the player's performance, two or three should be enough. As those are the most common multiple-ending scenarios used in games, it should come as no surprise that the average number of endings in multiple-ending stories is two or three. But if you've got a more creative use for your endings and the time and money to create them, there's no reason you can't have more. *CHRONO TRIGGER* may feature more endings than average, but there are some games with far more!

Why, Exactly, Are We Doing Multiple Endings?

In production meetings, the desirability of multiple endings is often championed by marketing. They state that putting the bullet point on the back of the box that the game has "three endings" implies that the game is greatly replayable and thus delivers more value for the dollar. This trade-off is always compared to the increased production cost to create the content for those multiple endings, which can be significant.

It is a sad fact, however, that most games that are purchased are, historically, not finished by the purchaser at all – and an even smaller percentage of players finish a game multiple times. There are players who do so, and those players certainly are the types of customers who are loyal fans, so there is certainly a return on investment from the point of view of the developer and the publisher. But it has never been convincingly demonstrated that the technique of multiple endings increases sales in any measurable fashion.

I mentioned previously the experience of talking with *Dragon Age* players. I asked them after they had discussed the multiple endings whether they would have purchased the game anyway if the game had not explicitly stated that it contained multiple endings. Their reply was inconclusive, and they meandered around the topic as they discussed it. Their main concern was how, if there were not multiple endings, the game might dilute their sense of agency without them. We spent some time analyzing the story and came to the conclusion that, indeed, inability to choose a path of action that affected the ending would have diluted the experience for them. And second, they were willing, as a group, to sacrifice a definitive theme if it meant retaining their sense of agency. This is a small sample, and by no means definitive, but it is a window into the evaluation of an interactive product. They agreed that expression of an author's point of view is valuable, and in fact have enjoyed stories in other media that delivered a powerful point of view (the film *American Beauty* came up in the conversation as a good example of a story that, if it had allowed multiple endings, might have been diluted by that choice). Perhaps it may be true that the interactive medium may not be the place to deliver a powerful theme. I don't think we've come to any solid conclusion either way.

—Chris

Case Study: *STAR OCEAN: SECOND EVOLUTION*

Developer:	Square Enix Co., Ltd.
Publisher:	Square Enix, Inc.
Writers:	Masaki Norimoto, Masayasu Nishida
System:	Sony PSP
Release Date:	January 20, 2009 (US)
Genre:	RPG
Original Version:	*STAR OCEAN: THE SECOND STORY* (PlayStation, 1999)

The *STAR OCEAN* series has a mixed history. The first game did well in Japan but never made it to the United States until it was remade for the PSP as *STAR OCEAN: FIRST DEPARTURE* many years later. Its PlayStation sequel, however, did arrive in the United States and went on to become the most popular game in the series. Despite that, its direct sequel remains a

Japanese exclusive and the third and fourth games in the series, though moderately successful, have met with somewhat mixed reviews. Through all that, the series' intriguing mix of sci-fi and fantasy elements, along with its fast-paced and additive real-time battles and deep skill and item creation systems, have helped it maintain a loyal following.

FIGURE
8.6

SECOND EVOLUTION's **world features a unique mix of fantasy and science fiction.**

STAR OCEAN: SECOND EVOLUTION is a PSP remake of *STAR OCEAN: THE SECOND STORY* that features numerous additions, including a new character and a large amount of additional voice work. The story takes place in the far future, long after mankind set out to explore the vastness of space, seeking out new planets and races. Claude is a young member of the Earth Federation who, while exploring some ancient ruins, is accidentally transported to the undeveloped planet of Expel, a medieval world with little technology but powerful magic. There he saves Rena, a local orphan girl, and is mistaken for the legendary hero of light. Although he insists that he's not the hero, Claude agrees to investigate a strange meteor that recently crashed into the planet both to help Expel's citizens and to try and find a way to contact the Federation and return home. Naturally, the meteor is anything but ordinary and their quest to stop the sinister Ten Wise Men leads Claude, Rena, and their companions all across both Expel and the high-tech world of Energy Nede.

The story itself is interesting and features a large cast of memorable characters, including the teenage inventor Precis and the morose dragon-possessed swordsman Ashton, but it also includes several features that specifically set it apart. First, at the start of the game, players are given the choice between having Claude or Rena as their main character. Although the decision doesn't really change the story, there are brief points in the game at which the two separate and some other events vary slightly depending on whether they're being viewed from Claude's or Rena's perspective. Additionally, some endings are harder or easier to get, depending on the chosen character. The second unusual storytelling feature is private actions. When entering towns, the player has the option to initiate a private action instead of exploring the town normally. During private actions, the player's party splits up, with the player retaining control over the main character (Claude or Rena) while the rest of the heroes explore and go about their business on their own. Tracking down and talking to the various heroes during private actions leads to a variety of different scenes and conversations that serve as the game's primary means of character development. There are a very large number of private action scenes, which make for an enjoyable way to learn more about and grow closer to the characters outside the main story.

FIGURE
8.7

Talking to and forming relationships with other characters is a very important part of the game. © Square Enix, Co., Ltd. All rights reserved.

Finally, there is the primary reason we're talking about *STAR OCEAN: SECOND EVOLUTION* right now: the endings. *STAR OCEAN: SECOND STORY* originally featured a whopping eighty-six unique endings, with *STAR OCEAN: SECOND EVOLUTION* raising the number to somewhere around one hundred. You're probably wondering how any one story could possibly have that many different outcomes and, in fact, it doesn't. Claude and Rena's journey to stop the Ten Wise Men ends the same way every time you play. However, the majority of the ending scenes focus on what becomes of the different heroes afterward. Each hero has an ending in which he or she goes off on his or her own, at least one friends or couples ending for every other hero, and often one or two special endings as well. There's also a special bonus ending that can be unlocked under certain conditions. Upon beating the game, the player is treated to several of the possible endings (between four and eight) depending on how friendly and/or romantically attracted the various heroes are to each other. These friendship and romance values are determined by what the player says during various private actions and which characters are together most often in battle, though they can also be manipulated through the use of certain rare items. The values themselves are hidden from the player, so unless he or she goes into the game knowing about them and makes a significant effort to track and modify them, the ending selection will come across as entirely natural, perhaps even leaving the player unsure of why specific matches were chosen.

The sheer number of endings is impressive, and it can be fun for players to see their favorite characters pair off at the end. However, because there are so many endings, they're all extremely short (many containing only several lines of dialog) and some overlap quite a lot. Furthermore, the hidden friendship system makes it tricky to keep track of how much the various characters like each other, and because of the way the system is set up, certain endings are extremely difficult to get. This can lead to a lot of frustration for players trying to get specific endings, especially if they don't use a guide and do a lot of preplanning. A final issue is that even with multiple save files and a lot of planning and value manipulation, players must complete the entire game numerous times in order to see all or even most of the possible endings – something that none but a very dedicated few are likely to do. In the end, as unique and enjoyable as *STAR OCEAN: SECOND EVOLUTION*'s ending system can be, there are many who question whether it might have been better to just stick with the "canon" character pairings (based on information from the sequel) and provide longer and more satisfying endings for each of them. But, whether or not you appreciate *STAR OCEAN: SECOND EVOLUTION*'s ending system, its fun characters, enjoyable plot, and unique private actions make its story a very memorable one.

Determining Which Ending the Player Sees

By now, you've seen examples of several methods that games use to determine which ending the player can see. For example, there's the straight-up method used in *Blood Omen* that provides the player with a clear choice, often at or near the end of the game, and directly determines which ending the player receives, and *CHRONO TRIGGER*'s timing method, with the ending depending on the point in the story at which the player decides to defeat the final boss. These two methods are the most direct, as they not only make it clear to the player how the ending is chosen, but allow him or her to easily and directly control that choice. Other popular methods – such as the good and evil system (whereby the hero becomes good or evil based on the player's actions) in games such as *Bioshock* (discussed in a case study later in this chapter), *Dawn of Sorrow*'s performance-based endings, and *STAR OCEAN: SECOND EVOLUTION*'s hero relationship system – are less obvious to the player and/or harder for him or her to manipulate, often requiring the player to start the game from the beginning with very specific goals in mind to order to achieve certain endings. Even games that use a fairly clear choice to determine the ending don't need to place that choice right near the end of the game or make it clear that the decision has serious ramifications.

When it comes to deciding which method you should use, the choice should be fairly obvious because certain types of systems lend themselves better to different types of endings. A story with good and evil endings, for example, would work best with a good and evil system or possibly a clear decision point while endings focused on different character relationships could use a system similar to that of *STAR OCEAN: SECOND EVOLUTION*. In the end, it's all about ensuring that the system supports the types of endings you're going to have along with the rest of the story and gameplay.

Case Study: *Growlanser II: The Sense of Justice*

Developer:	Career Soft
Publisher:	Working Designs
Writers:	Shinjiro Takada, You Haduki
System:	Sony PlayStation 2
Release Date:	December 7, 2004 (US) (as part of *Growlanser Generations*)
Genre:	Strategy RPG

Despite having a strong following in Japan, only a few *Growlanser* games have been released in the United States. *Growlanser II* and *III* were the first to arrive here, coming several years after their Japanese release in Working Designs' *Growlanser Generations* collection, and Atlus released *V* shortly after, but the rest have unfortunately remained Japanese exclusives. The series' most popular elements include its non-grid-based battles, ring weapon customization system, and highly stylized artwork. Many games in the series also feature a character relationship system similar to but less complex than the one found in *STAR OCEAN: SECOND EVOLUTION*.

Sense of Justice technically uses a branching path story rather than a multiple-ending one. However, aside from the decision that determines the game's ending, the only other choice that significantly alters the main plot doesn't becomes available unless the player receives a top ranking on every mission in the first portion of the game, a feat that's virtually impossible on a first playthrough, making it unlikely for most players to ever find it.

The hero of the story is Wein Cruz, a knight of the kingdom of Burnstein who dreams of rising in the ranks until he has enough influence to try and prevent wars such as the one that raged during his younger years. At the same time, his friend Maximillian Schneider sets off to try and achieve the same goal through political means. Unfortunately, Wein's first mission as a commander ends with him and his comrades framed for a crime they didn't commit, forcing them to go on the run in an effort to prove their innocence. Several major twists occur as the tale progresses, including a strange encounter with a girl from Wein's past, the secret plot of the mercenary Wolfgang, and Maximillian's ultimate plan to create a peaceful world. The characters and dialog are enjoyable throughout, and things frequently aren't what they seem, ensuring that players remain interested through the course of the adventure. And, in a refreshing change from many game stories, there's no single villain manipulating everything from behind the scenes but rather several separate threats that must be dealt with over the course of the story.

Like in *STAR OCEAN: SECOND EVOLUTION*, *Sense of Justice*'s endings are based on character relationships, the one exception being the special ending for those who discovered and followed the well-hidden decision point I mentioned earlier. However, instead of presenting endings for every possible character pair-up, *Sense of Justice*'s endings focus entirely on Wein and the party member he becomes closest to. This focus, combined with a New Game+ mechanism, makes getting all the different endings a far more realistic goal than in *SECOND EVOLUTION*. His relationships with his comrades strengthen or weaken based on the player's responses in certain conversations as well as finding and participating in a variety of optional story scenes that can be triggered by visiting certain areas at specific times during the game. Unlike in *SECOND EVOLUTION*, the characters' relationships are quite easy to keep track of, as the status menu displays every character's current level of affection for Wein. To make it even easier for the player to achieve his or her chosen ending, there's a point about 80 percent of the way through the story at which Wein has a day off and can choose to spend it with any one of his comrades. If the chosen character's affection for Wein is high enough, he or she will agree and the day's activities, along with the eventual ending, will be decided. Having the decision point earlier in the game makes for a somewhat more natural progression than a last-minute choice and also allows the story to show Wein and his chosen friend/girlfriend growing closer prior to the ending. However, it also means that even if the player develops strong relations with every character and creates a save point prior to his or her choice, he or she will still have to play through the final portion of the game each time he or she wants to obtain a different character's ending. In a nod to romance over friendship, the player is required to get the endings for all three of the game's female heroes before any of the male heroes' endings become available, which can be disappointing for some players. One final surprise, and a strong incentive for obtaining every ending, turns up in *Growlanser III*, when after undertaking an optional quest, the player is given the ability to import his or her party from *Growlanser II* (who otherwise don't appear in *III*'s story), though aside from Wein, only characters whose endings were seen are able to make the transfer. Aside from providing a cool cameo and a chance for *Growlanser III* players to obtain some powerful characters and items early in the game, it provides one of the best incentives I've ever seen for players to actively seek out every different character and ending. Though rather hard to find, it's touches like this one – combined with excellent stories and fun gameplay – that make *Growlanser Generations* worth tracking down.

Multiple-Ending Stories and Sequels

In multiple-ending stories, it's quite common for the various endings to contradict each other, sometimes considerably. Although this isn't an issue in individual games, in an industry with such a heavy focus on series and sequels, it can cause quite a lot of problems. In *Growlanser II* and *STAR OCEAN: SECOND EVOLUTION*, for example, different characters can become romantically involved or just end up being really close friends. But what if those characters appear again in the sequel? Who should they be paired with? An even tougher decision comes in games such as *Blood Omen*, in which the different endings are not only strongly opposed but lead to major repercussions throughout the entire game world. There are several different ways to deal with this issue, each of which has its own advantages and disadvantages.

The first is to pick a single specific ending and declare it to be canon. From that point on, that ending is what truly happened and the one on which all future games are based, and the others are nothing more than things that could have been. In games featuring the classic good, bad, and neutral set of endings, the good ending is generally used. In games using other types of endings, it really comes down to the writer's preference, though looking into which ending was most popular among fans is a good idea as well. This is a popular method used by series including *Legacy of Kain* and *Star Ocean*. It's a quick and easy solution that allows you to continue on with the world and characters from the first game. However, fans of a particular ending (for example, those who feel that Kain really should have sacrificed himself at the end of *Blood Omen*) may be upset that the story didn't go the way they wanted. Creatively, this can be problematic as it says to the players "we know we gave you two choices but only one really mattered."

If you don't want to tie yourself down to a particular ending, the other easy way out is to dodge the issue entirely. Just because a game is a sequel doesn't mean that it must feature the same characters or even take place on the same world. Many series, such as *FINAL FANTASY*, feature new worlds and characters in each game, with only a few common threads linking them together, making this a very popular approach. If you want to keep your sequel in the same setting and the different endings of the first game didn't feature massive world-changing ramifications, you can still dodge the issue by having the sequel take place in a different time period and/or feature different characters. In *Growlanser III*, for example, the cast of the previous game show up only if the player completes a certain optional quest, and even then they have little dialog and no important role in the story, so the question of who Wein ended up with never becomes an important issue.

A less popular and trickier but still workable approach is not to use any of the first game's endings and instead combine elements from all of them to create a new ending, which then becomes the canon. Although this allows you to reuse your favorite elements from multiple endings, it requires more work, as you need to write an entirely new ending to go off of. It also tends to confuse fans, though they usually manage to piece together the events of the new nonexistent ending eventually.

The final option is the toughest, requiring a lot of extra work from the entire development team, but also provides the biggest payoff for the choices the player made in the previous game. If your sequel is going to be released on the same system as your previous game, or the new system is backward-compatible, you can allow players to import their old save file, with the game playing out differently based on which ending they received in the first game. Depending on the types of endings used in the first game, the extra work required can range anywhere from rewriting a few lines of dialog to creating several almost entirely different stories. However, in an effort to keep the additional workload at a reasonable level, the rare games that use this approach usually do their best to keep the endings close enough that significant story changes aren't required. For fans of the series, carrying over their story decisions from the past game shows them just how much their choices mattered and can be a big selling point. On the downside, it can also discourage new players, who may feel like they can't really play the new game unless they play the original first, and can potentially hurt replayability, as replaying two entire games takes a lot longer than replaying one.

Case Study: The *Mass Effect* Series

Developer:	Bioware
Publisher:	EA
Writers:	Drew Karpyshyn, Mac Walters
System:	Microsoft Xbox 360, PC
Release Date:	November 20, 2007 (*Mass Effect*, US); January 26, 2010 (*Mass Effect 2*, US)
Genre:	Action RPG

FIGURE
8.8

Mass Effect takes place in the far future, when humanity has spread into space. *Mass Effect* Images, © 2010, Electronic Arts Inc. All rights reserved. Used with permission.

Bioware's epic sci-fi series has quickly grown to become one of their most popular franchises. Like all Bioware games, *Mass Effect* features a long, complex story; well-developed characters; and a massive number of optional quests and tasks for the player to undertake. Although the heavily streamlined battle and character development systems in the second game irked some fans, both *Mass Effect* games launched to near-universal praise and expectations for the third and final volume of the trilogy are very high.

The *Mass Effect* series follows Commander Shepard, an experienced human solider in the late twenty-second century, when space travel and planetary colonization have become commonplace. Though humans are one of the less influential species in the universe, Shepard soon gains an opportunity to change that by becoming the first human Spectre (a type of special agent with freedom to go anywhere and do as he or she pleases, answering only to the highest levels of government). Shepard's appearance and gender are chosen by the player, who is – in an interesting twist – also able to pick between several possible origin stories for the hero. Although these decisions don't significantly affect the main story, they do alter the dialog in various conversations and make certain optional quests available or unavailable. Thanks to the planned backstories and well-written dialog, Shepard manages to avoid the generic hero stereotype that plagues most RPGs featuring player-created heroes. However, as a result, the player's control over Shepard's personality is limited to acting as a paragon (a law-abiding, by-the-book hero) or a renegade (a get-the-job-done-by-any-means-necessary antihero).

FIGURE
8.9

While hunting down a rogue Spectre in *Mass Effect*, Shepard learns of an ancient alien race called the Reapers, who secretly foster the technological advancement of other races only to suddenly wipe them out once they've progressed to a certain point. Unfortunately, there are few who believe him, forcing Shepard and his ragtag crew to search for a way to stop the Reapers on their own. The planet-hopping adventure features a diverse cast of races and characters, along with a detailed universe and mythology to explore. Shepard is able to make numerous choices when reacting to different characters and situations and can even pursue a romantic relationship with one of several members of his crew. However, these decisions have little to no effect on the main plot, and even the ending – which features several variations depending on the result of two choices Shepard makes – changes only slightly, leaving *Mass Effect* to straddle the line between a multiple-ending story and an interactive traditional story. This approach does have its advantages, allowing players to customize Shepard and his behavior to better suit their preferences and providing a strong illusion of control, while still allowing for a well-structured, writer-controlled story.

Mass Effect 2 picks up shortly after the first game, when Shepard's ship is suddenly attacked by a powerful enemy. Though his crew manages to escape, Shepard himself is caught in the crash and thought to be dead. Two years later, he wakes up under the care of Ceberus, a human group with a questionable history, that brought him back from the brink of death. Their leader wants Shepard to investigate the disappearance of large numbers of human colonists, which he believes is the work of the Reapers.

FIGURE
8.10

Mass Effect 2 **features many new characters, though many from the first game make appearances as well.** *Mass Effect 2* **Images, © 2010, Electronic Arts Inc. All rights reserved. Used with permission.**

Featuring a mostly new cast of characters that are just as interesting and fun as the first and many more worlds to explore, *Mass Effect 2* provides another engaging planet-hopping journey throughout the universe. The story has even more twists than the first and often takes on a much darker tone as well, with slavers and twisted human experimentation playing significant roles. Once again, players are able to play the paragon or renegade and woo one of several crew members along the way. As in the first game, the majority of choices the player makes have little to no effect in the long run, but some of the choices – particularly those near the end of the game – have significant ramifications later on, making the game (barely) a branching path story.

FIGURE
8.11

Battles are fast-paced and intense. *Mass Effect 2* **Images, © 2010, Electronic Arts Inc. All rights reserved. Used with permission.**

Players are also able to import their save data from the first *Mass Effect*, which carries over their customized Shepard along with a record of the important decisions he made and ending he received in the first game. As most of the major characters and areas from *Mass Effect* play a much smaller role in *Mass Effect 2*, this data doesn't significantly alter the main story, though it does change some events and conversations. This continues to let the players feel that their choices matter and provides a strong illusion of control, while maintaining the structured story. A similar system is planned for *Mass Effect 3* as well, allowing characters to complete the entire trilogy with their custom character. Although carrying over the results of decisions from past games made for a lot of extra work for Bioware's writers, it allows the series to achieve a degree of consistency rarely seen in series using anything but interactive traditional stories, making *Mass Effect* an excellent example of the most player-centered way of solving the multiple-ending dilemma.

The Strengths of Multiple-Ending Stories

Multiple-ending stories can serve several purposes. First and foremost, they allow the players to gain some degree of control over the plot, which can – in theory, anyway – help ensure that the story plays out in the way they'll most enjoy. (For an in-depth discussion on whether this is really the case and why, see Chapters 12 and 13, along with the research data in Chapter 14.) The more endings there are, the higher chance there is that there will be at least one the player likes, possibly avoiding unsatisfying ending situations like the one in *Arc the Lad II*. Multiple endings can also increase a game's replay value by encouraging players to restart the game and try for a different ending. In some games, they also serve to support and enhance core game concepts such as *STAR OCEAN: SECOND EVOLUTION*'s relationship system and *Castlevania: Dawn of Sorrows*'s exploration-based gameplay. Multiple endings may also drive players to play a game in ways they normally wouldn't, such as playing as an evil hero instead of a good one or striving to complete a particularly difficult task in order to achieve a certain ending.

Case Study: *Disgaea: Afternoon of Darkness*

Developer:	Nippon Ichi Software
Publisher:	NIS America
Writers:	Yoshitsuna Kobayashi, Sohei Niikawa
System:	Sony PSP
Release Date:	October 30, 2008 (US)
Genre:	Strategy RPG
Other Versions:	*Disgaea: Hour of Darkness* (PS2, 2003); *Disgaea DS* (DS, 2008)

FIGURE
8.12

Disgaea's **unique story focuses on Prince Laharl's bid to conquer the Netherworld.**
© 2006-2011 Nippon Ichi Software, Inc © 2011 NIS America, Inc. All rights
reserved.

Japanese developer Nippon Ichi is known for creating some of the deepest and most hardcore strategy RPGs in existence, with nearly endless character and item development, battle systems built to be carefully dissected and exploited, and optional challenges that require players to push their party to extreme levels of power in order to succeed. However, fans of their games are quick to point out that much of the appeal comes not just from the gameplay, but from their unique characters and hilarious stories. Nippon Ichi's flagship franchise, the *Disgaea* series, embodies both of these traits. *Afternoon of Darkness* is an enhanced port of *Hour of Darkness* (the first game in the series) that features many additions, including new bosses and a bonus what-if story starring fan-favorite character Etna.

The story takes place in the Netherworld, a hell-like dimension, where the demon Prince Laharl has just awakened from a two-year nap to discover that his father, the mighty overlord King Krecheskoy, choked to death on a pretzel, leaving the Netherworld in chaos as hordes of powerful demons battle to claim the throne. Unwilling to let someone else become overlord in his place, Laharl sets out with his questionably loyal retainer Etna and a squad of underpaid prinnies (which can best be described as evil penguins) to beat down the upstarts and cement his claim to the throne. Along the way, he battles and occasionally befriends a wacky cast of characters, including the pesky "Dark Adonis" Vyers (who, much to his chagrin, is renamed Mid-Boss by an unimpressed Laharl), bumbling angel trainee Flonne (who was sent from Celestia to assassinate the overlord), and the overly heroic Captain Gordon, Defender of Earth. In between the zany antics and humorous dialog, *Disgaea's* story manages to work in a few surprise twists and a nice, if slightly corny, moral about the importance of love and friendship, even among demons, who many (themselves included) believe to be too evil to care about such things. The clash of ideals between demons such as Laharl and Etna, who hold things like ruthlessness and betrayal in high regard, and Flonne and Gordon, who value kindness and heroism, is handled in a mostly lighthearted way, but there are occasional serious moments as well. Over the course of the game, it's fun to watch Laharl's progress from a spoiled brat to a powerful overlord and finally to a person who truly understands love and compassion, though in a somewhat demonic way.

FIGURE
8.13

Disgaea is full of crazy characters and hilarious dialog. 2006–2011 Nippon Ichi Software, Inc. © 2011 NIS America, Inc. All rights reserved.

Disgaea contains numerous endings. Most of them are humorous in nature, but they all build on various characters and/or game elements to great effect. Though not all of the endings are easy to find, they all fit in very logical places throughout the game. Some focus on what-if scenarios. Losing a battle to Mid-Boss, for example, shows an ending where the oft-beaten underdog at last reigns supreme; another ending shows what would happen if Laharl pursued the traitorous General Carter to Earth instead of letting him escape. Others, however, show the results and consequences of Laharl's actions. If he's deemed to be suitably cruel (determined by how many of their own allies players have killed in battle), he's given the option to kill certain enemies rather than spare them, leading to bad endings in which his own allies attack him in turn. The main ending also plays on the story's themes of love and friendship, concluding on a rather sad note unless the player successfully reached the end without killing any allies, in which case – having fully learned the meaning of love and compassion – Laharl holds back at a crucial moment, sparing his enemy and allowing the best possible ending to take place.

FIGURE
8.14

The importance of love and kindness plays a key role throughout the story. 2006–2011 Nippon Ichi Software, Inc. © 2011 NIS America, Inc. All rights reserved.

The way *Disgaea*'s endings focus on interesting what-if scenarios and tie heavily into the story's themes works wonderfully, fully showing the way that multiple endings can expand and enhance a story. However, *Disgaea*'s approach isn't without problems. The game itself offers no hints as to how to achieve the different endings (though one NPC does break the fourth wall to suggest that there is more than one way for the story to end). Although this isn't a big problem for most of the endings, which serve as fun extras and are easy enough to stumble across with a little exploration and experimentation, reaching the end of the game without killing any allies is a moderately difficult task. In strategy RPGs featuring abilities with large areas of effect, it's quite common to find one or two allies standing in the blast radius of an attack that will also strike quite a lot of enemies. Strategically, it can be best for the allied character to take one for the team rather than hold off on the attack, especially when the injured ally can be healed after the battle. Even for players trying to avoid such a scenario, it's easy enough to accidentally hit an ally with any number of attacks if the player isn't paying close attention to exactly what's in his or her target range. This could easily lead to many players never seeing or even realizing the existence of *Disgaea*'s best ending, which is a problem because it not only wraps up a couple of otherwise unexplained plot threads, but is also the canon ending that the stories in the rest of the series build on. This is *Disgaea*'s biggest weakness and also one of the key weaknesses of multiple-ending stories in general, but is still only a minor flaw in an otherwise excellent game.

The Weaknesses of Multiple-Ending Stories

First, a general warning. At the end of the day, after putting hours upon hours into a particular game, players want an ending that provides at least a moderately satisfying conclusion to the story. As previously discussed, the ending doesn't need to tie up every single plot thread or be entirely happy, but it shouldn't be completely depressing, vague, or abrupt, either. Though this is a big enough problem in interactive traditional stories, players expect multiple-ending games to have at least one good ending. If they put in the extra time to see every ending only to find out that all of them are bad, they're going to be understandably upset.

When it comes to multiple-ending stories, one thing you need to ask yourself is which ending the player is most likely to see. Keep in mind that many people play through a game only once. If their first playthrough results in a bad ending, they may not be willing to replay the entire game (especially if it's a long one) just to try for a better ending. They may not even realize that there is a better ending and may walk away from the game feeling decidedly unsatisfied. This is an especially big problem in games such as *Disgaea* and *Bioshock* in which a single mistake can render the best ending impossible to achieve without restarting the entire game. In general, the shorter a game is and/or the more fun the gameplay, the greater the chance is that players will be willing to replay it to get different endings, but there's still no guarantee that they'll do so, and it needs to be clear to them that there are other endings to find. Furthermore, although the most common ending doesn't necessarily have to be the best one, it should at the very least provide a somewhat satisfying conclusion to the story so that players who see only that ending won't be upset.

Games such as *Blood Omen* avoid that problem by allowing players to easily choose which ending they want to see at or near the end of the game, so that at most they need to replay only a very short portion of the game to see each ending. This approach, however, leads to another weakness of multiple-ending stories. If the player is allowed to simply reload his or her last save and watch all the different endings one after another, they tend to lose their impact. One ending may show the hero bidding a tearful farewell to his lover, who sacrificed herself to save him, but if players know that they can just reload and watch another ending in which she survives, the scene loses much of its shock value and emotional impact. The player can also get bored watching all the different endings back to back if they're too similar. In some cases, the player may also realize that the hero's actions in many of the endings contradict his or her beliefs and personality as shown in the other endings or even the rest of the game. On the other hand, if the player has to replay most or all of the game to get a different ending that at least reduces (though doesn't entirely negate) the loss of emotional impact and also lessens the chance that the player will see enough of the endings to get bored or spot any serious consistency issues, though it also drastically reduces the number of players who will see more than one ending.

Finally, although this isn't a hard and fast rule, the more endings a game has, the shorter and more repetitive most of those endings will generally be. Although there are some notable exceptions to this rule (*Chrono Trigger*, for example), the amount of extra time and effort required to create each additional ending means that it will probably always hold true for the majority of games that use multiple-ending stories.

Case Study: *Bioshock*

Developer:	Irrational Games
Publisher:	2K Games
Writer:	Ken Levine
System:	Sony PlayStation 3, Microsoft Xbox 360, PC
Release Date:	August 21, 2007 (US)
Genre:	FPS

The spiritual successor to the cult classic *System Shock* series, *Bioshock* did away with many of the typical FPS conventions, presenting a dark and disturbing tale devoid of wars or alien invasions with a heavy emphasis on atmosphere and a deep combat system that rewards experimentation and unusual strategies. Proving that doing things differently can pay off, it rapidly became a surprise hit, selling millions of copies and receiving near-universal acclaim from players and critics alike.

When a passenger plane goes down in the middle of the ocean one night in 1960, Jack, the lone survivor, swims from the burning wreckage and comes across a small island. The only structure is a tower containing an elevator, which takes him far below the sea to the underwater city of Rapture. Built in the 1940s by business tycoon Andrew Ryan, Rapture was founded on the principles of famed writer Ayn Rand, with the goal of allowing business, art, and science to flourish, free from the oppressive restrictions imposed by politics, religions, and morals. A marvel of design and engineering, Rapture thrived as its citizens made rapid advances in many fields. However, by the time Jack arrives, something has gone horribly wrong. Most of Rapture's inhabitants are dead, and those who survived have become murderous mutants known as splicers, who roam the halls, seeking out the few remaining pockets of normal humans while the city slowly crumbles around them.

Jack is guided over the radio by a man named Atlas, who promises to help him find a way to safety if Jack in turn helps Atlas and his family escape from Rapture. Though weapons are surprisingly common, as Jack begins to explore the city and piece together its troubled history, he soon discovers that guns alone aren't enough to survive and gains the ability to use plasmids as well. In one of Rapture's more notable developments, plasmids and gene tonics use a substance known as ADAM (discovered by a Rapture scientist named Dr. Tenebaum) to rewrite human DNA, granting almost magical powers such as telekinesis, pyrokinesis, and teleportation. However, ADAM has its dark side as well, with overuse leading to horrendous mutations and a loss of sanity. But that was only one reason for Rapture's downfall. Frank Fontaine, a mobster and the only supplier of ADAM, also contributed, setting up false charities as a front for twisted human experiments in order create the creepy ADAM-harvesting Little Sisters and their hulking guardians, the Big Daddies. Even Andrew Ryan himself, the founder of Rapture, contributed greatly to its destruction. Forsaking his own ideals, he became a tyrant, violently taking over Fontaine's businesses and then tearing the city apart in a war against Atlas and his supporters.

The use of audio diaries to explain Rapture's backstory is an interesting one and adds a very personal touch, allowing the player to see the city through the eyes of the people who lived during its darkest times. The only downside is that finding them all can be rather difficult, requiring a considerable amount of searching if players want to uncover the full story. Throughout his explorations, Jack also has several run-ins with some of Rapture's surviving citizens, most of whom are only marginally saner than the deadly splicers tracking them, and is frequently lectured over the radio by Atlas, Dr. Tenebaum, and Andrew Ryan. Jack himself, however, is very much the silent protagonist, not speaking a word throughout the entire game, even during the shocking plot twist that takes place when he finally meets Ryan. And, as the entire game is played from a first-person perspective, he lacks body language as well. This is, in my opinion, the weakest point in *Bioshock*'s story, making Jack more of a generic "guy with a gun" than a true character that players can grow to like and sympathize with. That aside, *Bioshock*'s story explores the dark depths of human greed and depravity in one of the most unique and compelling settings in gaming, making for a disturbing yet intriguing experience.

As a multiple-ending story, *Bioshock* contains three endings, which can be classified as good, bad (or evil), and neutral. The ending received is based on Jack's treatment of the Little Sisters, the young girls who roam about the city extracting ADAM from dead bodies. Each girl is guarded by a hulking Big Daddy. Although this powerful guardian will ignore you if you leave him alone, he becomes merciless when threatened, and bringing him down is no easy feat. Doing so, however, will leave the Little Sister unprotected. As Jack grabs the struggling child, the player is given the option to harvest her (killing the girl and receiving a large amount of ADAM) or saving her (removing her genetic modifications so that she can return to a normal life while gaining a small amount of ADAM). This makes for a very straightforward good and evil mechanic. Saving the girls is good, but leaves Jack with less ADAM to improve his plasmids and gene tonics; harvesting them is evil but makes Jack far stronger. Unfortunately, the theory isn't supported by the gameplay, as saved Little Sisters periodically give Jack gifts containing large amounts of ADAM, making the difference between the good and evil paths rather minimal, though players are unlikely to notice this on their first playthrough.

The endings are somewhat problematic as well. The bad ending (achieved by completing the game while harvesting every single Little Sister) briefly shows Jack taking over Rapture and leading an army of splicers to conquer the surface world. Although very short, it does effectively show the type of monster that Jack could become after his journey through Rapture, though it doesn't make for a very satisfying conclusion to the story. The good ending (gained by saving every Little Sister in the game) has Jack instead bringing the former Little Sisters to the surface and raising them until they have families of their own. Though still short, it allows the story to go out on a much more satisfying note. The neutral ending (gotten by harvesting some Little Sisters while saving others) is unfortunately the same as the bad ending, but with slightly different narration. Though players who go through the game harvesting every Little Sister might expect some sort of dire consequences eventually, for players who harvested only one or two Little Sisters while saving the others, Jack's dark actions in the neutral ending are inconsistent and disappointing. And because getting a different ending requires replaying the entire game from the beginning, it discourages many players from trying over in hopes of obtaining a better outcome. But despite the occasional blemish, *Bioshock*'s unique setting and compelling story make it an experience that no one with an interest in game storytelling should miss.

Summary

Multiple-ending stories are very similar to interactive traditional stories, with the notable difference being that players are – either consciously or unconsciously – allowed to choose from two or more possible endings. There are many different types of endings that can be used, including endings based on the hero's morality, based on character relationships, based on the player's performance during the game, and based around various what-if scenarios. Though most multiple-ending stories limit themselves to two or three endings (generally a good, bad [or evil], and neutral ending), there's no set limit to the number of endings a story can have. However, because each ending takes additional time and effort to create, it's important to ensure that they add enough to the experience to be worth it.

Choosing between endings gives players a degree of control and choice not found in interactive traditional stories, though it can be debated whether doing so significantly improves or detracts from the overall experience. Care also needs to be taken so that players who play through the game only once still receive a satisfying conclusion. This can be done by placing the deciding point near the end of the game so that players can reload and try again if they don't receive an ending they like, but it has the drawback of significantly reducing the emotional impact of each individual ending, a problem that plagues most multiple-ending stories to some degree.

Finally, sequels to multiple-ending games create additional challenges, as you need to decide which ending, if any, to make canon. There are other ways to approach the issue; some games, such as *Mass Effect*, allow players to carry over their progress and ending from the previous game into the sequel, though doing so requires a considerable amount of extra planning, writing, and design.

Things to Consider

1. List five games you've played that use multiple-ending stories (and if you haven't played that many, just list the ones you have).

2. Pick two of the games from your list. How many endings do they have? How do they determine which ending the player receives?

3. In both games, were you happy with the first ending you received? Why or why not?

4. Did you want to replay one or both games in order to see the other endings? Why or why not?

5. Do you think that the additional endings enhanced or detracted from the games' stories? Write a short explanation of your reasoning.

Nine

Branching Path Stories

FIGURE
9.1

Fully Traditional Stories

Interactive Traditional Stories

Fully Player-Driven Stories

Multiple-Ending Stories

Open-Ended Stories

Branching Path Stories

Branching path storytelling.

While multiple-ending stories only allow the player to choose the game's ending, branching path stories insert multiple decision points throughout the story, allowing the player to make a series of choices as he or she progresses through the game. Though some of these decisions have little to no lasting effects on the main plot, others can change it significantly, causing it to branch off in another direction entirely (hence the name). Branching path stories have multiple endings, but unlike in multiple-ending stories, the player doesn't follow the same path to reach all of those endings. Because of this, they allow for far greater player freedom and control, granting the player significant power at multiple points throughout the story rather than just at the very end.

What truly makes branching path stories unique is that unlike open-ended stories and fully player-driven stories (covered in Chapters 10 and 11), they're built around a very rigid structure of decision points and branching paths leading off those points. Though the player makes a choice at each branching point, the writer retains strict control over the points themselves and everything that takes place in between them. Though it can be difficult to write, a well-done branching path story can provide the perfect bridge between the more structured, writer-focused storytelling styles and the more open, player-driven ones, telling a carefully controlled story while still providing the player with a number of important decisions. This combination of well-structured story and player choice has helped branching path stories gain popularity (see Chapter 14), and they've recently been used in some very high-profile games.

Multiple Branches Multiply the Cost

Though it is absolutely true that branching path stories can be glorious (and I have designed two of them), there is one big issue when building them: cost. Game publishers being a prudent lot, they really want to pay only for content that will be *seen* by the game player. And because multiple-path stories aren't just words on the page when created but voice-over dialog as well as locations, characters, and so on, there is a real chance with these games that content will be created that the player may never see – even with repeated playthroughs.

When you're a writer, pressure gets brought to bear on your team to design for these multiple paths, but also to reuse material created for one story purpose when sending a player on another side path, which can negate the exciting nature of these alternate paths. Most successful versions of games like this are written stories with limited graphics and other audio visual elements, as these elements can quickly become very expensive to create.

Aidyn Chronicles: First Mage used a typical method to mitigate this issue. We had one main storyline without much branching. The story nodes were location-based, meaning that the story advanced when the player traveled to certain cities. There was technically nothing stopping the player from skipping ahead (we blocked paths with boulders in only a couple crucial locations when the story would truly unravel if the player got *too* far ahead), but players had to complete certain tasks in a certain order to move the story forward, and the NPCs that would facilitate that advancement were only in particular cities.

We branched the story via the make-up of the hero's party. Along the way, the player could add/subtract traveling companions from his or her party, not only to increase a certain set of skills so as to meet the opposition more effectively, but also to alter the way in which the story unfolded. These party members would carry with them story elements, and these story elements would play out only if those members were actually *in* the party at the time.

As an example, one party member was the hero's girlfriend. Well, she would turn out to be the hero's girlfriend at the end of the story if she were in the party at that time and hadn't died along the way, but during the game the romance would be blooming. That relationship would grow in one way if the hero's party didn't have a competitor for her affections, and a completely different way if the hero had added a second female as a party member. After that NPC was added to the mix, she and the original girlfriend would fight over the hero as the game progressed, and eventually the hero would be put in a position in which he would have to choose which girl to go with.

This is an example of how, on the A-story level of the main plot, the story didn't branch, but branched on the B-story level, yielding a different emotional tone to the game depending on the composition of the party.

—Chris

Case Study: *Choose Your Own Adventure* Books

Writers: The series featured 32 different authors; the two most prolific are R.A. Montgomery and Ed Packard, with 60 books each.
Publisher: Bantam Books (original publisher) and Chooseco (current publisher)
Release Dates: 1979–1998 (original series) and 2005–present (Chooseco reprints)

Though not the first books to make use of branching path stories, the well-known *Choose Your Own Adventure* series is responsible for popularizing the concept. Generally well received, *Choose Your Own Adventure* books were an extremely popular children's series in the 1980s and early 1990s, spanning over 300 volumes and selling more than 250 million copies, while also inspiring a wave of copycat titles. Though the popularity of branching path books eventually waned, leading to the series' cancellation in 1998, Chooseco began republishing them in 2005 with moderate success.

The series followed a very predictable structure. You (the reader) were on a great adventure. You might be a famous explorer, cunning general, master detective, or one of a variety of other professions, or you might just be an ordinary person who was in the wrong place at the wrong time. Regardless, something big is going on and you're right in the middle of it. As the story unfolds, you frequently find yourself facing various important decisions. There are two or three possible choices per decision, each one prompting you to turn to a different page to see the outcome. Quite often, your choice would lead to a grisly death, forcing you to flip back to the last decision point and try again, but at times your choices would lead you down different paths and, eventually, to one of the book's handful of good endings.

Though famous for their interactivity and novelty appeal, the stories in *Choose Your Own Adventure* books are extremely shallow, which is likely one reason for the demise of both the series and the style in general. Though it could be argued that many children's stories are shallow when compared to those geared toward older audiences, the *Choose Your Own Adventure* books simply didn't have the length required to tell a strong story. Each book averaged around 120 pages, with anywhere between 20 and 40 of those pages occupied by the various available endings. That left very few pages for any sort of serious plot or character development, especially as those remaining pages were divided between several story paths. In addition, the story paths and endings often contradicted each other, preventing any larger narrative development from taking place when they're combined. *Journey Under the Sea*, for example, is 117 pages long with 42 endings and revolves around a deep sea search for the lost city of Atlantis. Although the vast majority of the endings involve the hero dying or giving up the search, he can also discover that Atlantis is an ancient undersea civilization ruled by an evil king, an ancient undersea civilization split into two warring factions, a secret government research facility, an alien base, or a passage to the center of the earth. Some of the later titles reduced the number of endings and decision points, focusing more strongly on the story and consistency, but even the best *Choose Your Own Adventure* stories never approached the level of plot and character development found in ordinary children and young-adult books.

Despite their flaws, the *Choose Your Own Adventure* books are still fun to read and provide the perfect example of how branching path stories work. Games, however, have several key advantages, including much greater length and the lack of physical pages to flip (which make it easy to lose your place or cheat and jump to a section you haven't reached yet), which has allowed them to expand on and show the true potential of branching path storytelling. However, as Chris pointed out, the cost of creating a branching path story in games can be a significant drawback.

Creating Branching Path Stories

Branching path stories take a lot more work and planning to create than do similar interactive traditional or multiple-ending stories. You start off the same way, by creating a basic concept and outline for your story. After that, however, you need to look carefully at your story's structure and decide where the decision points are going to be, what purpose each branch is going to serve, and how the various branches combine and separate over the course of the story. Other important issues include ensuring that the branches aren't too similar to each other and that the story remains interesting and engaging regardless of which way it branches. Length can also become a major issue, as a 200-page interactive traditional story could easily take 300 or 400 pages or maybe more to tell as a branching path story. And when it comes to games, the writing is only the beginning, as each branch will have its own art, programming, and sound needs as well. We'll discuss all of these issues and how to approach them over the course of this chapter, but first it's important to understand a bit more about how branching path stories are structured.

Types of Branches

Each time the player makes a decision in a branching path story, the plot branches off in one of two or more different directions. However, not all branches are created equal. Branches can be divided into three distinct groups – minor, moderate, and major – each of which serves a different purpose in the structure.

FIGURE
9.2

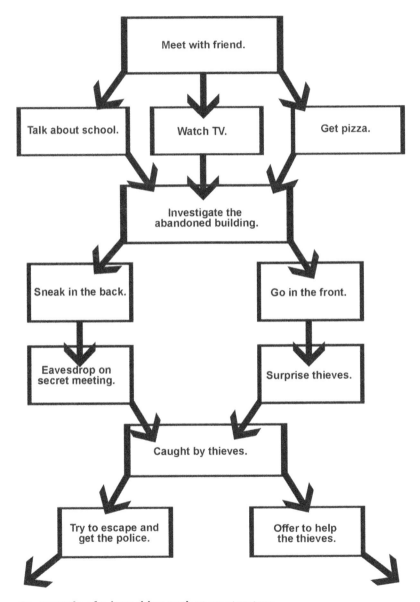

An example of a branching path story structure.

Understanding the differences and uses of each of these three branch types is critical when creating branching path stories. Figure 9.2 shows the structure of the opening section of a fictional branching path story. It contains all three types of branches and will be used to explain the primary differences between them.

Minor Branches

Minor branches rejoin the main branch very shortly after branching off. As such, they have little to no significant effect on the story and serve only to offer several different versions of a single scene. In our sample story, the first branch is a minor one. After the hero meets a friend, the player can choose to have the two of them talk about school, watch TV, or get pizza. Unsurprisingly, this isn't a very important choice, and all three lead to minor branches that converge when the hero decides to investigate an abandoned building. However, even though none of these branches have a lasting effect on the main plot, their scenes can be used to convey backstory, character development, or hints about future plot developments.

Moderate Branches

Moderate branches are the next step up. Like minor branches, they eventually rejoin the main branch, preventing them from having a significant impact on the main plot. However, they take far longer to rejoin the main plot than minor branches do, allowing them to present very different scenarios that lead to the same eventual destination. In our example, while investigating the building, the hero can choose to sneak in the back, which leads to his finding and eavesdropping on a meeting between thieves, or he can go in the front, in which case he runs into the thieves almost immediately. Either scenario eventually ends with our hero getting captured by the thieves, but it takes time for the paths to rejoin. As with minor branches, each moderate branch can contain interesting information not present in the other branches, just as choosing to sneak in the back is the only way for the hero to listen in on the thieves' meeting and learn of their plans.

Major Branches

Minor and moderate branches serve to modify their main branch; major branches break away entirely. Instead of rejoining the main branch later on, they form new main branches, each with its own set of minor branches, moderate branches, and endings. In our sample story, a major branch comes at the very end. After being captured by the thieves, the hero can try to escape so he can call the police or he can offer to join the thieves instead. It shouldn't be too surprising that this choice has major ramifications on the plot, causing what was a single main branch to split into two. In one, the hero goes on to fight crime; in the other, he seeks to become a master criminal himself. Though some of the same characters and situations may occur along both branches, the two remain separate for the rest of the game, creating two very different storylines.

Because major branches are the only ones that significantly alter the story, you can't have a true branching path story without at least one major branching point. Both minor and moderate branches, however, can be used in interactive traditional stories and multiple-ending stories, as they provide only minor modifications to the overall story. In fact, if you look back at the games we discussed in the previous several chapters, you'll see that many of them use minor branches, letting the player steer conversations or small events in different directions, and a few (such as *Mass Effect)* contain moderate branches that allow players to tackle certain quests or goals in two or more different ways.

One thing to keep in mind is that although most branching points are presented to the player as a clear choice between two or more options, that doesn't mean that the results need to be obvious as well. In *FRONT MISSION 3* (which we'll discuss in a moment), the first branch involves choosing whether the main character helps his friend with a delivery. On the surface, this seems like a very minor decision, but it's actually a major branching point, dividing the story into two very different main branches depending on which option is chosen.

As in multiple-ending stories, choices don't always need to be the result of a conscious action on the part of the player, either. In *Fate/Stay Night* (a visual novel game discussed in greater detail later in this chapter), there are several branching points at which the choice is made automatically based on how friendly certain characters are with the hero, which is determined by the choices the player made at various minor and moderate branching points earlier in the game.

Finally, though each branching point in the sample image uses only a single type of branch, there's no reason a single branching point can't have one option that leads to a minor branch, one to a moderate, and one to a major, or any combination of the three. Mixing things up will make your structure more interesting and a whole lot less predictable.

Case Study: *FRONT MISSION 3*

Developer:	Square Co., Ltd.
Publisher:	Square Electronic Arts LLC
Writers:	Kazuhiro Matsuda, Norihiko Yanesaka
System:	Sony PlayStation
Release Date:	March 22, 2000 (US), December 21, 2010 (Playstation Network rerelease)
Genre:	Strategy RPG

FIGURE
9.3

***FRONT MISSION 3*'s story is rife with warring factions and political intrigue.
© Square Enix, Co., Ltd. All rights reserved.**

FRONT MISSION is one of Square Enix's lesser-known franchises, particularly outside Japan, as only four out of ten games have been released overseas. Originating on the SNES and continuing on to current generation consoles, *FRONT MISSION* is set on Earth in the near future. Many of the world's countries have combined into a set of super nations that include the USN (North and South America), OCU (Japan, Australia, and much of Southeast Asia), and EC (Europe). Despite this new unity, wars and civil strife are common. The new weapon of choice is the Wanzer, a giant humanoid robot that comes in many different forms and can be heavily customized to suit the pilot's preferences. The gameplay places a heavy focus on battle strategy and Wanzer customization, with some games like *FRONT MISSION 3* encouraging players to disable and capture enemy Wanzers rather than destroying them outright. The series has been frequently praised for its depth, though the complexity has also been known to intimidate new players.

FRONT MISSION 3's heroes are Kazuki and Ryogo, a pair of young Wanzer test pilots in Japan. When Kazuki's stepsister is caught up in an attempted coup by the Japan Defense Force, who have stolen a newly developed super weapon named MIDAS, the friends set out to rescue her. They eventually end up traveling through much of Asia and Eastern Europe, working as mercenaries for hire while gaining allies and trying to track down and stop MIDAS. Though much of *FRONT MISSION 3*'s story is told via cut-scenes and character conversations, it does contain a rather novel way of fleshing out its characters and setting. Between battles, players have access to an in-game version of the Internet. Each party member has his or her own email address and receives letters throughout the game. Players can carry on the correspondences by choosing from various predefined replies, steering the conversations in the direction they choose. In addition, players can access a variety of "websites" that contain information related to the various locations, people, and corporations in the game. There's a massive amount of information available, greatly expanding on the setting and backstory, though many of the sites can be accessed only after Kazuki has learned of their existence from conversations, emails, or other sites. Some even require a good bit of searching and a little "hacking" in order to uncover. This makes for a fun optional way to delve further into the game's story and also rewards thorough players with some special Wanzer parts and other bonuses.

FRONT MISSION 3 uses a branching path story. The first branch occurs near the beginning of the game when Ryogo asks Kazuki to assist him on a delivery. At first glance, this seems like a very unimportant choice. However, it actually constitutes the game's only major branching point. If Kazuki stays behind, he'll receive Alisa's desperate email message the moment it arrives and rush to her aid in time to save her from her kidnappers, only to be framed for the destruction of a research base, forcing them to flee and seek a way to clear their names. But if he goes on the delivery, he won't see the email until he gets back and arrives too late to save Alisa, instead teaming up with a USN officer named Emma to chase after the people that took Alisa and MIDAS. Although both stories primarily revolve around Kazuki and Ryogo's search for MIDAS and have them traveling to many of the same locations, the details vary considerably. With the exception of Kazuki and Ryogo, each branch has its own set of playable characters. Furthermore, depending on which branch was taken, the pair will find themselves on different sides of various regional conflicts. In Alisa's branch, for example, Kazuki and his comrades join the DHZ (formerly China) in an effort to stop a USN-backed rebel movement. In Emma's branch, however, they join the rebels to help overthrow the DHZ's government. The events and conflicts in *FRONT MISSION 3* are rarely clear-cut, and many characters who are bitter enemies in one branch become close friends and allies in the other, making it difficult to say for certain which sides are in the right. It also ensures that players will need to complete both branches in order to fully understand the story, significantly increasing the game's replay value.

FIGURE
9.4

Different characters join Kazuki's party depending on which choices the player makes. © Square Enix, Co., Ltd. All rights reserved.

In addition to the single major branch, *FRONT MISSION 3* makes use of various moderate and minor branches as well. An example of a moderate branching point occurs when Kazuki's forces are tasked with assaulting an army stronghold in Emma's story. The player can choose to either break in through the front (a difficult but very direct route) or sneak in through the mountains (a longer but far safer option). Aside from the different sets of battles, the choice determines whether Kazuki will eventually recruit Jose or Li to join him. The main plot remains the same either way, but both characters have their own specialties, backstories, goals, and opinions on the events taking place throughout the rest of the game. Finally, many minor branches are spread throughout the game. These branches generally revolve around which route or strategy the player decides to adopt in certain situations and change little other than one or two battles (and the events surrounding them). Some, however, are determined by whether the player is able to complete certain goals in battle (such as destroying an enemy transport before it escapes). Though the effects of these branches aren't long-lasting, they increase player freedom in what is otherwise an extremely linear game and provide enough variety to mix things up a bit and further increase replay value.

FRONT MISSION 3's branching path structure allows the player to have a moderate degree of control over the progression of the plot while still telling a deep and well-structured story. In addition, the way its different branches focus on characters and situations on both sides of conflicts greatly expands on the story and setting, giving players a much broader perspective than they'd have in an interactive traditional or multiple-ending story. The only notable flaw in the game's story structure is that the decision at the major branching point seems so minor that players could easily underestimate its importance and put away the game after a single playthrough, never realizing that they're missing an entire half of the story.

Deciding Where to Place Branches

As with endings, have your story's basic concept and structure planned out before you start adding decision points and branches.

Minor branches are the easiest to add. Look for places in the story at which the hero will face a decision that won't have a serious impact on the main plot. Conversations are a good place to put them, as you can let the player steer the subject toward the matters that interest him or her most or allow the player to approach a topic in several different ways (kind, rude, crafty, etc.). Battle strategies such as deciding to sneak past or engage enemies are also a good place to work in minor branches, though the exact method will very heavily depending on the type of gameplay and battle system in your game.

Moderate branches require a bit more forethought. A good set of moderate branches should be placed at a point in your story where they can safely split off from the main branch for a while – only to rejoin it later. Giving the player a choice between two alternate routes to the same destination (taking the long route over the mountains or the short dangerous one through the caves) works well, as does providing multiple ways to approach a certain goal. For example, if the hero needs an artifact that is owned by a very rich man, you could provide a choice between sneaking into the man's manor and stealing it, performing a task for the man in return for the artifact, or earning enough money to buy it outright. All three of those options would take a decent amount of time and bring the hero into contact with different characters and situations, but they'd all eventually rejoin once he gets the artifact.

As major branches are the biggest and most important ones, their placement needs to be approached with the most care. First, you need to identify points in your story where a certain decision or action on the part of the hero has the potential to wildly change the plot. Next, you should think about what the key differentiating factor between each major branch should be. In *Front Mission 3*, it's who Kazuki ends up working with to stop MIDAS (Alisa or Emma), while in *Fate/Stay Night* (which we'll discuss a little later on) it's which girl Shiro falls in love with (Saber, Rin, or Sakura). Naturally, there's far more that differentiates the major branches than that, but these key factors begin a series of events that go on to affect the entire story. Although romances and alliances are two common key differentiating factors, other possibilities include the choice between good and evil, whether certain characters live or die, and which hero becomes the "main character." Once you have your key differentiating factor in mind, take another look at your list of potential branching points and narrow it down to ones that fit well with the types of stories you want your major branches to focus on. For example, because the two major branches in *Front Mission 3* are based on who Kazuki partners with, the decision point revolves around whether he arrives at the research center in time to save Alisa or comes later on, at the same time Emma is there. In *Fate/Stay Night*, the decision points for the major branches are tied into how Shiro acts around the three girls. So give it some thought and decide which potential branching points best support your major branches. One more interesting thing to note is that you can approach your major branch structure in two ways. The first is *Front Mission 3*'s method, in which players sooner or later reach a point where the story splits into two or more main branches and they have to choose one in order to continue. The second is *Fate/Stay Night*'s method, in which there is a "default" main branch (Saber's) and any additional main branches can be reached only if players fulfill certain specific conditions doing the first part of the default branch (in *Fate*'s case, that means saving Rin from Saber or being especially nice to Sakura).

There's one final thing you should consider when planning each of your branches. What does this branch add to the story? Branches do exist to give the player choices, but if those choices lead to uninteresting results, you're more likely than not to bore the player rather than engage him or her. Branches can provide a different perspective, different dialog, different quests, and even entirely different takes on the story as a whole, but unless a branch is interesting and/or enjoyable and at least moderately different from the other potential branches, it should be left out. If you have a decision point with three branches and only two of them lead to interesting scenarios, you can expect at least a third of your players to miss out on the interesting parts and be forced to slog through a dull and boring section. This is especially important with major branches. Although players can forgive some boring minor or moderate branches, because they'll end and rejoin the main branch sooner or later, a major branch significantly changes the rest of the game, so it's critical that each one provides an experience that's fun and interesting enough to keep players entertained until the end.

How Many Branches Should a Story Have?

As with endings, there's no hard and fast rule as to how many branches you should put in your story. If you followed the instructions in the previous section and put together a list of potential decision points and branches, you should have an idea of just how many branches your story can potentially have. However, you'll probably want to reduce that number a bit. First, as we just discussed, get rid of any branches that don't provide interesting and/or enjoyable additions to the story. Then look at your abbreviated list and start thinking about your production schedule. As mentioned in the last chapter, every additional ending you add to your story takes extra time, effort, and money to write, model, code, and so on. Branches are the same. Minor branches are usually fairly quick and simple to create (though this can vary considerably based on their exact content), but the longer and more unique a branch is, the more work is required to create it. Moderate branches naturally take quite a lot more work to create than minor branches, but they can't even begin to compare with the time and effort required to create additional major branches, especially as each major branch will need its own set of minor and moderate branches. You'll be able to reuse some material across multiple branches (the game engine, certain areas and characters, etc.), but the time and cost needed to add extra branches still grows very quickly. With that in mind, it's a good idea to consult with the lead designer and/or producer (unless you yourself are filling one or both of those roles), review your schedule and budget, and then go over your list of potential branches one more time and remove everything except for the best and more important ones.

Japanese Visual Novel Games

We talked a little bit about Japanese visual novel games back in Chapter 7 during the case study of *Higurashi: When They Cry*; now it's time to explore the genre in a bit more depth. Visual novels (or sound novels, as they're sometimes called) are a popular game genre in Japan. They're primarily released on the PC, but many titles are later ported to consoles such as the PlayStation 2 and DS. Due to their relatively low production costs, visual novels are generally created by small teams of independent game developers. They often begin as hobby projects, with their creators later going on to form official development studios if their first game proves successful. The most popular visual novels frequently spawn anime (animated television series), manga (comic series), and massive amounts of merchandise – including soundtracks, figurines, and much more – with some visual novel developers such as Type-Moon and Key becoming extremely successful.

Despite their popularity in Japan, only a handful of visual novels have been released outside the country, and most of the more popular ones, such as Type-Moon's *Tsukihime* and *Fate/Stay Night* and Key's *Kanon*, *Air*, and *Clannad*, have yet to be released outside Japan. There are numerous reasons for this, including the small independent nature of most visual novel developers, worries about translation accuracy, concerns about how Western gamers will react to the gameplay style, the adult content found in some visual novels, and a general misunderstanding of the American market by many people in Japan. Though the situation is slowly improving, it's hard to say if we'll ever see official English releases of the vast majority of visual novels, which is highly unfortunate because they contain some of the best branching path stories in gaming.

> Though most visual novels aren't released outside Japan, there are a few available from MangaGamer (http://www.mangagamer.com) and JBox (http://www.jbox.com), though it should be noted that JBox specializes primarily in adult-oriented dating sims rather than visual novels and that a large portion of MangaGamer's catalog is also made up of highly adult-oriented titles rather than story-focused ones.
>
> If you can't read Japanese but want to try out some of the more popular story-focused visual novels such as *Fate/Stay Night* and *Kanon*, there are some fan-made translation patches available online that can be used with the Japanese retail versions of the games. Though importing the games and tracking down the correct patch takes a bit of work, it's currently the only way people without advanced Japanese skills can experience these excellent stories.
>
> Note that although anime and manga adaptations of some popular visual novels have been released in the United States, they contain highly abbreviated versions of the original stories, often losing much of their depth and leaving lots of unresolved plot threads.

So what exactly is a visual novel game anyway? A visual novel is a type of game that is in many ways similar to reading a book. The story is told through large blocks of text, generally written in a first-person perspective from the main character's point of view. However, unlike e-books, visual novels contain background images that change based on the hero's current location and facial and/or full-body portraits of any character or characters he's talking to. The artwork usually isn't animated, but each character has enough poses that he or she still appears to be reacting accurately to the situation. The text and visuals are further complemented by a full set of sound effects and background music and, in some games, voice acting. This turns what would be an e-book of sorts into a full audiovisual experience – hence the term *"visual novel."*

But where does the game part come in? Visual novels (with a few rare exceptions such as *Higurashi: When They Cry*) use branching path stories. On the surface, they're fairly similar to those found in *Choose Your Own Adventure* books. Every so often, the player will be presented with a choice, with the story branching accordingly depending on his or her decision. Also similar to the *Choose Your Own Adventure* formula, it's quite common for many wrong choices to lead to the hero's unfortunate demise, forcing the player to back up and try again. However, the branching path stories in visual novels represent significant improvements over those found in *Choose Your Own Adventure* books. First, some decision points are hidden from the player, with the game automatically selecting a branch based on the player's past decisions. For example, in one part of *Fate/Stay Night* the hero, Shiro, is seriously injured and close to death. If, over the course of the game, he was friendly enough to Ilya (a mysterious girl he encounters at various points), she'll come to his rescue. If not, he'll be left to fend for himself. Things like that would be far more difficult to track in a physical book. Other features, such as a large number of save slots and the ability to rapidly skip through sections that have already been read, make it easy for players to fully explore the story and try out all the different branches. But most importantly, being a digital product, visual novels don't face the length restrictions found in physical books. When taking into account all of *Fate/Stay Night's* different branches, the total word count is more than that of the entire *Lord of the Rings* trilogy. A book of that size would be huge, and the need to constantly flip through the pages to follow different branches would make it a chore to read. However, this significant increase in length allows visual novel games to tell stories as long and complex as those found in any good novel while still using a branching path structure. The focus on deep stories with mature themes and consistent plots throughout all the branches further sets them apart from *Choose Your Own Adventure* books.

If you're interested in exploring the world of visual novels, it should be noted that there's a rather large subgenre that is based around hentai (adult) games. These visual novels focus far more on the adult elements than on the story and can be highly pornographic in nature. Even a lot of the story-focused visual novels such as *Fate* and *Kanon* tend to contain a few token sex scenes (just as R-rated Hollywood movies do). But because these scenes generally have little to no importance to the main plot, they can be skipped over without consequence. Quite a lot of story-focused visual novels are also released in two versions: a regular, unedited one and an "all ages" edition that is nearly identical except for the removal of the sex scenes. *Kanon All Ages* and *Fate/Stay Night Realta Nua* are two examples of these "all ages" editions.

Case Study: *Fate/Stay Night*

Developer: Type-Moon
Publisher: Type-Moon
Writer: Kinoko Nasu
System: PC
Release Date: January 30, 2004 (Japan)
Genre: Visual Novel

Fate/Stay Night is one of Japan's most popular visual novels – a position it's managed to hold throughout the years since its release, thanks in part to an anime, manga, movie, novel series, several spin-off games, and a variety of related merchandise. But the most important reason behind *Fate*'s continuing popularity is its intriguing story and memorable characters.

Fate's story spans a two-week period of time known as the fifth Holy Grail War. The Holy Grail War is a contest of sorts in which seven magi each summon a Servant (powerful familiars based on heroes of legend such as Hercules and Gilgamesh) and fight to the death for the right to control the Holy Grail, a magical relic with the ability to grant any wish. This particular Holy Grail War is unusual, having begun decades ahead of schedule.

Before the war, Shiro Emiya is a seemingly ordinary Japanese high school student who lives on his own after the death of his guardian, Kiritsugu (who rescued the young Shiro from a devastating fire ten years before). Unknown to those around him, Shiro is also a mage, albeit a very weak and inexperienced one. He learned the basics of the art from Kiritsugu before his death, but never received full training; he can do little other than slightly strengthen various objects. Though disappointed by his lack of progress, he continues to practice in hopes of realizing his dream of using the art to help others, becoming a sort of superhero. Although he knows nothing of the Holy Grail, Shiro's life is turned upside down when a strange twist of fate puts him in control of Saber, a young woman and master of the sword who is rumored to be the strongest Servant of all. Shortly after, he saves the life of Rin Tosaka, a classmate who is heir to a prestigious family of magi and Master of the Servant Archer. In thanks, she tells him about the Servants, the Grail, and the war. Though Shiro has no interest in the Grail or fighting, he agrees to join in order in protect the townspeople from the other, far more ruthless, magi who are competing.

The story quickly grows far more complex. All Masters and Servants have their own reasons for seeking the Grail, many of which belie dark troubled pasts. Shiro's determination both to not kill and to protect everyone, along with his lack of magical skills, puts him at a serious disadvantage. Even though Rin and Saber see his ideals and dream as foolish, Shiro defends them to the end, determined to die rather than betray them. Meanwhile, Saber is wrestling with her own past, which is tied into the heroic identity she keeps hidden from everyone, Shiro included, and is desperate to find the Grail so that she can correct her greatest mistake. And that's barely scratching the surface. *Fate*'s tale is shocking, emotional, and often very dark, grappling with issues including murder, rape, loyalty, betrayal, and the morality of sacrificing a few to save many.

As previously mentioned, *Fate*'s English fan translation contains more words than the entire *Lord of the Rings* trilogy, spread over three major branches and numerous minor and moderate ones. Though many branches lead to Shiro's untimely demise, finding every bad ending is actually a worthwhile pursuit in and of itself, as they're followed by humorous scenes featuring the other characters discussing what Shiro did wrong and offering hints on what to try next time, while also unlocking special bonus content. There are forty bad endings and five full endings (one on Saber's branch and two each on Rin and Sakura's), and because the correct choice isn't always the one that seems most logical, it's impossible to completely avoid death. Fortunately, the ability to save at any time and rapidly skip over completed sections of the story makes it easy to experiment and try different options.

The three major branches – dubbed Fate/Stay Night, Unlimited Blade Works, and Heaven's Feel – each tell a very different side of the story, and it's impossible to understand everything that's taking place behind the scenes in the Holy Grail War without completing each one. Despite retelling the same basic story, each major branch is considerably different, focusing on different characters (both friends and enemies) and showing vastly different ways in which the story could play out. Fate/Stay Night is Saber's story, the default main branch, and the one that players have to complete first. It focuses on Shiro and Saber's backstory, while introducing players to the Holy Grail War and many of the important characters. Completing it opens up the decision point leading to Unlimited Blade Works, which focuses on Rin and Archer while also delving deeply into Shiro's motivations and the dangers of his naïve ideal. Getting either of the good endings in Unlimited Blade Works opens the decision point leading to Heaven's Feel. It's the longest and darkest of the main branches, with a focus on Shiro's friend Sakura, her brother Shinji, the Servant Rider, and Berserker's master Ilya.

Each branch tells a very important part of the story, and it's not until after the completion of Heaven's Feel that players will fully understand each character's histories and motivations and the true nature of the Holy Grail. All told, finding every ending (good and bad) and following every branch (minor, moderate, and major) can easily take over 60 hours, but it's a worthwhile investment for such a deep and multifaceted story. Although forcing the player to go through the three major branches in a predetermined order does somewhat limit player freedom, it also removes the need to reiterate the same character introductions and exposition in each branch, which prevents players from getting bored by repeatedly rereading the same material and allows each progressive story revelation to build on the ones that came before, making the small reduction in player freedom worthwhile.

There are many games that use branching path stories well, but it's visual novel games like *Fate* that show the true potential of the style first popularized in the old *Choose Your Own Adventure* books, allowing players to make choices and fully explore multiple aspects and perspectives of the story while maintaining well-structured plots with the depth and complexity normally reserved for far less interactive storytelling styles.

The Strengths of Branching Path Stories

As shown in the previous case studies, the greatest strength of branching path stories lies in their ability to provide players with a large number of important choices while still giving the author a considerable amount of control over the progression of the story. This allows for lengthy and complex stories with good structures and pacing (things that become increasingly difficult to control in heavily player-driven stories). Meanwhile, the interactivity itself gives players a moderate amount of control, rather than just the illusion of control present in interactive traditional stories, and allows both the player and the writer to explore many different aspects and alternate tellings of the story. Though they don't give the writer complete control and lack the ease of creation found in interactive traditional stories, while also lacking the larger degrees of player freedom found in open-ended stories and fully player-driven stories, a well-done branching path story strikes an excellent balance between player freedom and a well-structured plot. Despite their shortcomings, in many ways they form the best possible combination of both sides of the storytelling spectrum.

Case Study: *Heavy Rain*

Developer:	Quantic Dream
Writer:	David Cage
Publisher:	Sony Computer Entertainment
System:	Sony PlayStation 3
Release Date:	February 23, 2010 (US)
Genre:	Adventure

Though best known for their recent PS3 hit *Heavy Rain*, developer Quantic Dream also created the cult classics *Indigo Prophecy* and *Omikron: The Nomad Soul*, both of which are known for their excellent stories. Thanks to its realistic graphics, emotionally charged story, and a strong marketing campaign, *Heavy Rain's* success has greatly exceeded expectations, finally bringing Quantic Dream's name into the public eye.

Part adventure game, part interactive film, *Heavy Rain* takes place in an unnamed American city and follows four characters in their attempts to discover the identity of the illusive Origami Killer, a serial killer who abducts and then drowns young boys. Ethan Mars is an architect who lost his oldest son in a traffic accident two years prior. He never got over the tragedy, causing him to become estranged from his wife and younger son, Shaun. However, when Shaun mysteriously disappears and all signs point to the Origami Killer, Ethan puts everything on the line to get him back. His chance encounter with Madison Paige, a newspaper photographer with a serious case of insomnia, leads her to aid him and begin her own investigation into the killer's identity. Meanwhile, the Origami Killer is also being pursued by Scott Shelby, an aging private eye hired by the victims' families, and Norman Jayden, an FBI profiler working with the local police.

Though the four characters' stories frequently intertwine, they never actually team up, with each pursuing his or her own methods of finding the killer and the game switching between characters at the start of each chapter. The gameplay itself is a mixture of standard adventure fare (conversing with other characters and engaging in some light puzzle solving) and extended quick time events (scripted cut-scenes in which the player frequently has to push certain buttons to help the hero succeed in whatever he's doing). Despite the use of a PS3 controller, the button combinations used in these scenes do a good job of representing what the character is physically doing, whether it's firing a gun or gently rocking a baby to sleep. The addition of support for Sony's new Move motion controller helps to make these events even more realistic. One of the most unique aspects of *Heavy Rain's* gameplay is that regardless of whether the player successfully hits all the button prompts, the scene will continue, with the events changing based on the player's success or failure. Though quick time events have become commonplace, especially in action games, failure to hit the proper button usually results in the event failing, forcing the player to restart it. But *Heavy Rain* keeps going, no matter what. Even if one of the heroes dies an early death, the story will continue on without him or her.

Despite suffering from a few plot holes, *Heavy Rain's* story manages to be emotional, profound, and disturbing. It draws players in like few other games, making them strongly feel Ethan's desperation as he pushes through a crowded mall calling out to his missing son and Madison's shame when a sleazy night club owner forces her at gunpoint to perform a private striptease act. It also brings up a large number of interesting moral dilemmas. Shortly into the game, Ethan is given a set of challenges by the Origami Killer that he must complete to receive clues to Shaun's location, all in the name of seeing just how much he's willing to sacrifice to save his son. Early challenges test Ethan's bravery and willingness to risk serious injury; some of the later ones become true tests of Ethan's and, by extension, the player's beliefs and convictions. As discussed in Chapter 3, one challenge tasks Ethan with killing a man. Although Ethan is desperate to save Shaun, seeing his intended victim kneeling at his feet begging for a chance to see his own child again gives him serious second thoughts. Later on, the final challenge presents Ethan with a vial of deadly poison that when drunk will kill him in one hour, leaving him just enough time to save Shaun and say his final goodbye. Ethan is free to back out of any or even all of the challenges, and it is possible for him to find and save Shaun without completing all of them, but that's something that neither Ethan nor the player knows at the time, making each decision a matter of life and death and leading to a lot of interesting discussions among players about what they would choose if faced with a similar situation in real life. The game's last major plot twist, involving the unmasking of the Origami Killer, is another shocking scene that has led to an enormous amount of discussion and makes for an emotionally charged lead-up to the final confrontation and ending.

The sheer number of reactive events and the way they match the players' actions, rather than forcing players to retry them until they do it right, create an incredibly strong sense of control, making players feel as if their every decision and button press matters. Unfortunately, playing through the game additional times shatters this illusion, as players will soon realize that most things they do actually don't have any effect on the story beyond the current chapter – and even then, the effect is often minimal. Most branching points are minor, with only a couple moderate branches and one major one. That isn't counting the branches that take place if players allow one or more of the heroes to die or fail in their search, as keeping them alive and on the right track is surprisingly easy (with numerous chances to recover from poor button presses and faulty leaps in logic), and even if they do die, their remaining story scenes are merely dropped from the rest of the game, with the only significant change to the rest of the story being the events of the final chapter and the ending scenes the player receives. To some extent, this is a good thing, as it allows the story to retain its tight pacing and careful structure. However, players may be somewhat disappointed upon discovering that the game doesn't quite live up to the "everything you do matters" hype. Regardless, its emotional story and

> unique gameplay make *Heavy Rain* one of the most interesting and innovative games in years. The replay value is questionable, but this player's first playthrough was an extremely engaging and exhilarating experience and the shocking scenes and difficult moral decisions are sure to remain on players' minds long after the credits roll.

The Weaknesses of Branching Path Stories

Branching path stories are in many ways an excellent synthesis of the structured plots of interactive traditional stories and the freedom of more player-driven forms of storytelling, but they're not without problems. The first is their creation process. As you probably realized when reading through this chapter, planning out all the different branches and decision points and ensuring that each one is interesting and serves a purpose in the overall story isn't easy. If you haven't realized that yet, just give it a try for yourself and you'll soon see what I mean. And, as previously mentioned, the more branches you add to a story, the more time and effort (and, by extension, money) it takes to complete. This can be somewhat negated by creating shorter stories and/or reusing a lot of assets, but some players will be annoyed by short stories (regardless of how many branches they have), and reusing too many assets can lead to your main branches feeling overly similar, which is sure to bore many players.

The structure itself also shares a problem with multiple-ending stories, namely, a potential loss of impact. Important story events such as the hero's failure or the murder of an important character lose quite a lot of their emotional impact when players know that they can just reload from an earlier save and take a different branch in order to prevent it. After all, what's a death or crushing defeat when you can just turn back time and pretend that it never happened? You can avoid this result entirely by making your more emotionally charged moments unchangeable, though that may leave some players wondering why you bothered giving them choices in the first place if they can't change some event. Or you could place the branching points that influence those events long before the actual event takes place, so that the player won't be so quick to jump back and try out a different branch, though this only lessens the problem and doesn't remove it entirely.

Another potential problem lies in the fact that it's not always easy for players to tell what the results of their decisions are going to be before (and at times even after) the fact, such as Kazuki's delivery decision in *Front Mission 3*. In cases like this, players may end up on a branch they don't like with no idea of what wrong choice sent them there. This can lead to quite a lot of frustration, especially if a player needs to replay a significant portion of the game in order to turn the story down a more enjoyable branch.

Finally, branching path stories tend to require players to complete most – if not all – of their different branches before they can fully understand the story. Though this is fine for hardcore players who are determined to thoroughly explore every nook and cranny of their games, it's important to remember that many players will play through a game only once or maybe twice and may never see quite a lot of the branches that you put so much time and effort into creating. This raises the question of whether adding all of those branches is really worth the effort – something we'll discuss more in Chapter 13.

Case Study: *THE BOUNCER*

Developer: Square Co., Ltd.
Publisher: Square Electronic Arts LLC
Writers: Seiichi Ishii, Kiyoko Ishii
System: Sony PlayStation 2
Release Date: March 5, 2001 (US)
Genre: Beat 'Em Up

FIGURE
9.5

At the beginning of every battle, the player can choose to play as Shion, Volt, or Kou.

Square's first PlayStation 2 game was a large departure from the epic RPGs that made them famous. Though the graphics, music, and voice acting are generally well regarded, the story and gameplay drew very mixed responses from fans. For starters, *THE BOUNCER* is short, with a single playthrough requiring only several hours at most. There's also very little exploration and only light RPG elements, with the game mostly made up of cut-scenes and FMVs interspersed with beat 'em up–style brawls.

The story revolves around Shion, Volt, and Kou, three bouncers working at a bar named Fate, and Dominique, a teenage girl whom Shion took in after finding her wandering the streets alone in the rain. At the start of the game, Dominique is kidnapped by a group of strange ninja-like assailants, causing the three friends to run off in pursuit. Their journey leads them to the powerful Mikado Corporation and its cruel and calculating CEO Dauragon, and eventually into space for a final showdown. The plot has a strong Hollywood action movie vibe with lots of fast scenes, chases, explosions, and battles against increasingly strange and powerful martial artists. As such, it's a lot of fun and has a couple of genuinely interesting twists, but also gets a bit ridiculous at times (thanks to things like the space flight and Dauragon's assistant, a woman who can transform into a panther).

THE BOUNCER has a strong action movie vibe. © Square Enix, Co., Ltd. All rights reserved.

The most interesting aspect of *THE BOUNCER*'s story is the way it uses branching path storytelling. At the beginning of each battle, the player is given a choice of which of the three bouncers to control directly, with the others being handled by AI. Only the chosen bouncer receives stat boosts and new attacks from the battle, and the subsequent cut-scene is also told from that particular character's perspective. For example, after the opening brawl, Kou calls someone on his cell phone to help track down Dominique's kidnappers. If the player chose Shion or Volt, he hears only Kou's side of the conversation; players who chose Kou get to hear both ends. Almost all of these constitute minor branches, with only a couple of moderate ones when the three heroes split up for a short time. However, players need to play through the game at least three times in order to learn all about Shion, Volt, and Kou's pasts and their connections with the Mikado Corporation. The only real major branch occurs at the very end of the game and determines, along with their decisions at some earlier minor branches, which ending the player will see.

Although being able to play the story from three different perspectives is interesting and significantly increases the replay value, each character's path is extremely similar, making those replays feel somewhat repetitious. Players who are put off by this, or who simply don't have the time or inclination to play through the game multiple times, will also miss out on quite a lot of important story elements, including the heroes' backstories and the identity and motivations of enemy characters such as Kaldea (the panther lady) and Echidna (a Mikado employee who has a history with Volt). Some players enjoyed having lots of incentives to play through the game multiples times; others strongly disliked having to replay it so many times to fully understand the story, especially as each character's path is so similar. In the end, although *THE BOUNCER* remains a fun and enjoyable game, it also exemplifies some of branching path storytelling's inherent problems.

Summary

Branching path stories use a structured, writer-controlled story combined with a number of decision points and branches to provide players with a degree of control over the direction and progression of the plot, a style first popularized in the *Choose Your Own Adventure* books. Though most branches are minor or moderate and stray from and/or alter the main branch for only a short period of time, major branches break away completely, creating new main branches of their own and taking the story in entirely different directions.

Deciding where to put your decision points and branches can be difficult and takes a lot of planning, as does ensuring that the story remains interesting and enjoyable no matter what choices the player makes. The additional amount of time, effort, and cost needed to create each branch is also a very important factor, especially considering that many players complete a game only once or twice and may never see quite a lot of the branches.

When done correctly, branching path stories can create an excellent combination of well-structured, writer-controlled plots and player freedom – something that is demonstrated especially well in Japanese visual novel games. However, they can suffer from a loss of impact similar to that found in multiple-ending stories. There's also the danger that players will become upset if they get struck on a branch they don't like or have to replay the game too many times in order to fully understand the story. This is especially problematic if the different branches use too many of the same elements, making them feel overly similar. Despite this danger, branching path stories still remain one of the most promising forms of player-driven storytelling.

Things to Consider

1. List five games you've played that use branching path stories (if you haven't played that many, just list the ones you have).

2. Pick two of the games from your list. Make a simple flowchart of their branching structure, using a strategy guide or online FAQ as a reference (if the games are really long, chart out only a portion of them). Mark each branch as minor, moderate, or major.

3. Pick one of those two games. Are there any branches that you consider to be boring and/or unnecessary? Explain your reasoning for each of those branches.

4. Did the presence of the different branches make you want to replay the game so that you could see the other outcomes? Why or why not?

5. Do you think the use of a branching path structure significantly enhanced or detracted from the game's story? Explain your reasoning.

Ten

Open-Ended Stories

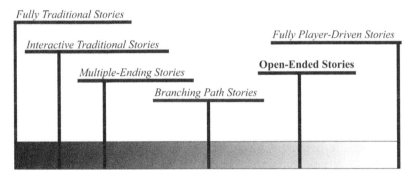

FIGURE
10.1

Fully Traditional Stories

Interactive Traditional Stories

Fully Player-Driven Stories

Multiple-Ending Stories

Open-Ended Stories

Branching Path Stories

Open-ended storytelling.

Open-ended stories are something of an evolution of the branching path formula, but several notable things set them apart. First, branching path stories retain a strong writer-controlled structure that moves the player from decision point to decision point; open-ended stories are far more player-driven. Players have numerous ways to approach nearly every quest and situation and are often free to progress through the game any way they want. Even important story scenes can often be done out of order or even skipped entirely. The decision points in open-ended stories also tend to be far more organic than those in branching path stories, with the branch chosen based on the player's actions and speech, rather than a clear-cut choice.

Outside the main plot, open-ended stories tend to feature a large world (or country, city, or the like) that players are more or less free to explore during most parts of the game. While doing so, players will encounter a myriad of different optional quests and activities that they can choose to take on or ignore. Many games with open-ended stories also feature a morality system, with players' actions changing their moral alignment and affecting how various NPCs act toward them.

Because of their extreme complexity, open-ended stories can be very tricky to write, and in fact, frequently feature shorter and simpler main plots than games that

205

use less player-driven forms of storytelling. To make up for this, a heavy focus is placed on developing the setting and providing the player with numerous optional activities to keep him or her busy. Open-ended stories can be considered the best way to tell a highly player-driven story in video games, even more so than fully player-driven stories (for reasons we'll talk about in the next chapter). As such, high-profile games using open-ended storytelling are generally the poster children for industry figures who argue for the superiority of highly player-driven stories. But despite this, the style comes with many challenges and quite a lot of innate weaknesses, making it very challenging to use and somewhat limiting its popularity among players (see Chapter 14).

Structure Without Sequence

As you will see throughout this chapter, the real challenge in game stories of this type for the writer doesn't lie in the typical "How can I make this quest interesting?" issue, but rather high above that, in the realm of "Have I created an interesting enough world so that the players can create compelling stories for themselves?" This is a new kind of challenge for the writer. We are used to creating both the setup as well as the reversal leading to the climax, and then sorting out all the details of the journey from one stage to the next. In this type of story, the player does the sorting. Most stories of this type are simple because of this design constraint. Yet-to-be answered questions for writers in this structure are

• How do you truly surprise a player in this kind of structure?

• Can dramatic tension be kept at an appropriate level in this kind of story?

At this point in the history of game writing, I think the jury is still out on those two concerns. Or we haven't gotten our act together yet.

—Chris

Case Study: *Fallout 3*

Developer:	Bethesda Game Studios
Publisher:	ZeniMax Media
System:	Sony PlayStation 3, Microsoft Xbox 360, PC
Release Date:	October 28, 2008 (US)
Genre:	Action RPG

FIGURE
10.2

Despite the destruction, the Capital Wasteland is a rich and vibrant setting.
Fallout 3 © 2008 Bethesda Softworks LLC, a ZeniMax Media company. All rights
reserved.

The *Fallout* series' complex battle system, nuclear war–ravaged Earth, and
dark stories made them some of the more popular PC RPGs in the late
1990s. However, when series creator Interplay sold the rights to Bethesda,
creators of *The Elder Scrolls* series (one of which is discussed later in this
chapter), fans were worried about the new direction *Fallout* would take.
Fortunately, though *Fallout 3* did adopt some of the presentation and
gameplay elements of *The Elder Scrolls*, it stayed true enough to the world
and story of the previous games to please longtime fans while also
attracting many new players with its large world and more action-oriented
gameplay.

Fallout 3 takes place in the year 2277, two hundred years after a nuclear
war decimated modern civilization. Since then, the world has become a
dangerous place, filled with violent mutants, ruthless slave gangs, and
several warring factions trying to become the new leaders of the age. It's
not a world for the weak or inexperienced. However, there are pockets of
survivors who have lived on unaffected by the terrifying changes that
swept the world, hidden away inside massive vaults before the bombs fell.
The hero, an unnamed man or woman created by the player, grew up in
one such vault, having never seen the outside world. However, when his
(we'll just pretend the hero is a man for this discussion) father goes
missing, the hero ventures out of the confines of the vault and into the
Capital Wasteland, the ravaged remains of what was once Washington, D.C.

The hero's quest to find his father brings him into contact with many of
the wasteland's warring factions including the Brotherhood of Steel (a cultish
military group), the Outcasts (former Brotherhood members), and the
Enclave (the corrupted remnants of the U.S. government) as he learns more
about his father's past, his groundbreaking research, and the history of
the world itself. The hero, however, lacks the complex backstory that

characterizes most main characters in less player-driven stories, and even the main plot itself tends to be overshadowed by its setting. Though there is a series of main quests to follow in order to advance the story, deviating from the path is easy and encouraged. The Capital Wasteland is a large area with a diverse collection of towns, dangerous locals, and survivors. With so much to see and do, it's easy to forget about the story missions and go off to explore the world, run some deliveries, seek out caches of rare soda, and engage in countless other optional tasks. The game uses a point-based karma system, which measures how good or evil the hero is based on the player's actions. Freeing slaves, for example, is good and will raise your karma; capturing people and selling them to the slavers will lower it. Some characters react differently to the hero based on his karma score, and most quests feature multiple completion methods, some of which are significantly more good or evil than others. The story missions have many similar choices, but the only major branching points come very late in the game and affect little other than the brief ending. However, it should be noted that the *Broken Steel* downloadable content (DLC), which serves as an epilogue to the main story, does accurately portray the results of the player's earlier choices.

FIGURE
10.3

A lot of effort was put into making *Fallout 3*'s characters unique and interesting. *Fallout 3* © 2008 Bethesda Softworks LLC, a ZeniMax Media company. All rights reserved.

The main plot itself isn't particularly deep or complex – it does have its moments and features quite an interesting cast – but there are always new things to find and do in the Capital Wasteland. Learning more about its history and environs via conversations with NPCs and uncovering lost recordings can be quite engaging. Players also have the ability to mold the hero to fit their preferences, be it smart or strong, good or evil, open or cunning, or somewhere in between.

Fallout 3 also makes good use of DLC, with five separate packs. Three serve to expand the setting and let the player explore some areas outside the Capital Wasteland proper, one adds some depth to the backstory by allowing the hero to participate in a virtual reality reenactment of a key historical event, and the last one serves as an epilogue and allows players to see how their choices near the end of the story go on to affect to the Wasteland and its inhabitants.

In the end, *Fallout 3* is an excellent example of open-ended storytelling. It provides the player with a moderately engaging main plot and a large and intriguing area to explore with numerous people, quests, and activities that can be approached in many different ways based on the player's preferences. It also manages to avoid a lot of the major pitfalls that tend to plague games using open-ended stories (which we'll talk more about later on). This makes it one of the best current games using open-ended storytelling and a very good introduction to the style.

Creating Open-Ended Stories

If you thought that branching path stories required a lot of planning and structural work, you haven't seen anything yet. Open-ended stories tend to have far more minor and moderate branches than even the most complex branching path stories. The number of major branches doesn't increase nearly as much (in fact, many open-ended stories have very few major branches) and they're often a bit on the short side, but all the minor and moderate branches add up fast. The decision points in open-ended stories also tend to be far less clear-cut, so you'll need to think about less obvious ways to send the player down different branches. In addition, you'll need to write two or more different variations of most dialog and conversations, based on what type of personality the player has decided to give the hero. After all, people are going to react much differently to a famous hero than they are to a dreaded villain, and those are only two possible character types. Chances are good that you'll have to write alternate versions of many quests as well, depending not only on the hero's morality but whether he or she prefers confrontation, stealth, diplomacy, or the like.

Split Personality

Think about this for a minute. Every scene ideally needs to be redesigned from top to bottom for at least two extreme character types. And of course there are all the possible gradations in between. You're constantly at risk of pushing the player out of the reality as the NPC adopts a tone with the player that seems incongruous with the player's actions. Though the advantages of this type of gameplay are obvious, it makes scene creation extremely difficult.

209

Dramatic scenes are basically arguments. The argument may be friendly or fierce, but when you begin creating a dramatic scene, the first question you need to ask is, "What does each character want?" Ideally, there should be some tension between the two distinct wants, even if the tension is simply that one character wants to talk while the other character wants to leave. This conflict can ramp all the way up to such situations as one character wanting to get married while the other one wants to break up.

Now that you know what the conflict is, you then need to figure how it resolves. In each scene you create, one character or the other must "win" the scene for the audience to perceive that the story has advanced in some small way during that scene. Bad scene design has the two characters wrestling their way through the scene with no obvious win or change at the end. The audience will at worst feel subconsciously that the scene was a waste of time, and at best that the scene was flat emotionally. Think of scenes in *Star Trek: Next Generation*, in which scenes often had no conflict at all. Remember how flat they mostly felt? Compare them to scenes in *Battlestar Gallactica*, where the conflict was almost always in your face, and how those emotions were almost over-the-top.

Okay, so you need conflict, and now you need resolution. To write the scene, we create a little microstory with ascending action, plot twists, and a climax, all in the short few minutes that these two characters are talking with each other. Those are the guidelines for good scene construction. However, in this kind of story structure, we don't really know where the player sits on a continuum of good to evil, so we can't predict how the NPC will feel about the player character when the scene begins. And because we don't know where the player sits on that continuum, we don't really know what the player wants, either. If not handled artfully, scenes written in this kind of story environment will tend to all feel like nothing happens in them and like they are a waste of the player's time. When faced with this challenge, game writers have in the past resorted to a stylized humor in order to give the scene some life, a kind of humor that might seem superficially like they are just being flip. But I believe the root lies in the conundrum of being uncertain what the stakes of the scene are at the moment it happens in the game, and what "wants" the player's character has, because the writer doesn't know what personality the player had adopted. The only solution I have encountered that works even slightly is to place at the top of the conversation some kind of interrogatory moment in which the dialog can determine the player's (or character's) emotional tone and act accordingly. But with too many of these moments, every bit of dialog feels structured the same.

It is a real dilemma for the writer.

—Chris

Furthermore, as the setting and backstory tend to play a much larger role than they do in less player-driven forms of storytelling, you need to spend a lot of time developing the history of your world and the personalities and backstories of as many NPCs as possible – even those who have little to no importance for the main plot. Lots of NPCs will be needed to dole out and otherwise play important roles in the myriad of optional quests that an open-ended story requires, so the writer's job is to ensure that those NPCs are interesting and believable and that their quests help to, in some way, further develop the story and/or setting.

A Halloween Parade of Personalities

Often the writer is faced with a dilemma related to the open-ended nature. If you try to make sure that the NPC relates to the main story and is performing the task the story demands of them (which is what you really want to do), you need contextual information that you don't have. So you default to "one-off" (humourous but not story related) NPCs, which can be very entertaining in the moment of encounter, but a steady diet of such NPCs can risk having the game feel very disconnected.

—Chris

Now, let's take a look at the three key elements that make up an open-ended story.

The Main Plot

Just like in all the story types we've already discussed, open-ended stories still need a main plot that focuses on the hero's epic quest to do ... something. Save the world, probably. Because that hasn't changed, all the information in the previous chapters still applies. Furthermore, in open-ended stories, you can actually get away with having a much shorter and simpler main plot than with most other story types, as all the optional quests and activities will help distract the player and fill in the gaps. More importantly, with all the writing you'll need to do for that optional stuff, you probably won't have the time (or budget, for that matter) to create a main plot with the length and depth of *FINAL FANTASY XIII* or *Fate/Stay Night* – especially when you consider that you'll probably need to create at least two or three variations of the dialog for each conversation, quest progression, and the like so that they can change based on the type of hero the player creates.

The biggest problem you're likely to encounter when working on your main plot is the pacing. Unlike interactive traditional, multiple-ending, and even branching path stories, in which the writer maintains at least a moderate amount of control over the story's progression, in open-ended stories, the player is the one in control. As such, it's very difficult, if not impossible, to maintain a steady pacing when the player is frequently encouraged to wander off and is often free to approach important story-related quests in a multitude of different ways and orders. Often the best you can do is try to ensure that the main plot itself maintains a good pace, as long as the player follows it in one of the intended ways.

The Branches

As with branching path stories, once you've got your main plot planned out, you need to go over it, think of places where it could branch off and what would happen on each of those branches, and then sort through your list and single out the best and most interesting branches to actually add to the story. In an open-ended story, however, you need to pay far more attention to minor and moderate branches. In the end, nearly every quest and mission – both optional and story-related – should contain a branching point leading to one of two or more minor or moderate branches based on things like the hero's moral alignment, intelligence, and fighting style (or lack thereof). And as I said in the last chapter, it's very important to make sure that things stay interesting and entertaining – no matter which branch the player ends up on. Also, although you can send the player down different branches as the result of a conversation at times, try to make most of your decision points less obvious, with the correct branch automatically being chosen based on the player's past actions (has he or she been friendly or unfriendly to quest-related NPCs, is he or she seen as good or evil, and so on) or simply how the player decides to approach the problem at hand (when told about the relic in the rich man's house, does the player sneak in through a window, break down the front door with guns blazing, or approach the rich man to try and make a deal?).

Major branches are actually far less of an issue in open-ended stories. In fact, many of them contain only a single major branching point late in the game that determines which ending the player receives – a far cry from games like *Front Mission 3* and *Fate/Stay Night*, in which major branching points are found early on and change the vast majority of the game. Although increasing the number of major branches and spacing them throughout the game greatly increases the importance of the player's decisions and the amount of replay value, when it comes down to it, with the vast number of minor and moderate branches and optional activities that need to be made, developers usually don't have the time, manpower, and/or budget to also create multiple nearly full-length main branches, especially considering that those main branches also need their own sets of minor and moderate branches. So it's generally best to keep your plans for major branches relatively simple.

The Distractions

By "distractions," I'm referring to the large number of optional quests and other things the players can do to occupy themselves that aren't directly related to the main plot. In *Fallout 3*, for example, there's a wide variety of quests that include freeing or capturing slaves, finding stashes of the rare Nuka Cola Quantum to sell to a collector, and running dozens upon dozens of other optional tasks for the citizens of the Capital Wasteland. *Grand Theft Auto IV* (which we'll talk about a little later in this chapter) has numerous "random encounters" where the hero can run into various NPCs (many of whom were first met as part of the main story), triggering cut-scenes and/or optional quests. It also features chains of brief mini-quests like stealing certain cars for a wealthy collector, working as a taxi driver, and hunting down various wanted criminals for the local police. Then there's the relationship system, via which the hero, Nico, can befriend and/or date various characters. These characters will then help him in a variety of ways, but only if he maintains a good relationship by frequently taking them out on enjoyable outings.

While these activities don't need to tie directly into the main story (and their creation is often more the job of a designer than a writer), they should all fit well within the world and the specific setting. Nico is a criminal living a bachelor's life in the big city with his cousin, a taxi driver. Keeping that in mind, it's only natural that he'd steal cars, go on dates, and drive a taxi from time to time. The hero in *Fallout 3*, on the other hand, is a more generic character defined by the player's actions, so the quests have less to do with him and more to do with the characters he meets and the condition of the world in general. Because ghouls, slavers, and other threats roam the Wasteland, it makes perfect sense that other people would have problems with them and be looking for a skilled fighter to help them out. You don't need to infuse all of these tasks with a whole lot of story elements, but it's a good idea to use them to expand on the world and setting. If you have a well-defined hero like Nico, use the "distractions" to better show his personality, goals, and backstory. If you're using a generic hero, focus on developing the personalities and backstories of your NPCs. Use some of them to better explain the world/country/city in which the game takes place, expanding on its inhabitants, culture, political climate, and history. Although it's easy to just toss in a bunch of random things to keep the player busy, tying them into the story in one way or another will make them feel more like a natural part of the game and its setting, rather than a tacked-on activity, and will make your world feel much more interesting and alive.

Case Study: *Fable II*

Developer:	Lionhead Studios
Publisher:	Microsoft Game Studios
Writers:	Peter Molyneux, Rich Bryant, Dene Carter, Mark Hill
System:	Microsoft Xbox 360
Release Date:	October 21, 2008 (US)
Genre:	Action RPG

FIGURE
10.4

Even in the early parts of the game, the player is given many different ways to approach each task. *Fable II* © **2008 Microsoft Corporation. All rights reserved. Used with permission from Microsoft Corporation.**

Designer Peter Molyneux is a very vocal supporter of highly player-driven stories in games. And although even many of his biggest fans admit that he has a tendency to promise a lot more than he can deliver, the *Fable* series contains some of the most innovative open-ended stories available.

Fable II's main plot is short and rather simplistic, a fact that Molyneux himself has readily admitted and has worked to improve upon in *Fable III*. In Fable II, set in the land of Albion, the hero is a young street urchin named Sparrow. Shortly into the game, his (or her, depending on whether the player chose a male or female Sparrow) sister Rose is killed by the tyrannical ruler Lord Lucien and Sparrow himself is wounded and left for dead. He's saved by a mysterious fortune teller, who informs him that he carries the blood of an ancient hero and must find and unite the heroes of strength, will, and skill in order to defeat Lucien and bring peace to the land. The quest to gather the heroes and stop Lucien is broken up into several sections, spanning 20 years of Sparrow's life. With a few exceptions, the important characters mostly follow standard archetypes and the plot's handful of twists are all fairly predictable. Instead, the main focus is on letting players explore all Albion has to offer while molding Sparrow to suit their personality and play style.

Fable II presents players with a huge amount of freedom. Albion is a large kingdom with many places to explore and numerous optional quests to undertake on behalf of its citizenry. Almost every quest has both a good and evil method of completion, allowing players to strive toward becoming the ultimate hero, ultimate villain, or something in between. Nearly every property in the game can also be bought and rented out by the player, providing a steady stream of income and other bonuses, such as reduced prices at shops the player owns. Buying out all of the property in various towns and cities can also lead to the hero being appointed mayor or even king over different parts of Albion, though these titles are more for show than anything else, leaving out most of the practical matters that would normally be associated with running a town or country.

The player can also woo and marry the woman or man of his choice, set up a household, and raise a family. Other less wholesome practices such as adultery and polygamy are also possible, as is divorce if Sparrow's spouse discovers that he's been engaging in such deviant behaviors. Though an interesting diversion, and fitting in a game that strives to let the player do it all, the entire system is rather shallow. Wooing the girl or guy of your dreams is a very easy matter, comprised of flirting briefly, giving a good gift, and then presenting the chosen character with a ring at an appropriate spot – a far simpler task than that found in dating sims or even some other open-ended story games such as the *Harvest Moon* series, in which winning the heart of your desired spouse is a lengthy and difficult process. Running your household is also simple, with Sparrow's spouse requiring little more than a nice house, a lot of money, and the occasional visit to remain happy. Having children doesn't really change matters one way or the other, though it does lead to a couple of optional quests later on.

FIGURE
10.5

Sparrow's appearance is shaped by the player's actions, and can range from angelic to monstrous. *Fable II* © 2008 Microsoft Corporation. All rights reserved. Used with permission from Microsoft Corporation.

Sparrow himself (or herself) has a good/evil scale (much like *Fallout 3*'s karma system) as well as a purity/corruption scale that changes based on the player's actions throughout the game. It should be noted that the two are not directly related, and it's perfectly possible to have a good but corrupt or evil but pure Sparrow. Being particularly good, evil, pure, or corrupt opens up various special quests that the player can undertake and changes the way Albion's inhabitants react to Sparrow. Sparrow's physical appearance is also affected. A good Sparrow appears handsome and heroic; an evil one is pale, twisted, and frightening. Similarly, a pure Sparrow will gain a healthy complexion and a halo; a corrupt one sports diseased skin and horns. Several other stats also affect Sparrow's appearance, making him appear stronger, taller, and/or more magically inclined.

The good and evil scale is pretty straightforward. Things like lying, stealing, and killing innocents are evil; helping others and giving charity are good. The purity and corruption scale is a little less obvious. Sparrow becomes purer by doing things like maintaining a vegetarian diet and using a condom during sex and becomes corrupt by eating meat, drinking, and general debauchery. Some of the designers' decisions could certainly be questioned, such as whether meat should really be seen as corrupt and why the corruption gotten from hiring a prostitute is more than offset by the purity gained from using a condom during the encounter, but the system is fairly easy to figure out and stays consistent throughout the game. The real problem with many of the good and evil systems used in games is how easy it is to cheat them, which is especially apparent in *Fable II*. As previously mentioned, engaging in corrupt acts such as adultery or hiring prostitutes can easily be negated by things like using condoms or eating a few pieces of tofu. So, as long as Sparrow practices safe sex and eats plenty of tofu, everyone in Albion will consider him a model of purity, regardless of what impure and debauched acts he participates in. The good and evil scale is also easy to manipulate. Becoming fully evil is as simple as slaughtering a group of helpless villagers, which makes sense. However, as good and evil are on a simple sliding scale, the murderous Sparrow can then become a paragon of good simply by giving a large sum of gold to a needy beggar. In real life, such an act may make the beggar love you, but it certainly wouldn't do much to improve your standing in the eyes of everyone else. This quick bounce between ultimate good and ultimate evil can be repeated as many times as the player wants, robbing the system of any sense of consequence or realism.

One last interesting story decision in *Fable II* is the way in which Sparrow interacts with NPCs and story scenes. Instead of using branching dialog such as in *Fallout 3*, Sparrow communicates by using various physical gestures. These gestures range from the sensible (such as motioning for someone to follow) to the ridiculous (hand puppets, farting, and the like). Depending on which gestures Sparrow uses, different NPCs will react in different ways. It's a unique change from the usual dialog systems, and some players really enjoy playing around with the different gestures. However, the whole concept can feel rather ridiculous at times (especially considering what many of the gestures entail), and often makes Sparrow come across more as a crazed mime or village idiot than a destined hero. Sparrow is also free to move around and use his various gestures during most of the game's cut-scenes, though this can best be considered interactivity for interactivity's sake, as it serves no real purpose other than giving the player the option to run away and cancel the cut-scene partway through (which, in the end, is also pointless, because the cut-scene will just replay when the player returns to the area).

In the end, *Fable II* provides players with a large world to explore and a nearly endless number of ways to pass their time, though at the cost of a rich, well-paced narrative. Similarly, it gives them considerable control over Sparrow's development, personality, and actions, but as a result, he has little background, personality, or consistency. These are the types of trade-offs that you routinely have to face when writing open-ended stories (the matter of whether they're worth it is something we'll discuss in Chapters 12 through 14). It should be noted that Lionhead Studios is aware of these issues and tried to improve them in the recently released *Fable III*.

Depending on your own preferences, *Fable II*'s open-ended story can be seen as either a masterpiece of free choice and player-driven storytelling or a failed experiment showcasing everything that's wrong with the style. But, regardless of your views, for better or worse, it clearly accomplishes its goal of putting the player, not the writer, in control.

The Strengths of Open-Ended Stories

The strength of open-ended stories is their freedom. When compared to interactive traditional, multiple-ending, and branching path stories, open-ended stories provide players with an enormous amount of freedom to say and do as they please. Though there are still limits (they can't go anywhere or do anything that wasn't specifically placed in the game by the designers, writers, art team, and programmers), the amount of freedom and choice available in games like *Fable II* and *The Elder Scrolls III: Morrowind* is immense. The player still has a main plot to follow when he or she wants to, but the real fun in open-ended stories comes from developing your character and exploring every little thing the game world has to offer, especially when there are so many different ways to go about it. For those who are convinced that player control is the most important part of game stories, the freedom of open-ended stories speaks for itself. It's the ultimate strength. For those who don't believe that highly player-driven storytelling is such a good thing, the strength of the style comes not from the story itself, but from the large detailed world in which that story takes place.

All the World's a Stage

Indeed, the real arena in which the writer can succeed in these types of stories is not in the micro sense (isn't it interesting how *Fable* deals with the dialog question?), but rather in the way the world is architected. If we look at the design issues when we create a scene (look for conflict between the characters, and then drive that conflict home by the end of the scene, resolving it in some way), the same guideline applies to overall story design. The writers' job in a world like this is to create a world where the conflict is built in, which is where *Fallout 3* succeeds. The conflict in a ravaged postapocalyptic world is evident in every encounter. An ill-chosen setup in a game like this can be impossible to overcome, regardless of how cleverly your dialog is written.

—Chris

Case Study: *Grand Theft Auto IV*

Developer:	Rockstar North
Publisher:	Rockstar Games
Writers:	Dan Houser, Rupert Humphries
System:	Sony PlayStation 3, Microsoft Xbox 360, PC
Release Date:	April 29, 2008 (US)
Genre:	Sandbox, Action Adventure

Though many games are responsible for the development of the so-called sandbox genre (characterized by giving the player a large setting [sandbox] where he can do as he pleases), it owes much of its current popularity to the *Grand Theft Auto* (*GTA*) series, particularly 2001's *GTA III*. Despite its title, *GTA IV* is actually the eleventh game in the series. Like in previous *GTA* games, *GTA IV* places the player in the role of a criminal out to make his way in the world and accomplish his goals by any means necessary. Murder, extortion, drugs, and, of course, theft are all business as usual. Some of the *GTA* games have been praised for their stories, but the real star of the show is the setting and the freedom players have to explore, interact with others, and cause general chaos and mayhem.

    GTA IV tells the tale of Nico Bellic, a European war veteran turned smuggler who has just come to live with his cousin Roman in Liberty City (based heavily on New York City). There he hopes to both pursue the American dream and find the man who betrayed his unit back in their army days.

But as Nico soon discovers, he can't leave his old life behind so easily. Roman quickly introduces him to Liberty City's seedier side, leading him to perform missions for many of the city's biggest crime bosses. As time goes on, Nico and Roman make friends and enemies with many colorful characters and come face to face with the best and worst humanity has to offer. Nico himself is a surprisingly complex character and reacts in a consistent and believable way despite the extreme situations he finds himself in. The main plot is fairly long and well paced, though there are very few points when the player actually has a chance to change the story, and only the last of those can be considered a major branching point, with the players' decision determining which of the two endings they receive. When combined with its well-defined main character, *GTA IV* is rather close to a multiple-ending story; at one point I did consider classifying it as such. However, although the main plot doesn't quite fit the norm for open-ended stories, the rest of the game most certainly does.

The entirety of Liberty City is open for Nico to explore from early on. Though there's always a clear chain of story missions for players to follow when they wish to advance the plot, it's easy for them to take a back seat to all the distractions found throughout the city. Most NPCs are generic pedestrians, but there are special characters scattered throughout the city (often people Nico met during previous story missions) who are available for interaction, leading to cut-scenes and/or optional quests. Nico can also befriend certain characters and date several different women. Each friend and girlfriend has his or her own personality, likes, and dislikes, and maintaining good relationships encourages them to aid him in a variety of different ways. Nico can also take part in a number of setting-appropriate optional missions, such as stealing rare cars, working as a taxi driver, and even hunting down wanted criminals. All of these tasks, though they have little to no affect on the main plot, fit perfectly within the world and story of the game, making them feel like a perfectly logical and natural extension of Nico's life in Liberty City. However, players looking to make things a bit crazier are free to steal a variety of different vehicles and create general chaos and mayhem throughout the city while trying to stay out of the clutches of the police.

Though it lacks a generic highly customizable character like those found in *Fallout 3* or *Fable II* and gives the player relatively few opportunities to change the main plot, *GTA IV*'s approach to open-ended storytelling allows it to tell a much more moving and character-driven tale than either of those games. And with the large amount of freedom presented to players throughout the rest of their adventures in Liberty City, few if any will complain about the relatively small number of important decisions presented to them in the main plot, making *GTA IV* an excellent fusion of traditional and player-driven storytelling styles.

The Weaknesses of Open-Ended Stories

The weaknesses of open-ended stories are shared by most highly player-driven forms of storytelling. As with multiple-ending stories and branching path stories, the story can easily lose much of its emotional impact when players know that they can easily go back and try again to get a different (hopefully better) outcome. And, just like in branching path stories, a wrong choice on the player's part can quickly send the story in a direction that he or she doesn't like. This is an even more serious problem in open-ended stories, because – as the branching points tend to be less obvious – it can be very difficult for players to figure out where they went wrong and how to change it. This can be helped by giving the player relatively little control over the progress and outcome of the main plot, as in *Grand Theft Auto IV*, though doing so sacrifices a good deal of the player choice and freedom that are often considered to be the most important part of open-ended storytelling.

As previously mentioned, due to time and budget constraints, the main plots of open-ended stories are often relatively short and simple when compared to those of similar games using less player-driven forms of storytelling. This is due to both the massive amount of time and effort required to create all the different optional activities and branching paths and the fact that the more branches and player choices you add to a story, the harder it becomes to tell a long, complex tale with any sort of proper progression or consistency (something we'll discuss more in Chapter 13). Whether this is actually a problem depends on developer and player preferences, but it's worth keeping in mind that it's extremely difficult – perhaps impossible – to create stories with the depth, complexity, and emotional impact of titles such as *FINAL FANTASY VII* or *Metal Gear Solid 3* using open-ended storytelling.

From a storytelling perspective, the tendency of open-ended stories to feature generic customizable heroes is also a problem. Generic heroes lack not only a defined appearance but a solid personality and backstory as well. Despite players' ability to customize the hero to their liking, this lack of any sort of defined traits or characteristics makes it extremely difficult for players to truly identify or empathize with the hero. This is the reason that although heroes like *Fable II*'s Sparrow and *Fallout 3*'s vault dweller feature a nearly endless number of customization options, you never see them winning any game character popularity polls. As shown by *Grand Theft Auto IV*, open-ended stories don't need to rely on generic hero characters; however, having a well-developed main character such as Nico greatly reduces player freedom and control.

Finally, when the player is given so much freedom, it becomes exceedingly difficult to ensure that the story has any sort of proper pacing. You can try to pace the main plot fairly well, but with so many different distractions vying for players' attention, there's really no telling where they'll go and what they'll do next. It's not uncommon for players of games with open-ended stories to get so distracted with all the optional activities available that they never even bother to finish the main plot. The fact that, as previously mentioned, most open-ended stories have rather simple main plots doesn't help in this regard. Even worse, with such large worlds to explore and so many things to do, it can become quite easy for players to lose track of the main plot entirely and wind up unable to figure out how to continue it. Fortunately, most developers have realized that problem and many newer open-ended story games such as *Fallout 3*, *Grand Theft Auto IV*, and *Fable II* feature different ways to ensure that players can always easily find their way to the next important quest or story scene. In some games, however, such as *The Elder Scrolls III: Morrowind*, the player is given so much freedom that it's actually possible for him or her to derail the main plot entirely, making it difficult or even impossible to complete.

Although the large degree of player freedom and control is open-ended storytelling's biggest strength, as you can see from the problems we just discussed, that very freedom also leads to a host of weaknesses. Some can be reduced or negated with good writing and design; others are an unavoidable part of the style itself that must be kept in mind when creating open-ended stories. In the end, it's best to keep these weaknesses firmly in mind and emphasize the setting over the main plot and the hero, as open-ended storytelling is far better suited to providing an interesting and detailed world for the player to explore than it is to providing a deep and moving storyline (as evidenced in Chapter 14).

Case Study: *The Elder Scrolls III: Morrowind*

Developer:	Bethesda Game Studios
Publisher:	ZeniMax Media
Writers:	Ken Rolston, Douglas Goodall, Mark Nelson
System:	Microsoft Xbox, PC
Release Date:	May 1, 2002 (US)
Genre:	Action RPG

FIGURE
10.6

Morrowind presents players with a massive world to explore. *The Elder Scrolls III: Morrowind*® © 2002 Bethesda Softworks LLC, a ZeniMax Media company. **All rights reserved.**

Bethesda's *Elder Scrolls* series has always prided itself on providing an extremely high degree of player choice and freedom combined with some of the largest game worlds ever created. This makes the *Elder Scrolls* games the very epitome of open-ended storytelling. The series began in 1994 with *The Elder Scrolls: Arena*, but it was *The Elder Scrolls III: Morrowind* that led to the series' current popularity, in part due to its release on the original Xbox, on which RPGs of any kind were a rarity.

Large and extremely ambitious, *Morrowind* places its player-created hero on the large island of Vvardenfell, where he or she is tasked with investigating strange happenings and ensuring the security of the Empire. This soon leads the player to discover the evil plans of the near-immortal Dagoth Ur and his followers. In order to stop them, the hero must fulfill a set of ancient prophecies and become the legendary champion known as the Nerevarine. The prophecies are fairly straightforward (the majority of which involve gaining the support of various factions throughout the island) and the plot never gets any more complex than completing them and gathering the items needed to destroy Dagoth Ur. The majority of these tasks can be completed in any order, and there's no long, detailed ending when they're completed. The hero is simply rewarded for his or her efforts and set free to continue exploring Vvardenfell without having to worry about the threat posed by Dagoth Ur and his followers.

The brevity and simplicity of the main plot was frequently cited as one of *Morrowind*'s weakest points, along with its rather boring battle system and poorly designed journal interface, which made it extremely difficult for players to keep track of the myriad of quests available, thus causing many to lose track of the main plot entirely (an issue that was significantly improved in the first expansion pack, though only in the PC version of the game). Despite all of these problems, *Morrowind* was mostly well received, due to the vibrancy of its world and the seemingly endless number of optional tasks and activities that the player can undertake.

FIGURE
10.7

The player is free to talk to, help, rob, murder, and otherwise interact with an enormous cast of characters. *The Elder Scrolls III: Morrowind*® © 2002 Bethesda Softworks LLC, a ZeniMax Media company. All rights reserved.

Despite being relatively small when compared to the explorable areas present in the first two *Elder Scrolls* games, Vvardenfell is a massive island featuring diverse terrain and numerous towns, cities, caverns, and other features to find and explore. From almost the beginning of the game, players are free to roam about the entire island as they please, with the only potential limiting factor being the strength of the monsters that inhabit certain areas. There's an enormous number of optional quests to find and complete, many of which combine to form short, self-contained stories of their own. Some are quite easy to find; others require traveling to out-of-the-way locales or fulfilling certain stringent requirements before they become available. A few, such as the set of vampire quests, can be almost impossible to trigger unless the player has prior knowledge of their existence and requirements. It's also possible for the hero to become a member (and eventually leader) of many different factions, all of which feature their own quests, duties, and benefits. Furthermore, the setting itself is extremely well developed, with a diverse cast of characters and over three hundred in-game books (with a combined amount of text equivalent to several full-length novels) from which the player can learn all about the world's races, history, mythology, religions, and the like. In the end, it's the island itself, and the vast number of interesting people and places therein, that players most enjoy and remember about *Morrowind*.

Players in *Morrowind* are even allowed to derail the main plot entirely. Unlike the other games we've discussed in this chapter, *Morrowind* allows the player to kill any character in the game, no matter how important that character may be to the main plot. In this way, it's actually possible to render the main plot impossible to complete. Fortunately, there are a few safeguards in place to reduce the chances of this happening. Killing an important NPC causes the game to display a warning message, hinting that the player should reload the game from his or her last save. And as long as the player didn't kill one specific NPC, there's an alternate way for him or her to rejoin and complete the main plot, regardless of how many other important characters the player killed, though this alternative path is risky and rather difficult to find. It should be noted that it's also rather easy for the player to purposely or accidentally incur the wrath of certain factions spread throughout Vvardenfell, which can in turn make certain parts of the game significantly more difficult.

Morrowind will long be remembered for its world and the enormous amount of freedom it gives players. Despite its many faults, it does an excellent job of keeping the focus on its strongest and most enjoyable elements and provides a perfect showcase for all the key strengths and weaknesses of open-ended storytelling.

Summary

Open-ended stories provide far more player freedom and control than any of the styles previously discussed. In many ways, they're similar to highly complex branching path stories, but there is a much heavier emphasis on minor and moderate branches and the decision points tend to be far less obvious and based heavily on the player's actions rather than a response to a prompt. Many open-ended stories also make use of some sort of morality system that affects the way NPCs react to the hero, though such systems are often easy to manipulate, allowing the player to bounce back and forth between the two extreme ends of the scale almost at will.

Defining features of open-ended storytelling include expansive worlds that the player is free to explore for most of the game and an extremely large number of optional quests and activities he or she can take part in. Because of how much time and attention are spent developing the setting and optional content, the main plot is often deemphasized, with most open-ended stories having relatively short and simple main plots featuring generic player-created heroes. Some games, such as *Grand Theft Auto IV*, go against this trend, offering deeper plots and well-defined heroes, though doing so sacrifices a considerable amount of the player control and freedom found in other less plot-focused games like *Fable II* and *The Elder Scrolls 3: Morrowind*. Which of these approaches is best is a matter that's frequently debated and one that we'll cover more in Chapters 12 through 14, but as a general rule, the more freedom that is given to the player, the less emphasis can be placed on creating a deep, structured, and emotional main plot, and vice versa. Other reasons for this include schedule and budget constraints, as the large amount of optional content required by open-ended stories takes a considerable amount of time and effort to create, leaving far less to spend on other parts of the game and its story.

The freedom offered in open-ended stories is their biggest strength, allowing players to do what they want when they want, and allowing writers to focus on creating highly detailed worlds and settings. However, it's also their biggest weakness, significantly weakening the structure, pacing, and emotional impact of the main plot and making it easy for players to get lost or sidetracked. In the end, depending on whether you consider player freedom or a well-structured story to be the most important aspect of game writing, open-ended storytelling can be seen as either one of the best or worst styles available.

Things to Consider

1. List five games you've played that use open-ended stories (if you haven't played that many, just list the ones you have).

2. Pick two of the games from your list and create simple outlines of their main plots. Compare them to the main plots of the games discussed in your answers to previous chapters' questions. What differences do you see in their length and structure?

3. Do one or both of those games use a morality system? If so, how does the hero's morality affect the rest of the game? How easy is it to change the hero's moral alignment?

4. Pick one of the two games. Do you think the use of an open-ended story structure significantly enhanced or detracted from the game's main plot? Explain your reasoning.

5. Do you think the use of an open-ended story structure significantly enhanced or detracted from the game's world and setting? Explain your reasoning.

Eleven

Fully Player-Driven Stories

FIGURE
11.1

Fully player-driven storytelling.

At last we've reached the far right end of the spectrum and the most player-driven form of storytelling possible. When compared to all the other storytelling styles we've discussed, fully player-driven stories are a bit of an oddity. All the other storytelling styles were defined by the amount of control, or lack thereof, that the player has over the progression and outcome of the main plot. That control can be anywhere from entirely nonexistent to relatively high, but either way, the main plot is still there to guide players through the game and tell some sort of story. As vital as the main plot is, it also restricts player control and freedom, forcing players to at least somewhat follow a set path through the game. That's why fully player-driven stories don't have any main plot at all.

Now you're probably wondering how you can have a story without a main plot. And, to some extent, you can't. However, instead of using a main plot created by a writer and/or designer, the main plot in fully player-driven stories, such as it is, is composed of the player's actions within a given setting. As such, some fully

227

player-driven stories, such as *The Sims*, have little need for writers. Others, however, like *Animal Crossing* rely on writers to create the world, characters, and general setting with which the player can interact. What the player does in that setting may be entirely up to him or her, but the writer still needs to give that setting and its inhabitants names, backstories, personalities, and the like.

A Story by a Committee Is a . . .

I fall into the camp of those who believe that fully player-driven stories do not define themselves as stories per se. Though I earlier stated that story is change due to conflict, I also subscribe to the philosophy that story exists in the gap between expectation and result. Here's what I mean by that.

At every single moment in a story, the audience is expecting something to happen next. In their heads, they are predicting where the story will go a millisecond before it gets there. They have assembled in their head everything they know about the characters, everything they know about the setting, everything they know about human nature, and everything they know about the plot. And they have computed what will happen next on every level of the story, from what Indiana Jones will say next to whether he will be able to prevent the Ark from being loaded on that German submarine to whether he and Marion will get back together. And, in a fascinating twist of human psychology, the audience wants to be both *right* and *wrong* about their predictions.

The audience wishes to be right so they can show off how smart they are to both themselves and their friends. Because, you see, being smart about stories translates to wisdom about life in general as well as demonstrates a creative bent.

The audience wishes to be wrong because they love being surprised by stories. In fact, being surprised by stories is perhaps the most singularly delicious aspect of story enjoyment. To not see something coming in a story means that the writers have done their job, been clever, been creative in the extreme, and, most importantly, been *entertaining*. If you don't believe this, just think back to the heady days just after *The Sixth Sense* was released in theaters and try to remember how moviegoers were imploring you to go see it but emphatically refused to tell you how it would end so that they didn't spoil it for you. Surprise is the Super Bowl Championship of storytelling.

In order to surprise an audience, you must stay ahead of them. Successfully having laid down a perfectly plausible future path for the characters and then having changed direction enough to surprise the audience – a combination of being organic and artful – comes from the structural foundation the writer has laid in all the beats and scenes leading up to this moment in the story, and does not happen by accident or randomness, but instead by careful planning.

The writer has set up an expectation in the audience but delivered a different result. This is crucial to entertaining writing, and it is why I enjoy stories. How this can occur in a fully player-driven story I cannot fathom, as the creator and the audience are one and the same. Although I can certainly enjoy playing by myself, and I can make up little scenarios in my head during that experience, those episodes of make-believe, though entertaining, are not as enjoyable for me as audience member as stories I consume written by someone else.

—Chris

Case Study: *The Sims*

Developer: Maxis
Publisher: Electronic Arts
Designers: Will Wright, Claire Curtain, Roxy Wolosenko
System: PC
Release Date: February 4, 2000 (US)
Genre: Simulation

FIGURE
11.2

The Sims lets you create entire families with their own personalities and interests. *The Sims* images © 2010 Electronic Arts Inc. All rights reserved. Used with permission.

In the world of computer game designers, there are few names more famous than Will Wright. This legendary game designer was the driving force behind much of Maxis's popular *Sim* line of games including classics such *SimCity*, *SimEarth*, *SimCopter*, and *SimAnt*, along with his more recent hit, *Spore*. Wright's early simulation games mostly focused on the big picture by having players create and manage an entire city, planet, ant colony, or the like; *The Sims* brought the focus narrower and closer to home. Instead of controlling an entire group or complex, it challenged players to create and manage the life of a single human being, or Sim. Despite many describing it as more of a toy or virtual dollhouse than a true game, *The Sims* became a huge hit and unseated *Myst* to gain the title of bestselling computer game of all time (for a while, anyway).

Since then, *The Sims* has received numerous expansion packs, sequels, and spin-off games. Some versions have changed the formula a bit, even going so far as to work in a main plot of sorts, but the original game has no story, no set goals, and no victory condition. Players are free to set goals of their own, such as getting their Sim a good job, starting a family, or just saving up enough money to buy a hot tub; however, these goals exist only in the mind of the player and aren't recognized or acknowledged in any way by the game itself.

FIGURE
11.3

As in real life, socialization is an important part of any Sim's life. *The Sims* **images © 2010 Electronic Arts Inc. All rights reserved. Used with permission.**

Players start out by creating a Sim and building a house for that Sim. The building tools are very comprehensive and there's an enormous number of materials and items available for players to build their ideal home. Although some of these are far too expensive for new Sims to afford, players can work toward buying them later on. Once the initial creation process is complete, the Sim is ready to go about his or her daily life. Sims go off to work (or school, depending on their age) every day, but the game focuses exclusively on their home life. Although Sims have enough AI to go about some tasks by themselves, it's up to the player to control most of his or her Sim's actions and ensure that the Sim eats well, exercises, maintains proper hygiene, and so on. Properly managing a Sim's social life is also an important part of ensuring that the Sim remains happy and content. Players can invite other Sims (either ones they created or a collection of premade ones) to their Sim's house for parties and other social gatherings – it's even possible for two Sims to get married and have children.

There's no real plot, no dialog (Sims converse in a made-up language known as Simlish), and very little writing at all. Instead, *The Sims* is all about giving players near complete control so that their actions can tell the life stories of their Sims. Many people would probably argue that *The Sims* doesn't have a story of any kind, and in some ways that would be correct. However, the large amount of fan fiction, comics, and movies that players have made chronicling the lives of their Sims shows that there is a story to be found, if only in the minds of the players. Nevertheless, *The Sims* expertly embodies the key principles of fully player-driven storytelling: specifically, creating an engaging setting and rules of interaction to govern activities within that setting and then letting players loose to do as they please and create their own stories.

Toy or Game?

Although this might seem simply a semantic argument, *The Sims* to me – while amazingly engaging to millions of consumers – is a toy, not a game. A beautifully conceived and implemented toy, but a toy nonetheless. Nothing wrong with a toy: toys can be and are the most amazing things to play with, and the persons who play with toys will always conceive of stories to accompany their playtime. And as long as game designers supply the proper context for the play, the best stories to come out of those experiences will be those created by the players.

—Chris

Creating Fully Player-Driven Stories

Because of the lack of a main plot, the creation process for fully player-driven stories is a bit different from that of the other styles we've talked about. You can pretty much forget about structure, pacing, endings, branching paths, and the like. Things like backstory and character types, however, can still be useful. In the end, when you don't have a main plot, your only real concerns are creating a setting and the rules governing how players interact with that setting.

Creating a Setting

In interactive traditional, multiple-ending, and branching path stories, the setting – no matter how unique and interesting it may be – tends to take a back seat to the main characters and their journey. If you think about the stories in games such as the *Metal Gear* and *FINAL FANTASY* series, you'll see that in most cases you could take the characters and place them in a different city/country/world without having to make many serious changes to the main plot. Sure, things would be a bit different, but the majority of the story is tied up in the characters, not the specific setting, and would remain unaffected. Even in open-ended stories, in which the setting plays a much more important role, the main plot is still there.

In fully player-driven stories, however, you need to avoid thinking of the setting as the backdrop for your story and instead approach it as a fully realized world that players can enjoy exploring and interacting with. The settings used in some open-ended story games such as *Fallout 3* and *The Elder Scrolls 3: Morrowind* are actually large and detailed enough that they could easily become fully player-driven stories if the main plot were removed, so all the setting-related advice from the previous chapter still applies. Whether your setting is an entire planet or just a single town, you want it to be interesting and fun to explore, with lots of things for the player to see and do. Also, keep in mind that most settings are nothing without the characters that inhabit them. Just because there's no main plot doesn't mean your fully player-driven story can't be full of characters for the player to talk to, work for, befriend, fight, and the like. In fact, with no main plot, it's the NPCs that serve to give a fully player-driven story much of its charm and personality.

Naturally, it's also important that your setting supports a lot of different activities to keep the player entertained. Similar to the distractions found in open-ended stories, but even more important because there's no main plot to back them up, these activities can include virtually anything – fighting, fishing, treasure hunting, socializing, or even short quests and mini-games. As long as it fits the setting and makes for a fun way to pass some time, go for it. If you're both a writer and designer, you'll probably be planning most of this out yourself. However, if you're just a writer, you'll most likely be limited to writing text and dialog for activities created by the designer.

Creating Rules of Interaction

With your setting planned out, the next thing to consider is what the player will be able to do in that setting. You may have already given this some thought when designing NPCs and planning out activities for the player to do, but in many cases at least half the fun in fully player-driven stories comes from the player messing around with the world and its inhabitants and finding his or her own forms of amusement. To facilitate this, you need to decide exactly what the player can and can't do in the world. Note that this is really the designer's role, not the writer's, so depending on your exact position on the team, you may or may not have much to do with this phase. However, even if you're not involved in planning the rules of interaction, you should study them and try to keep in mind exactly what the player can and can't do so that you can tailor your writing accordingly.

Actions Speak Louder than Words

The best example of actions speaking louder than words that I can think of is the MMO game *Eve*. *Eve* is truly the poster child of this design/writing philosophy.

The single most powerful choice a writer of a game-story makes is this: "What is the player going to do from minute to minute during play?" because in a game, the player is making the decisions, and decisions (and their repercussions) lead to an emotional response – a response potentially far more powerful than an empathic one traditional media delivers. This is why we want to write for games, no? We do it in order to deliver a more compelling experience. Well, at the risk of acting as a sort of wake-up call: in an interactive medium, words don't cut it so much. They can be cool, and they can deliver in games some of what they could deliver in novels, but they are weak sauce compared to things the player does. So if you intend to have a lasting effect on the games you write for, try to get in the design room as early in the development process as possible so that you can suggest game activities for the player. And by this I mean literally everything, from whether the player can jump to what kinds of attacks the player has in addition to the standard writerly-things such as what kinds of missions the player can go on. Now, the game designers aren't going to give up this kind of responsibility so easily, mind you, but you know that your input here – with all of your instincts and knowledge and experience in the areas of creating emotion in your audience – creates impact through these decisions instead of, well, writing words that many players aren't going to read anyway.

Eve's decision to let the players operate their spaceships inside a PvP (that is, player-versus-player) world is not only a bold decision story-wise, but a great decision, given the size of their development team and their development history. It allowed them to not have to worry so much about content creation at a time when they might not have had the capacity to deliver that content. But the best part of their decision was this: they built the conflict into their world design, and allowed the world to change due to the players' actions. "Change through conflict." From an MMO perspective, this was possible only because they set their universe on one server, so that the player actions were contained within that single place and had the ability to affect the entire player base at once. Brilliant choice.

—Chris

Depending on the type of game you're trying to create, the rules of interaction can be fairly simple or extremely complex. In many fully player-driven stories, such as the ones we discuss in this chapter, they tend toward the latter. For

233

example, say that the hero approaches a door. The rules of interaction may say that he can knock on the door or open the door, as long as it isn't locked (or they might say that he can't interact with the door in any way – it all depends). But that's just the beginning. In real life, the hero could try to break down the door with his own strength, bash through it with a rock or axe, attempt to pick the lock, burn the door down, melt through it with acid, or choose any of a number of other possible options. Now let's get back to that in-game door. Do you want the player to be able to pick the lock, bash down the door, or burn through it? If so, you need to plan for those possibilities and include them in the list of ways the hero can interact with doors. For another example, when the hero approaches an NPC, you need to decide whether the hero has the ability to talk with her (and if so, what types of things he can say), attack her, kill her, bribe her, serenade her, and the like.

For any given situation, there's a nearly infinite list of possible interactions, so it's important to narrow them down to a more reasonable number. Naturally, interactions should be appropriate for the setting and hero (if the hero is an elephant, flying probably isn't an appropriate interaction). They should also encompass the things that players will most likely want to do. For example, most players will probably want the ability to talk to NPCs, but they might not care whether they have the option to challenge every NPC to a game of leapfrog. Most importantly, every type of interaction you decide to allow will need to be designed, programmed into the game, animated, and so on. As you've probably guessed, all of this takes time, effort, and money. If you try to add in too many possible interactions, you'll soon find yourself overwhelmed. Bug testing can also become a huge problem when players decide to try using the different interactions in unexpected ways (such as serenading a door or unlocking an NPC). There's a reason why many highly complex fully player-driven story games take so long to develop.

The Problem with Fully Player-Driven Stories in Video Games

As we just discussed, at any point in time there is a practically infinite number of possible actions that any person can take. Right at this very moment, you could keep reading this book, take a break to make a sandwich, get up and go to the movies, read the rest of the chapter while standing on your head, or dance the hokey pokey while singing show tunes – and that's barely scratching the surface. I could write an entire book listing the many different things you could do right this minute and still not mention them all. Of course, many of these potential actions are highly unlikely to take place. Reading while standing on your head isn't very comfortable or practical and you may not know the hokey pokey or like show tunes. And, even if you do, you may be too embarrassed to sing them or just think that the whole idea is too stupid to entertain. But that doesn't mean you *can't* do it. Even if the odds of you deciding to are very low, it's still possible. If you're wondering where this is going, think back to how every potential player interaction you add to a game takes additional time, effort, and money. Now, when combined with the fact that the potential types of interactions that could be added are infinite, or nearly so, you should see the problem. No matter how many options and interactions you add to a game, how many conversation topics and lines of dialog you write, and how many areas you create, there will always be things that the player can't do or say and places he or she can't go. Sure, most players probably won't care about many of the things that get "left out," but somewhere there's going to be a player who's disappointed that there's no hokey pokey show tune option.

And that brings us to the inherent flaw in video games using fully player-driven stories. No matter how much time, effort, and money are poured into a game, it's impossible for the player to ever have the amount of freedom and choice that's present in any real-life situation. Simply put, creating a perfect fully player-driven story in video games can't be done. That doesn't mean you can't make an enjoyable game that allows the player a large degree of freedom. You can. You just need to realize the limitations both of the medium and your development team.

In the end, a perfect fully player-driven story is possible only if you have a real live person acting as a moderator. To get an idea of how that works, let's take a look at a game that uses perfect fully player-driven storytelling.

Case Study: *Dungeons & Dragons*

Original Designers: Gary Gygax and Dave Arneson
Publisher: Wizards of the Coast
Release Date: 1974 (Original), 2008 (4th Edition)

Although far from the only tabletop role-playing game available, *Dungeons & Dragons* (*D&D*) is the most well known and is widely regarded as one of the primary influences behind not only tabletop RPGs but RPG video and computer games as well. Combining elements of fantasy novels, battle strategy, games of chance, storytelling, and even improvisational theater, *D&D* challenges players to create characters and take part in fully player-driven stories under the watchful eyes of a dungeon master, or DM.

D&D is composed of a series of books, including three core volumes (*Player's Handbook*, *Dungeon Master's Guide*, and *Monster Manual*) and a very wide assortment of supplementary works. These books contain a detailed description of a setting (including its world, races, religions, gods, wildlife, and the like) and all the relevant rules of interaction (how characters get stronger, perform tasks, fight, learn new skills and magic, and the like). Players use this information to create a character (such as a half-human, half-elf ranger who is smart and fast, but weak, and is able to converse with dragons) and learn how to play the game (which dice to roll when attacking and defending, how to craft a new bow), but it's the job of the DM to truly learn and master the material contained in the books.

The DM serves as the game's master, writer, and narrator. He or she creates a story, explains the setting to the players, and controls the enemies and NPCs. For example, when players enter a town, the DM might say something like, "You're in a small village next to a forest. There are a few dozen wooden buildings including a general store on the left and a tavern to your right. Several people are milling about. An old woman in a tattered dress is walking toward you." Although the DM usually creates a main plot for the players to follow, it's up to the players to decide how to accomplish the goals set before them. And that's assuming they decide to follow the plot in the first place, as they can easily ignore it and get sidetracked doing other things.

The advantage of having a human running things is that a good DM can quickly change the game and ensure that NPCs react properly, no matter what the players decide to do. Using our town example from the previous paragraph, it's quite likely that the players will decide to see what the old woman wants, go to the store to restock their supplies, and/or stop by the tavern for drinks. Most DMs will have considered all those possibilities and planned for them. But there's no guarantee that the players will do any of those things. Perhaps the players will decide that they want to go look for a weapon master for training, go on a murderous rampage, or start doing an impromptu acrobatic performance. It's then the DM's job to change the story and tell the players the results of their actions. With enough imagination, a DM can think up the results of any action the player could possibly take, adjust the story as needed, and keep things more or less on track, giving the player complete and total freedom to do and act as he or she pleases. It's this freedom that sets *D&D* and other tabletop games apart and that has helped them maintain a loyal following despite the rise in popularity of video games and other forms of multimedia-rich interactive entertainment.

As you can see, a perfect player-driven story – even one with a main plot – is possible if you have a live person available to run things and modify the story on the fly. But is there any way to replicate this in a video game? At present, not really. Although it's technically possible to have a human moderator filling a DM-like role in a video game, the need for one moderator per player (or player group) and for the moderator and player to be on at the same time makes it highly impractical for commercial games. In addition, unlike in *D&D*, where the players can go anywhere and do anything that they and the DM can think of, a player in a video game can't go anywhere that wasn't previously planned for and modeled and can't do anything that the game's programming doesn't allow for.

There is one way that you could theoretically create a perfectly fully player-driven story in a video game without the need for a human moderator. In theory, a suitably advanced AI could take on the DM's role. If the AI were smart enough to understand both the story and whatever actions the player could conceivably take, it could then fill in the gaps and modify things as needed, even creating new characters and areas on the fly. Of course, all of that is only theoretical. At this point in time, it's often hard enough to make an AI that can guide an NPC from point A to point B without getting stuck on a tree in between. An AI with human or near-human levels of comprehension is purely the realm of science fiction. And even if such an AI did exist, it's hard to say whether the stories it made would contain the same skill and creativity as those of a good human writer.

There's considerable debate among AI programmers and future technology analysts as to how long it will take us to create such an AI. Although the most optimistic estimates place the date within the next decade or two, others question whether it will ever happen, citing the fundamental differences between the workings of computers and the human brain. I'm by no means an AI expert, but my own knowledge of the field and a look at the accuracy of other predictions by some of the more optimistic members of the debate have led me to believe that the creation of such an AI – if it's even possible – is a very distant event (several decades at least, and probably much longer). If such a thing does happen, it will significantly change the role of the writer in video games, possibly even removing the need for one entirely, though getting replaced by an AI probably isn't something we'll have to worry about during our lifetimes.

Massively Multiplayer Online Games (MMOs)

MMOs have come a long way, developing from a small niche market into one of the industry's most popular genres, though not one known for its storytelling (see Chapter 14). MMOs come in many forms; the most popular by far is the MMORPG (massively multiplayer online role-playing game), which encompasses hit titles including *Ultima Online*, *Everquest*, *Guild Wars*, and *World of Warcraft*. Although I suspect most of you are quite familiar with the genre, for anyone who isn't, MMOs are games that are played online in virtual worlds inhabited by anywhere from thousands to millions of other players. Most MMOs feature a strong emphasis on player cooperation during the PvE (player-versus-environment) portions of the game, with large groups of skilled players required in order to defeat the toughest challenges. It's also common for MMOs to include PvP (player-versus-player) elements, though whether players are free to attack each other in any area or only in designated PvP zones varies by game.

The story structures in MMOs vary but usually fall into one of two categories. The majority of MMOs use fully player-driven stories. They provide players with a large world to explore (often complete with a long and detailed history), along with lots and lots of enemies to kill, items to find, and quests to undertake. Some include numerous additional activities as well, such as crafting items, buying property, cooking, and the like. Although there's usually no main plot, it's common for MMOs to place players in the midst of a major conflict (though their role in the events is often extremely minor), and some contain chains of several quests that combine to form a short story with the player as one of its major characters.

Fully player-driven stories are the most common type used in MMOs, but there are also a few popular titles that use interactive traditional stories. *Guild Wars* is a good example of this style. Though it still contains a large world and wide variety of quests, there is also a set of missions (larger plot-related quests) that must be completed in order for the player to progress in the story and gain access to additional quests and other parts of the world. Once all the missions have been completed, however, the game changes into a fully player-driven story, leaving the player free to explore the world, complete quests, hunt for rare items, and so on.

Case Study: *World of Warcraft*

Developer:	Blizzard Entertainment
Publisher:	Blizzard Entertainment
System:	PC
Release Date:	November 23, 2004 (US)
Genre:	MMORPG

FIGURE
11.4

Traversing a frozen expanse in *World of Warcraft's Wrath of the Lich King* expansion. World of Warcraft ®, Wrath of the Lich King™, and The Burning Crusade™ are trademarks and/or registered trademarks of Blizzard Entertainment, Inc., and hereby used with permission. Image used with permission. © 2010 Blizzard Entertainment, Inc.

Although it's far from the first MMORPG, *World of Warcraft* is the game that comes to mind when most people think of the genre. Shortly after its release, *World of Warcraft* took the industry by storm, dominating the market and rapidly become the most popular MMORPG available, a position it has successfully held ever since. Though it relies on many elements common throughout most MMORPGs, such as simple quests, item collection, crafting, and player guilds, *World of Warcraft*'s high level of polish, attention to detail, and frequent updates, along with its use of the setting from the popular *Warcraft* series of strategy games, have helped set it apart from other similar titles.

As with most MMORPGs, *World of Warcraft* uses fully player-driven storytelling. Upon starting the game, players build a custom character by choosing attributes such as race (orc, elf, human, and so on) and class (mage, warrior, druid, and so on) and decide whether to join the Horde or Alliance in their ongoing conflict. The character is then turned loose in the fantasy world of Azeroth. Many different quests and activities are available from the start and more open up as the player progresses and increases his character's level. As in most MMORPGs (and regular RPGs, for that matter), the bulk of these optional quests tend to involve killing certain enemies, collecting a certain amount of a specific item (often gotten by killing enemies), or delivering something to an NPC in a different area. The dialog the player has with NPC quest givers and the additional information found in the player's journal serves to add purpose and color to these tasks and also teaches the player about Azeroth's people, history, and current situation. In addition, many quests come in sets, forming quest chains that allow the player to take on an important role in a short story. For example, the *Wrath of the Lich King* expansion contains lengthy quest chains following various characters' efforts to find a way to defeat the evil Lich King Arthas. Although only a small part of *World of Warcraft* as a whole, the Lich King quests and certain other quest chains can actually be thought of as complete interactive traditional stories in their own right, with beginnings, progressions, and endings, complete with special characters, dialog, bosses, and cut-scenes. Though they make up only a portion of Azeroth's lore, such quest chains do much to expand the setting and backstory while also providing a more story-focused experience for players who have little interest in farming monsters for experience points and rare items.

One important thing that sets MMOs such as *World of Warcraft* apart from single-player games is that the player is far from the only hero in the land. Therefore, no matter how many times he kills the Lich King, he'll still miraculously return to challenge the next group of adventurers. Many quests can even be completed multiple times by the same player. Because of this, it becomes difficult to show any massive and/or world-changing events as a result of the player's actions. With so many players exploring the same world, it can't go changing every time someone completes a new quest. One solution to this problem involves the use of instances, which are unique copies of a portion of the world that are inhabited only by the player and his or her party. While in an instance, the results of the player's actions can safely be shown without affecting any unrelated players. However, once the player leaves the instance and returns to the main shared world, any changes made while in the instance are lost. This system allows many players to experience the same story elements while still sharing a world but requires the writer to always keep in mind what exactly can and can't be shown in the game in order for the story's progression to remain smooth and consistent.

FIGURE
11.5

A meeting of elves in the *Burning Crusade* expansion. World of Warcraft®, Wrath of the Lich King™, and The Burning Crusade™ are trademarks and/or registered trademarks of Blizzard Entertainment, Inc., and hereby used with permission. Image used with permission. © 2010 Blizzard Entertainment, Inc.

Another aspect that should be kept in mind when looking at *World of Warcraft* is the difficulty of individual quests relative to the rest of their quest chain. Defeating the Lich King, for example, is far more difficult than many of the quests leading up to that battle. As in all video games, it's only natural to have the difficultly gradually increase as the story progresses. The difference is that in single-player games things are fine-tuned so that the player can smoothly progress through the story from start to finish, yet a considerable amount of content in MMOs is targeted at players with specific levels or skills, or those in groups of a certain size. Although there's nothing wrong with this, as it helps encourage players to join groups and try out new types of characters, it's important to ensure that any player who successfully starts a quest chain has a reasonable chance of being able to finish it, instead of being forced to quit in the middle and missing out on the rest of the story. *World of Warcraft* does a pretty good job in this regard and presents many examples of strong flow and pacing throughout individual quest chains.

These are only a few of the challenges faced when creating an interesting and engaging setting that can accommodate a large number of players at once; though difficult, they can all be overcome with careful planning and design. A good MMO such as *World of Warcraft* makes sure to provide many interesting story elements and quest chains for players who prefer a more structured experience, but doesn't force too many of those elements on players who just want to ignore the story, fight monsters, and power up their characters. Though many different MMORPGs have offered their own unique approaches to this issue, none can claim the player base or enduring popularity of *World of Warcraft*, making it the perfect example of how fully player-driven storytelling can be used to create an immense and satisfying online gaming experience.

WoW Changed Everything!

Storytelling in MMOs has the potential to be delivered very differently than we have seen in most state-of-the-art MMOs, at least those designed on the *World of Warcraft* model. *World of Warcraft* was a seminal product because it showed that players would embrace a play model in which leveling speed (the speed at which the player's character gains levels and grows stronger) could be coupled with advancing through the storyline in an enjoyable manner. In short, that story could be consumed and enjoyed along with killing MOBs continuously over time, and players would like this change of pace. Remember, the only model we had seen before this was really *EverQuest*, which – contrary to its name – didn't have very many quests.

Server design and build processes currently dictate that all content on all player servers be identical. Stated in a different manner, with today's technology, you can destroy an enemy NPC on one server forever, while on another server, that enemy continues to live. You either get to kill these NPCs over and over again on each server, ad nauseam, or they are killed forever across all servers at the same time (that is, with a content update).

In that kind of environment, the way you can leverage story best is through factions, meaning, or having the players do quests to raise or lower their factional status with a certain political group in the universe to allow the players to gain access to quests, zones, treasure, and so on. In this way, identical content can serve both players without the status with that political group as well as those who have the status. Thus, the universe will change for those players yet stay the same for others.

—Chris

The Strengths of Fully Player-Driven Stories

Without a main plot or any sort of strict structure, fully player-driven stories offer the players far more freedom and control over their actions than any other type of storytelling. Within reason, the player is free to spend time doing whatever he or she wants, and can even create his or her own goals and story. There are few deeper or more comprehensive ways for players to explore a fictional world. Additionally, the large degree of freedom and experimentation – combined with all the optional quests and distractions usually found in fully player-driven stories – give them a near infinite amount of replay value, ensuring that players will always be able to find something to keep them occupied.

Case Study: *Animal Crossing*

Developer: Nintendo
Publisher: Nintendo
Writer: Kenshirou Ueda, Makoto Wada, Kunio Watanabe
System: Nintendo GameCube
Release Date: September 15, 2002 (US)
Genre: Simulation

Animal Crossing can be thought of as one of Nintendo's early attempts to appeal to casual players and nongamers, though it gained quite a few hardcore fans as well and spawned sequels on the DS and the Wii. Despite having no plot and little backstory, its charming characters are a testament to Nintendo's skilled writing and translation staff.

Animal Crossing begins when the player-created hero moves into a small town and takes out a mortgage from the local store to buy his or her first house. Much like *The Sims*, there's no real story beyond this setup – and no set goals, either. The player can work to pay off his debt to Tom Nook, the raccoon storekeeper, which leads to his taking on another larger debt in order to expand his house (a cycle that can be repeated several times until the house is fully upgraded), but even this is optional, as there are no deadlines or penalties for not doing so. Instead, the player is free to spend his days exploring the village and taking part in numerous relaxing activities such as fishing, searching for fruit, gardening, bug catching, digging for fossils, and shopping for new furniture and other items to improve his house (which is periodically rated on its overall design), just to name a few of the many different pastimes. There's even a set of old NES games (including classics such as *Super Mario Brothers* and *The Legend of Zelda*) that can be collected and played. Players can also devote time to improving the village itself by pulling weeds, picking up trash, planting trees and flowers, and the like, which can in turn attract more residents to move in.

It's these residents that give *Animal Crossing* much of its charm. There's a wide variety of possible residents (more than can live in any town at one time), each with their own likes, dislikes, and personalities. Interacting with them can lead to many amusing conversations and optional quests and befriending different villagers is the only way to get certain rare items. These interactions help make players feel like they're part of a real village with other residents who have their own lives and goals and are quite a lot of fun, despite the lack of any sort of deep plot or backstory.

Animal Crossing also makes use of the GameCube's internal clock, which ties into numerous features including the weather, yearly holidays, and special characters who visit your village from time to time. Players can also visit each others' villages to explore, collect and trade items, and even entice village residents to relocate to the other player's town.

Whether you like trying to hunt down all of the myriads of different items and collectables, or just want to relax with a nice, slow-paced game, *Animal Crossing* contains more than enough gameplay to keep players busy and entertained for months on end, no matter which activities they enjoy most. It proves beyond a shadow of a doubt that fully player-driven storytelling (most often the domain of serious simulation games and MMOs) can also be used to great effect in simpler, slower-paced titles.

The Weaknesses of Fully Player-Driven Stories

We already discussed some of the difficulties that come with creating a fully player-driven story and also talked about how, barring the creation of some sort of near-human AI, the style can never be perfected in video games, as there will always be some actions that the player is unable to perform. But these are not the only weaknesses to be found.

In many ways, the total player freedom and lack of a structured story – though they are the style's biggest strength – are a considerable weakness as well. Many players like having structure and want a game with clear-cut goals and a set ending. Although some players enjoy being free to mess around and do what they want, or are at least good at creating goals and a structure for themselves, others often find themselves lost. Faced with too many options, they can't decide what to do and become stuck and/or frustrated. Others initially enjoy the freedom, but after they spend a little time playing around with the various options and activities, quickly grow bored. With no specified goals to motivate them, they soon tire of the game and move onto other things. Some games, such as MMORPGs, deal with this issue by adding a large variety of game-recognized goals (levels, titles, quest chains, and the like) that the player can pursue or ignore at his or her leisure. This certainly helps and is, in fact, quite effective at hooking some players, but others still find the lack of an ending and complete story structure off-putting and have little interest in completing various arbitrary tasks when there are no real plot elements tied into them. For that type of player, collecting 12 diamonds in order to bribe the prison guard and rescue the princess is fine, but collecting 12 diamonds for 100 experience points and a check mark in his or her quest journal just doesn't provide the same motivation. Of course, some players are the opposite, and focus little on the story while obsessively completing every quest and earning every title, no matter how pointless, to earn bragging rights and prove their mastery of the game. There's nothing wrong with either attitude – it's just important to remember that both types of gamers exist.

Summary

Fully player-driven stories are the most player-driven type of storytelling possible. Instead of being built around a main plot, they're instead composed entirely of a setting (which can include NPCs, backstory, and/or short stories told via quest chains) and rules detailing the way in which the players can interact with that setting. This leaves players free to do what they want when they want and to create an entirely unique story of their own.

However, without a main plot, it's extremely important to be sure that the setting is interesting and contains enough activities and options to keep the player entertained. A lot of planning also has to go into deciding the rules of interaction so that the nearly infinite number of actions that a real person could take at any given time are narrowed down to those that are most fun and useful within the game. Limiting the options like this is currently the only way to create fully player-driven stories in games, but does impose strict limitations on the player, thereby reducing his or her freedom and control. The only way the style can be perfected is through the use of broader, less-structured systems (such as tabletop RPGs like *Dungeons & Dragons*) combined with a human moderator who can modify the story as needed based on the player's actions. Theoretically, a near-human AI program could fill that role, but it's highly unlikely that such an AI will be created in the near future (if ever).

Although the freedom in fully player-driven stories can't be matched, it can also spell trouble with regard to attracting players who prefer to have set goals, stories, and/or some kind of basic structure to help them decide how to proceed through the game. MMORPGs, many of which use fully player-driven storytelling, attempt to solve this problem by using things such as titles, character development, and story-based quest chains to give some structure and more of a plot than can be found in games like *The Sims* and *Animal Crossing*. However, none of these can replace a true main plot, and although they have proven popular with some players, they fail to interest others, showing that even at their best, fully player-driven stories really aren't for everyone (as evidenced in Chapter 14).

Things to Consider

1. List five games you've played that use fully player-driven stories (if you haven't played that many, just list the ones you have).

2. Pick two games from your list. Do one or both of them have any sort of plot or backstory? If so, in what ways is it conveyed to the player?

3. Pick one of your two games and list the different activities available within the game. Make your list as comprehensive as you can.

4. Does your chosen game have any set goals or accomplishments? If so, make a list of what they are and how to achieve them. Do you feel that these goals are an enjoyable addition to the game? Why or why not?

5. Do you think you would have enjoyed the game more if it included a full main plot? In what ways do you feel that the addition of a main plot would have improved or detracted from the game?

Twelve

The Argument for the Supremacy of Player-Driven Storytelling

Now that you have a strong understanding of each of the main types of interactive storytelling used in video games, it's time to return to the question that was first brought up in Chapter 1. Out of all these different storytelling styles, which is the best? Do the strict structure and careful pacing of the less player-driven forms of storytelling or the open structures and freedom of highly player-driven forms create the most enjoyable and moving stories?

In this chapter, we'll look at things from the perspective of the player-driven storytelling advocates and delve into the reasons behind their beliefs. In the next chapter, we'll do the same for the supporters of more traditional forms of storytelling. Finally, in Chapter 14 you'll see what the players themselves have to say on the matter.

Those of us who actively follow the game industry have heard much about the benefits of highly player-driven stories. It's the subject of a large number of papers, lectures, and interviews. Many notable industry figures such as Peter Molyneux (designer of the *Fable* series) are strong supporters of the move toward highly player-driven storytelling and are very vocal about its benefits and importance to the future of the industry.

Despite the vast amount of writing and discussion available on the subject, nearly all arguments for the supremacy of player-driven storytelling can be boiled down to four key points:

- The evolution of the art form
- Giving the writer greater freedom
- Strengthening the player–character bond
- Giving the players what they want

Instead of trying to examine and pick apart each individual argument, we'll instead focus on the points themselves.

The Evolution of the Art Form

You may hear many game designers saying that thanks to the interactivity allowed by modern computers and game systems, traditional storytelling is old-fashioned and that highly player-driven stories are the natural evolution of storytelling itself. However, they're far from the first to voice such opinions. In his 1967 essay *The Literature of Exhaustion*, John Barth described traditional storytelling as an art form that reached its peak long ago and can no longer evolve or advance in its present state.

Storytelling has been a part of human culture from the dawn of recorded history. Over time, the arts of writing and storytelling rapidly improved but are they really still doing so today? The works of great storytellers from hundreds and even thousands of years ago – such as William Shakespeare, Charles Dickens, and Homer – are still widely read and considered by many to be some of the best tales ever created. If we still attach so much reverence and skill to works that old, can we really say that the art of storytelling has significantly improved since their time? When we look at things from that perspective, it becomes easy to say that traditional storytelling reached its peak long ago and can advance no further as an art form. Traditional storytelling can still be used to create excellent stories, but nothing created using traditional storytelling methods will lead to any sort of progression or evolution in the art of storytelling itself.

Talent Elevates the Form

Modern dramatic forms of film, theater, and television *are* evolutions of the form. Each of those forms has evolved to meet the needs (desires) of the world of commerce they exist in and is doing so very nicely in terms of their art. Some of the best examples of the storytelling art are viewable today, and have been created in the last thirty years or so. Many professional writers agree that the very best dramatic writing is taking place in television, which – owing to the influence of the cable networks – has matured rapidly over the last fifteen years or so. It is interesting that although the "art" of that form is possibly at its highest, the size of the overall viewing audience is dropping, mainly due to the influence of interactive media, such as the Web and games.

The world of television was once a sea of shows like *Kojack* (which was fun, but formulaic) but is now inhabited by *Mad Men* and, before that *The West Wing* and *The Sopranos*, shows that took the formula and elevated it.

—Chris

If the impossibility of progression is true, then in order to push storytelling to new heights, it's necessary to disregard traditional styles and methods and experiment with new and different forms of storytelling. Player-driven stories can easily be seen as the evolution of and successor to traditional storytelling. Unlike traditional stories, they give freedom to both the player and author to explore multiple outcomes and side trails. They also, for the first time, allow the player to take on an active role in the story instead of being a mere viewer. This can, at least in theory, significantly increase the player's interest and immersion while ensuring that the story remains new and different no matter how many times it's replayed.

Supporters of this argument point out that player-driven storytelling is the true evolution of the art form and that their interactive nature puts video games at the forefront of the player-driven story movement. Therefore, game designers and writers should be focusing their efforts on this new and better form of storytelling, rather than falling back on the methods and styles of the past.

Giving the Writer Greater Freedom

Of the four key points in the argument for the supremacy of player-driven storytelling, giving the writer greater freedom is the least frequently mentioned but still bears discussion, as it provides a much different view than the artistic approach of the first point and the player-based approaches of the following two points. Specifically, this point states that regardless of the artistic merits of player-driven storytelling or the benefits it provides to the player, highly player-driven stories actually provide significant benefits to the writer as well.

In traditional storytelling, the writer is forced to commit to having the events of the story play out in a single way. With player-driven storytelling, however, the writer is free to explore multiple story progressions and endings. He or she may even feel that those extra branches and endings are necessary for players to gain a full understanding of the plot and characters, show multiple sides of a character's personality, and/or demonstrate the potential consequences of different choices that the hero could make. If that's the case, limiting the story to a single outcome would be a tremendous disservice to both the writer and the player. The writer would be unable to fully pass on his or her creative vision, and the player would be stuck with an incomplete story. In player-driven stories, the writer leaves players free to explore the different branches and outcomes as they see fit, whether they merely pick the options that best fit their personalities and preferences or are drawn to explore them all and uncover every last possibility in order to gain a complete understanding of the story.

In addition, trying to add too much backstory or supplemental information to a traditional story can easily ruin the pacing and make it difficult to maintain reader interest. In player-driven storytelling, however, backstory and supplemental material can be spread out across multiple branches, endings, conversations, and the like. This not only keeps it in more easily manageable portions, but ensures that players who have little interest in such extraneous details are able to avoid becoming bogged down by them.

Strengthening the Player–Character Bond

Throughout this book, we've talked about the importance of making characters interesting and believable, as this helps players come to care about and bond with them, sharing their triumphs, failures, joys, and sorrows. After all, if players don't care about the fate of the hero, there's much less reason for them to be interested in the story as a whole. This player–character bond is often seen as one of the most important aspects in game storytelling. Furthermore, the interactivity present in games – even ones using interactive traditional storytelling – often helps develop and strengthen this bond by making the player in many ways responsible for the hero's actions and survival.

If interactivity helps players bond with characters, it seems reasonable to assume that the more control the player has over the character's actions, decisions, and even personality, the deeper that bond will become. Following that line of reasoning, players should be able to bond much more closely with a generic player-created hero over whom they have complete control than with any sort of predefined character created by the author, no matter how good that character may be. Therefore, highly player-driven storytelling should significantly increase the player–character bond. Whether this line of reasoning actually holds true is another matter entirely (as previously mentioned, it's extremely rare for generic player-created heroes to come up when listing favorite video game characters) which we'll discuss in the coming chapters, but that's the way the point is argued.

Giving the Players What They Want

At the end of the day, games need to make money. Regardless of how good a game might be, if it doesn't sell, then its creators will be out of work. Therefore, making games that players will enjoy and want to buy is extremely important. There are many factors that contribute to a player's enjoyment of a game – story is only one of them. Exactly how important of a factor it is depends on both the player and the type of game (for example, stories tend to be a far more important part of RPGs and adventure games than music or puzzle games), but crafting a story that players will find entertaining, interesting, gripping, or some combination of the three is a big concern throughout much of the game industry.

Commerce Corrupts?

There is not a worker in any storytelling art form that is not feeling the pinch of commerce. If you want to argue that storytelling as an art form might need to evolve because people just aren't buying it as much as they are buying games, you might have a point. Again, as an observer of modern "traditional" linear storytelling, I think the work being done by today's writers is as artful as any of their ancestors. But today's audiences have much more choice with regard to media, and a much different experience of that media through devices new to the marketplace. On that level, storytelling needs to respond to this new evolution, which I don't think we have done yet as fully as we should. The reason? I believe writers, in general, are scared a bit to give up control to the audience.

—Chris

As previously discussed, there are many things that can ruin – or at least seriously detract from – a good story. Poor pacing can bore or overwhelm players. Unlikable and/or unbelievable characters can make it difficult for them to take a serious interest in the plot. Too much backstory can bore; too little can leave a story feeling incomplete. Plots that go in a direction that the player doesn't like can lead him or her to grow frustrated and upset (a certain romantic pairing in the *Harry Potter* series, for example, greatly angered many fans who wanted to see Harry end up with a different girl).

Hatred Is a Form of Love

I've always said that if they are arguing over a decision you've made in a story, at least they care. Better that than having them ignore you completely!

—Chris

These unexpected plot turns are especially problematic when it comes to endings. An ending that goes significantly against players' expectations and/or in a way that they think doesn't make sense for the story and characters can drastically reduce their opinion of the story as a whole. I can name a number of stories (in games, books, and movies) that I really loved ... right up until the ending. However, the endings of those particular stories were either so poorly done or so far removed from the way it seemed the story should have ended that they not only left me feeling extremely dissatisfied, but discouraged me from ever going back to reread, rewatch, or replay those stories, despite how much I liked them at first.

It's also human nature to think that in many cases we could do things better than the characters in our favorite stories if given the chance. Looking back, I'm sure you can think of many times when you've bemoaned a character for making a particularly stupid move, saying the wrong thing, or not picking up on a very important and obvious piece of information. In some cases, it's hard to say if our own instincts and intuition would have caused things to play out better or not, but at least giving us a chance would remove the frustration of watching the hero walk alone and unarmed into the room where the killer is hiding.

Game designers and writers want players to enjoy the story so they'll tell their friends and buy more games. Players want to enjoy the story so they don't feel like they wasted the time and money they put into it. But, as you can see, there are a multitude of factors that can easily ruin the player's enjoyment. In theory, giving the player more control should solve those problems. If the player is in control of the hero's personality and actions, there's no need to complain about the hero doing or saying the wrong thing. If the player is in control of the pace at which the story progresses and the amount of backstory he or she receives, he or she shouldn't have to worry about things going too fast or too slow. And, if the player is in control of the game's most important decisions, he or she can always ensure that the plot and ending play out in an enjoyable way.

Taking this to the next logical step, it could be said that what the player wants most from the story isn't to sit back and watch it unfold but to become an actual part of the story itself. If fiction is really an escape from reality, then living it should clearly be better than just observing it. Therefore, it's the job of game designers and writers to make the player as much of an active participant in the story as possible so that the player can fulfill his or her true desires and obtain as much enjoyment from the story as possible. If we assume that what players want most from a story is to become an active participant in it, then it's clear that highly player-driven forms of storytelling are the way to go. By this logic, it's true that traditional forms of storytelling have peaked and outlived their usefulness. Though they can be used to tell good stories, they're forever doomed to be an imperfect form. Linear and unchanging, they make the player a mere observer or grant only the most limited forms of involvement and can never fulfill a player's greatest desire and make him or her an actual part of the story. Only player-driven storytelling can grant this wish, making it the clearly superior style.

How Do We Do This?

I mentioned earlier the issue of surprising the audience. If player-driven stories are the solution – and because the player is, in essence, a co-creator – is what we gain in the art form by yielding some story control to the players worth what we lose when the performers/writers (the players) can't be surprised by what they do on their own in the story? This statement seems eerily reminiscent of the plotline of the movie *The Incredibles*. I suppose we'll see in the next chapter, eh?

—Chris

With that in mind, no further argument should be needed – assuming that we're right about what players want most. Though the logical progression works, it's all based on a series of assumptions about what players want most from a story. Do the majority of players really want to take on an active role, shape the hero to their own preferences, and control the progression and outcome of the story? Do they want the opposite? Do they even care? Perhaps even more importantly, regardless of whether players say they want more control over their stories, does giving them that control allow them to enjoy the story more than they otherwise would have? Over the next two chapters, we'll attempt to answer these all-important questions by looking at the arguments against the supremacy of player-driven storytelling and by researching what types of stories players really want and enjoy the most.

Summary

There has been much talk in the game industry about the alleged supremacy of highly player-driven forms of storytelling, most of which focus around the following four key points:

- Traditional storytelling can be said to have reached its peak as an art form and is no longer capable of significant growth or evolution; therefore, it's time to move on and focus on a new type of storytelling, such as player-driven storytelling.

- Player-driven storytelling gives the author the opportunity to greatly expand his or her story and to explore alternative versions of events, side stories, and the like.

- The large amount of player control and freedom in player-driven stories strengthens the player–character bond so that players will care more about the game's heroes.

- Most importantly, as there are many things that can reduce a player's enjoyment of a story, putting the player in charge and allowing him or her to control how the story progresses should, in theory, fulfill the player's wish to become part of the story and allow him or her to steer the story's events in the most enjoyable direction. This is something that more traditional forms of storytelling can never do and is the greatest advantage of player-driven storytelling.

However, quite a lot of these arguments are built around assumptions of what players want. If these assumptions are true, the points hold firm, but if they're false, then arguing for the supremacy of player-driven storytelling becomes very difficult. We'll carefully examine and test these assumptions in the following chapters to see how true they really are.

Things to Consider

1. Do you think that highly player-driven stories are superior to more traditional stories? Why or why not?

2. Briefly summarize your own thoughts on the four key points covered in this chapter.

3. Can you think of any additional arguments that could be used to support the supremacy of player-driven stories?

4. Do you believe that most players want to be given more control and freedom in video game stories? Why or why not?

Thirteen

The Argument Against the Supremacy of Player-Driven Storytelling

Supporting more traditional, less player-driven stories doesn't seem to be an overly popular position among members of the video game industry. At the very least, the pro-player-driven storytelling crowd is certainly the more vocal of the two by far. However, the pro–traditional storytelling side has many well-respected supporters of its own, and they have a strong set of arguments to back up their position. Although you can't really deny the superiority of player-driven storytelling if it's assumed that what players want and enjoy most is to become an active part of the story, whether those assumptions are actually true is highly debatable. In this chapter, we'll go over the key points of the pro–traditional storytelling arguments:

- The fine art of storytelling
- Time, money, and player interest
- Keeping the story interesting
- Loss of impact
- The illusion of control
- Giving the players what they want

The Fine Art of Storytelling

As we discussed in the previous chapter, it can be argued that traditional storytelling long ago reached its peak as an art form – especially considering that many of what are considered to be the best stories were written hundreds or in some cases even thousands of years ago. But even if that's true, is it such a bad thing? As anyone who follows video games should know, it's often not until a product (be it a game console, hardware device, or software program) has reached its peak that developers are able to utilize its full potential. Once all the bugs have been worked out and every aspect and feature is fully understood, developers know exactly what can and can't be done and how to best take advantage of every aspect, while avoiding the research and the trial and error process that filled their earlier projects, to bring out the best in the device or program. For a simple example, games that were released near the end of a console's life cycle (like *Kingdom Hearts II*) show an enormous technical improvement over those released early on (such as *The Bouncer*).

Building to What You Know Is Easier

I call this situation the Panavision Camera Effect. Here's why. Game development studios each create their own set of tools for their designers to use so as to get the game content (levels, characters, geometry) actually into the game. These tools facilitate adding story elements as well, including missions, quests, objects, and treasure. These tools are often very good, but they all work differently from each other (this is a by-product of their being built to facilitate a specific studio's working process). As a designer/writer, you get to tell only the kinds of stories that your tools allow you to. Broadly put, if your tool doesn't allow you to create dialog trees, you simply can't design your story so it has dialog trees. As we observed, experience with a development environment is the key to learning what can and can't be done in a particular environment, and learning how to squeeze out the most from that environment.

In the film business, most everyone uses a fairly standard camera made by Panavision, with a fairly standard set of lenses and a standard set of film stocks. So when a team assembles to shoot a new film, they all know their tools, because they've all used them many times before. The Panavision Camera Effect levels the playing field and allows the talents of the team to rise to the surface. In video game development, it seems as if just at the moment when the development teams learn exactly how to get the best out of a platform, the economic forces dictate that a new platform be put into the marketplace. Just as a writer/designer learns the ins and outs of a toolset, he or she changes jobs to a new studio or the studio "revs" the toolset to make it "better." These forces mean that most designers/writers are always *learning* their tools, but never *mastering* them.

—Chris

Why shouldn't storytelling be the same? It can be argued that traditional storytelling has survived so long in its current form not because humanity lacked the inspiration or technology to create more player-driven stories, but because traditional storytelling is a finely tuned and highly versatile form and is in fact the best way to tell most stories. And because the art of storytelling is already perfected, modern writers don't need to waste their time and energy chasing vaguely defined goals such as "evolving the art form" and can instead focus on what they do best: creating good stories.

Time, Money, and Player Interest

The Added Time and Expense of Creating Player-Driven Stories

On a more practical level, creating highly player-driven stories isn't easy. As we've talked about in previous chapters, doing so takes a lot of time and money. And, in the game industry, those things tend to be in short supply. Say we have a game using interactive traditional storytelling that has about twenty hours of gameplay. Now let's say that we want to take that basic game and change it to a branching path story with three main branches and numerous minor and moderate branches along the way. All of those additional branches are going to need a considerable amount of writing and design work. They'll also require additional programming, art, animation, sound, and testing. Although some elements can be reused across branches, the change from an interactive traditional story to a branching path story has probably doubled or tripled the workload. Changing that branching path story to an open-ended story would increase it even further.

Now, extra work means that the game will take longer to develop and may even require additional employees for the game to be completed within any sort of reasonable time frame. Those extra employees and working hours cost more money, and the longer the game spends in development, the longer it is before it actually ships and starts making money of its own.

Games using highly player-driven stories simply aren't very cost-effective when compared with those using more traditional forms of storytelling. And although a few developers and publishers can afford to spend several years and tens of millions of dollars working on their next game, most can't – especially when it's in no way guaranteed that the game will sell well enough to make that investment worthwhile.

Adding Interaction at the Expense of Other Elements

Because adding extra branches and types of interaction takes additional time and money, one way to try and make up for it is to cut costs in other ways, which often means removing or cutting back on other things in the game. As I mentioned in the earlier chapters, it's quite common for endings in multiple-ending story games to be rather short when compared to games using interactive traditional stories. Similarly, the main plots found in open-ended stories tend to be rather short and simple when compared to those using less player-driven storytelling methods. Although story elements are the most common things to cut out, optional quests, mini-games, and gameplay features can also be cut.

Consider our sample game, which – when using interactive traditional storytelling – took an average of twenty hours to complete. However, in order to have more time to work on all the extra content when it switched to a branching path story, it might become necessary to cut out some of the characters, story scenes, and quests. What started out as a twenty-hour game could now be a twelve-hour game. Of course, with three main paths of twelve hours each, the total play time is significantly greater than the original twenty, but it's quite possible that without the eight hours that got cut, the story simply isn't as interesting or well paced as it was before. Plus, there's no guarantee that players will play through the game multiple times.

To save time without cutting content, some developers reuse as much material as possible between their different branches. Although this approach can reduce the need for cuts, it raises problems of its own. Once again looking at our sample game, let's say that instead of cutting content, we decided to reuse as much material as possible. In the end, reusing material saved so much time that very little had to be cut and we've got our three main branches, each with about eighteen hours of gameplay. However, because we reused so much content, each of those branches has the player visiting the same areas, meeting most of the same characters, and completing many of the same quests. Although we didn't cut much, we didn't do a whole lot to differentiate the three main branches, either, which probably isn't going to provide a lot of incentive for players to replay the game. This was a common complaint about the game *Saga Frontier*. It featured seven unique heroes that the player could choose from, each with his or her own unique story. However, those stories featured many of the same towns, dungeons, enemies, and allies, as well as the same collection of optional quests, which made playing through every character's story highly repetitive, even though they all added something new to the overall plot and mythos of the game.

Making a game always involves trade-offs, though that fact can quickly become more obvious when trying to create a complex highly player-driven story. Sometimes these trade-offs will improve the game and other times they'll hurt it, but it's a very delicate balancing act and something that developers and publishers need to keep in mind when they want to keep adding additional content.

Who Is Going to See It All?

Let's say we decided to bite the bullet and spend the extra time and money necessary to complete our branching path story game with a minimal number of cuts and content reuse. This leaves us with a game with three highly unique main branches, each with a set of minor and moderate branches, and a total playing time of about twenty hours per main branch. But now that our masterpiece is complete, the real question is whether players will notice and appreciate all the extra work that went into it.

Although there are hardcore players who will play through a game dozens of times to uncover every last quest, conversation, cut-scene, and item, they're a very small minority. It's a rather unfortunate fact that many players play through a game only once before moving on to something different. Some don't even complete most of their games at all. This means that, disappointing as it may be, most players aren't going to play through our game three times to explore all of the major branches, much less the six or more times that would probably be required to see all of the minor and moderate branches. Furthermore, depending on how the branches are structured (their content and decision points), it's quite possible that the most players will devote their single playthrough to the same major branch. If that's the case, was it really worth so much extra time and money to create all those branches and extra content, when the vast majority of players will never see them?

Keeping the Story Interesting

Now that we've covered the points based on artistic merit and game development, it's time to focus on the heart of the matter: specifically, whether highly player-driven forms of storytelling create better and/or more enjoyable stories. Because games are made for the players and their enjoyment should be one of the key concerns, this is naturally a very important issue. If players really want and enjoy games with highly player-driven stories much more than those with more traditional stories, production costs and arguments about artistic merit should be less of an issue. But does the ability to interact with and influence events really make a story more interesting, engaging, and/or enjoyable? Let's look at some reasons why that may not be the case.

Story Structure and the "Ideal" Chain of Events

Let's start with a what-if scenario. In the bestselling novel *Harry Potter and the Sorcerer's Stone*, Harry's parents were murdered by an evil wizard when he was a baby, leaving him to be raised by his nasty aunt and uncle. This continues until shortly before Harry's 11th birthday, when a man named Hagrid appears, tells him of his wizard heritage, and presents him with an invitation to study at Hogwarts School of Witchcraft and Wizardry. While there, Harry makes friends and enemies, starts learning magic, and finds out more about his past. In the end, he even survives an encounter with the evil Lord Voldemort, the wizard who killed his parents.

Now let's pretend that we changed it to a branching path or open-ended story. What are things that the player might decide to change? The murder of Harry's parents certainly isn't a pleasant event and leads to Harry's miserable life with the Dursleys, so that seems like a good place to start. But then what would happen to the rest of the story? If Harry's parents survived, he would have grown up with a loving family and known about magic, witches, and wizards for his entire life. He also wouldn't have his iconic scar or be known as the only person to ever survive Voldemort's killing curse, making his reputation and status in the magical world considerably different. In the end, the entire story would be changed in significant ways. Would it still be a good story? Maybe. But then again, the loss of Harry's unique position as a newcomer to the world of magic and his fame for surviving Voldemort's attack would likely rob the story of much of its wonder and conflict.

Moving on, Hagrid's sudden and decidedly odd appearance – not to mention his shocking declaration that magic is real and Harry is a wizard – naturally left Harry rather confused and suspicious. So it wouldn't be too surprising if players suspected some sort of trap and had Harry turn down the invitation to Hogwarts. And then what? Following Harry's "adventures" at boarding school and with the Dursleys probably wouldn't make for a very exciting tale. At the very least, it would be a completely different story than the one that has captivated tens of millions of people worldwide. Then again, let's say that the player did allow Harry's parents to die and had Harry attend Hogwarts. Near the end of the book, during their confrontation, Voldemort offers Harry a chance to join him. In the book, Harry refuses, but what if the player said yes? Perhaps the player wants to see Harry become evil, is trying to stall for time until help arrives, or thinks that pretending to join Voldemort will give him a good chance to stab the dark lord in the back later on. This too would drastically change the rest of the story, and probably not in a good way. Although a story with Harry as the villain may be interesting to some, it would certainly have much less appeal than Harry as a hero. Considering Voldemort's character and motivations, it's also quite possible that he'd still try to kill Harry regardless.

The choices players make won't necessarily lead to a more enjoyable story. In fact, the opposite is much more likely. If you pay attention to story structures, you'll notice that many stories are interesting only because a very specific series of events takes place. If even one of those events was missed or handled differently, the hero would die, reach a dead end, or find himself following a much less interesting path. Even worse, it's often difficult to tell which choice is the "correct" one. Some can be fairly obvious (most people will probably realize that joining Voldemort is a bad idea), but others are less so (such as saving Harry's parents). This is especially clear in branching path stories such as the *Choose Your Own Adventure* books and visual novels like *Fate/Stay Night*, in which a very large number of the possible choices lead to a sudden bad ending. And although some of these bad choices are fairly obvious, others initially appear to be perfectly good courses of actions.

The Problem with How We Think

So what are the odds that a player will make a poor choice over the course of a story? From a purely statistical approach, when there are two options, the player has only a 50 percent chance of making the right choice. If there are three options, that drops to 33 percent and so on. Of course, that would hold true only if players make their decisions at random, but that's not the way things work. Players will use their intuition, common sense, and personal preferences when making decisions, so that should significantly increase their odds of making a good choice, right? Actually, no. In fact, when faced with a decision, people usually try to avoid things like danger, tension, and conflict. In real life, that's usually a good idea, but in a story it can make things pretty dull.

Maximizing Everyone's Pleasure

Then there's the type of gamer known as a "max/min" player. This type of player drives game-related decisions by trying to maximize his or her return in game rewards (experience points, treasure, whatever) while at the same time "minimizing" the expenditure of risk and time. Those players, generally speaking, avoid situations that may be more interesting story-wise, as those situations may take more time and be riskier. The challenge is to have the story appeal to them anyway, by doing things such as attaching experience points (XP) to achieving story advancement. This kind of design decision was one of the real advances of *World of Warcraft*, which said to the player, "The quickest way to level through this game is to do all the quests one after the other." This simple design decision elevated the story far above what had been possible beforehand.

—Chris

To demonstrate, let's think about a generic slasher/horror movie. In this movie, our generic bunch of stereotypical teenagers is camping out in the haunted woods when they stumble upon an ancient graveyard and remove the magical seal on one of the graves, accidentally reviving an evil serial killer. He then proceeds to chase them through the woods, killing them off one by one until the last couple of teens somehow manage to defeat him once and for all (or at least until the sequel). Now let's imagine what the player would do if this were a player-driven story of some type. It falls to reason that any player with half a brain would be smart enough to realize that camping in the haunted woods is a bad idea to begin with. He or she also would probably have the heroes steer clear of the graveyard, or at the very least leave the magical seal alone. Even failing at all of that, the player would certainly have the heroes stay in a group so that they could fight off the killer, rather than splitting up so they can easily be picked off one by one. After all, the player doesn't want the heroes to die. It's all common sense (something the characters in slasher movies tend to completely lack) and would certainly lead to the "best" possible ending, with all or most of the heroes surviving. But the resulting story certainly wouldn't be a slasher movie and would probably be pretty boring. A movie in which a group of teens think about camping out in a haunted forest but realize it's a bad idea and go bowling instead wouldn't be very exciting. Even if the killer did get free, having the heroes stay together and think about their actions would likely allow them to defeat him quickly and easily. In the end, the player is left with a story that, despite his or her careful control over the events, is rather boring and certainly not the bloody and spine-tingling thriller the player was hoping for.

Although not all story types rely on the hero's stupidity the way many slasher films do, it's quite common in storytelling for a mistake or failure on the hero's part to be a key element without which the rest of the story would change drastically or even collapse. Unless players use a strategy guide of some sort, the chances of them making all of the right choices throughout a game are extremely low. And because most players complete a game only once, the chances of them ever seeing the "best" path aren't good, especially if the less than ideal paths continue on for a long time before ending. Although following the advice in previous chapters and trying to ensure that only the most interesting and enjoyable branches and options make it into the game can help, the more choices and control you give to the player, the more difficult it becomes to create a unique and interesting branch for each possible decision he or she could make.

Trying to Correct a Mistake

It's highly unlikely that players will make all of the best possible choices on their first playthrough of a game using player-driven storytelling. So what happens if they make a wrong choice? Well, that depends on the game. In some games, such as *Fate/Stay Night*, the majority of wrong choices lead to a sudden bad ending. Naturally, there's nothing better than a "game over" screen to tell players that they did something wrong and need to try again. What really matters is how easy it is for them to go back and correct their mistake.

In branching path stories, the decision points are usually very obvious, so it's easy enough for players to reload from an earlier save file, go back to the decision point, and try another option that is, of course, assuming that they didn't somehow save over their file while on the wrong path, leaving them with no option but to restart the game. It can also be problematic if they didn't save their game recently and need to spend a considerable portion of time getting back to the decision point. Both of these issues can be blamed on player error, though a well-implemented autosave system can easily solve them. Many visual novel games even include a feature that lets players rapidly skip over previously completed sections in case they do find themselves replaying a considerable portion of the game just to get to a specific decision point (a solution that can work well for many types of game that are made up of clearly divided levels or scenes).

But it isn't always so easy. Some decision points aren't very obvious to the player, especially the ones that are based on general actions rather than specific decisions. Things like the relationship-based ending system in *STAR OCEAN: SECOND EVOLUTION* and the various behavior-based branches in games such as *Fallout 3* and *Mass Effect 2* are somewhat hidden from the player and can be hard to fully understand without the use of a strategy guide. This can make it very hard for players to determine exactly what it was that they did that caused the story to turn down an undesirable branch, making it very difficult for them to go back and fix things, especially because doing so often requires replaying a significant portion of the game.

Things become even more complicated when the consequences of a decision aren't made immediately clear. Even the results of a very obvious decision point can be difficult to identify if a large amount of times passes between the decision and its consequences. For example, in *Fate/Stay Night*'s Heaven's Feel branch, players will be unable to achieve the best ending unless they make certain specific decisions much earlier in the game (specifically, those that improve Shiro's relationship with Ilya). However, there are no immediate consequences if Shiro distances himself from Ilya early on, and should the player fail to befriend her, she simply won't show up to help Shiro near the end of the game. This leaves the player with no hint as to the important role Ilya plays in the best ending and how vital it is to get on her good side. Many decisions in *Heavy Rain* operate in a similar fashion. Important decision points such as whether Ethan becomes close to Madison or whether Jayden finds certain vital pieces of evidence about the Origami Killer's identity aren't made obvious to the player, with the game continuing normally regardless of the player's actions, but have a very large impact on the final parts of the story. Without the use of a guide, it's very easy for players to miss those pieces of evidence or make the wrong decision with Madison and never realize how much the story changed because of it. And even if they decide to replay the entire game, there's no guarantee that they'll realize the importance of those points or make the correct decision the second time around.

Although fixing a mistake can at times be difficult enough even with clear decision points where the consequences are immediately shown, it becomes far more challenging in games that use more open and natural forms of decision making. Having a very large number of decision points and branches further complicates matters, making it even harder for players to determine exactly where they went wrong – all of which is hardly conducive to an enjoyable experience.

Loss of Impact

Highly emotional moments in stories have a tendency to lose much of their impact when the players know that they can always go back and choose a different outcome. As an example, let's look at a moment from *FINAL FANTASY VII* that is frequently cited as one of the most shocking and emotional scenes in gaming history: the death of Aerith. Aerith is a flower girl living in the slums of Midgar who befriends Cloud early on; she also happens to be the last surviving member of the race known as the Ancients. Aerith is a very sweet, kind, and friendly girl and plays a large role in the story. She also proves to be an extremely useful party member, with excellent magic skills and some of the best limit break abilities in the game. These traits combined to make her a very popular character and caused many players to give her a permanent spot in their battle party. Her sudden murder at the hands of Sephiroth approximately halfway through the game shocked, saddened, and enraged players. That scene cemented Sephiroth's status as one of gaming's most infamous villains and started a seemingly endless chain of rumors and speculation about ways to revive Aerith (of which there aren't any, by the way). Her death is still talked about now, more than a decade after *FINAL FANTASY VII*'s release, and as I said before, is often considered one of the most emotional moments in gaming.

But if *FINAL FANTASY VII* had used a branching path or open-ended story, would Aerith's death still have had the same impact on players and the game industry as a whole? The answer is a resounding *no*. The very fact that there was no way to save or revive Aerith is what makes her death such a moving event. Just like in real life, death has a huge impact on people and society due to its finality. Had *FINAL FANTASY VII* used a branching path or open-ended story, instead of agonizing over Aerith's death most players would have merely shrugged it off, loaded their last save, and kept choosing different branches until they found one where she survived.

This loss of impact can be seen as a serious flaw in player-driven storytelling. How is it possible to tell a moving emotional story when the player can always backtrack and undo decisions that don't turn out the way he or she wants? Death, failure, mistakes? None of that really matters as long as there's a way to undo and avoid them. You could, of course, have a player-driven story that simply doesn't allow the player to avoid certain events (such as Aerith's death), but in many ways that defeats the purpose of player-driven storytelling. Players will be left wondering why you gave them control in the first place if you're not going to let them do anything about the moments they most want to change. Putting a very long gap between the decision point and the event can help, as many players won't realize the connection or won't want to replay so much of the game in order to change things, but that can frustrate players and lead to the problems described in the previous section. Some branching path games such as *Fate/Stay Night* and *Heavy Rain* manage to pull off fairly deep and emotional moments while still allowing for a moderate degree of player choice, but in both games those moments come more from the situations the heroes find themselves in rather than "changeable" events such as a character's death or a failure on the hero's part.

The Illusion of Control

It can be argued that players may often enjoy feeling like they're in control of a story, but – for the reasons we've just discussed – actually giving them a large degree of control can significantly detract from the story in many ways. Because of this, it's better to give them a strong illusion of control instead of actual control. This illusion of control can be created in many ways. A lot of games using interactive traditional storytelling create this illusion by giving the players a large amount of freedom outside story scenes and providing optional quests they can participate in. Even most branching path stories give players an illusion of control far greater than the actual amount of control they possess. *Heavy Rain* provides an enormous amount of player choice, though as discussed in its case study, most of those choices have little to no effect on the main plot (although this isn't immediately obvious to players). Similarly, despite all the decision points and choices available in *Fate/Stay Night*, there are only three major branches and a very large percentage of choices quickly lead to a bad ending.

Skilled use of the illusion of control will let players feel like they're in control (at least to a certain extent) while still allowing for a carefully structured and meaningful story. Because of this ability, you can argue that there's little reason to endure the expenses and difficulties required to give players a significant amount of true control.

Death by a Million Cuts

Technically speaking, game designers call this technique *indirect control*; it is the art, if you will, of presenting the players with a seemingly large number of choices but using psychology and visual design to influence their decision so that most of the time they make the choice you wish them to. Game designers aren't the only "evil" people who use these techniques – they are used all the time in theme parks, retail outlets, and elsewhere. Note how food stores put daily staples such as milk and eggs at the far reaches of the floor layout, indirectly forcing you to traverse much of the floor to get them? They aren't saying, "You have to consider purchasing items 'X,' 'Y,' and 'Z,'" but in effect, that is what you do en route to replenishing your fridge.

Unlimited choice seems like the ideal way to give your audience what they want, but actually it's a pretty bad way to design, because too many choices do not facilitate the user experience. How many people use only 10 percent of all of *Photoshop*'s thousands of options? Many, many *Photoshop* users do so, and many complain that the program is too complicated. Software development historically has gone through these kinds of cycles over and over again. A great product comes out that does a few things very well (say, a word processor). It takes the market by storm. Every year a new version comes out, adding "features" until finally it is so bloated that new users cannot figure out how to do even the simplest things. And then a competitor comes onto the marketplace that does a few well-chosen things well and clearly and grabs some of the market share away from the original. The original product hires a human-interface designer to figure out how to redesign the interface, making the most important features easy to find (often using indirect control) so that the product is once again easy to use.

—Chris

Giving the Players What They Want

Once again, as we discussed in the previous chapter, it all comes down to what the player wants most. Although supporters of player-driven storytelling say that what players want most from a story is to become an active participant and control it, supporters of traditional storytelling argue that what players want most is simply a good, enjoyable story. Both sides agree that players won't be happy with a story that they don't find entertaining and/or interesting. But although a large degree of player control could conceivably allow players to ensure that the story follows the path that they'll enjoy most, it's far more likely that most of them will make a mistake somewhere along the way and end up stuck on a less desirable branch. Therefore, because most players play through a game only once, it makes more sense to use traditional storytelling methods so that players can be sure to see the best possible story progression and outcome. Meanwhile, any desire the players have to change and affect the story itself can be satisfied by a strong illusion of control, giving them a lot to do without any risk that their decisions will detract from or derail the main plot.

Of course, once again, this brings up the question of what it is that players really want most. Is it control, or just a well-written story? Although it's easy to assume that the answer is one or the other, assumptions – no matter how well reasoned – aren't always correct, which is why we'll cover this issue in depth in the next chapter.

Summary

Though not as vocal as the pro-player-driven storytelling crowd, traditional storytelling has many supporters of its own, and they have some very strong arguments backing them up. First, it can be argued that because storytelling is such an old

266

and well-developed art, it has already reached its perfect form, and chasing vague ideals such as evolving the art form is a waste of time. Second, the added amount of time and money required to make highly player-driven stories can quickly become a serious concern, especially when it's taken into account that most players will play through the game only once and never see most of the branches and extra content. In addition, most stories are interesting only because of the occurrence of a specific chain of events. If players are given control, it's extremely likely that they will eventually make a wrong choice and steer the story in a less interesting direction, no matter how hard they try to avoid this outcome. And after they discover that they've made a mistake (assuming they notice at all), it can be very difficult and/or time-consuming for players to find the place where they went wrong and to go back and change it. Player-driven storytelling also makes it difficult for highly emotional scenes such as a character's death to have much impact, as the players know they can always go back and change things to get a different outcome.

As a result, it can be argued that giving players a strong illusion of control (through things like the gameplay and optional quests) is much better than giving them actual control over the story. This allows players to get what they want most – an enjoyable story – while still letting them feel as if they have an important role to play. Whether this is actually what players want most is debatable. In the next chapter, we'll look at what players themselves say in an effort to discover what it is that they truly want.

Things to Consider

1. Do you think that traditional stories are superior to more highly player-driven ones? Why or why not? Has reading this chapter changed your opinion on the matter?

2. Briefly summarize your own thoughts on the key points covered in this chapter.

3. Can you think of any additional arguments that could be used to support the supremacy of traditional stories?

4. Do you believe that most players want a well-written and enjoyable story above all else? Why or why not?

Fourteen

What Players Really Want: The Most Important Issue

As you've seen in the last two chapters, good arguments can be made for the supremacy of both player-driven and traditional storytelling methods in games. It's quite likely that you have your own thoughts on which side makes the better case. When I first began researching this subject, I found myself more in line with the pro–traditional storytelling group, but I also saw that both sides based many of their key arguments on assumptions of what players wanted and enjoyed most in stories (freedom and control vs. a structured and well-told story). The problem was that although everyone was saying "players want this" or "players want that," as far as I could tell, no one had done any serious research into what players actually wanted – the respondents were just going off their own personal opinions. And although voicing your own opinions is fine, it's rather rash and even a little arrogant to automatically assume that the majority of game players agree with your opinion, no matter how important of a position you do or don't hold within the game industry. With that in mind, I decided that the only way to truly answer the question of which type of storytelling was better was to ask the players themselves, so I put aside my own opinions and set out to find what players really want.

The Debate Continues

One of the most well-known figures in the debate is Raph Koster, designer of *Star Wars:Galaxies* as well as having worked extensively on *Ultima: Online*. Raph's bona fides in this area of game design are beyond question, and he is famous (or infamous, if you will) in this debate: in fact, he issued a challenge to designers in the form of this quote: "Designers, get over yourselves!"[1]

Here's the larger story from that article: "At the 2002 Game Developer's Conference, an audience member asked the panel on 'Building the Next-Generation PW' how he, as a writer, could ensure the integrity of his story in a PW. The reply came from panel member Raph Koster, the creative director on *Star Wars Galaxies* and former lead designer of *UO*: 'Get over yourselves; the rest of the world is coming. Okay? People value self-expression. Is 'story' going to go away? No. Is careful crafting going to go away? No. Are the professionals engaged in that going to go away? No. Well, except that IP—the concept of intellectual property—may, but that's a whole other side discussion. The thing is that people want to express themselves and they don't really care that 99 percent of everything is crap, because they are positive that the 1 percent they made isn't. Okay? And fundamentally, they get ecstatic as soon as five people see it, right?'"

Powerful stuff, and very true (at least in my experience with this community, it is true). In my industry jobs as well as in my role as an educator, I have observed this phenomena again and again, which I explain this way: there is a fundamental difference between those who have been paid by a publishing organization (which I define as a book publisher, movie studio, television network, or game publisher) to create stories and those who create stories for themselves and their close acquaintances. Many, many people think they can write creatively, and they certainly can. Do a Google search on "fan fiction" if you want to scare yourself a little bit. Almost every member of the Internet population can write creatively, and, generally speaking, they don't see much difference in quality between what they can and do create for themselves on the side in their spare time and what those making a living doing so can produce. It has been said by wiser people than myself that "Everyone has one novel in them, but the real test is whether you can actually finish that novel, and, having done so, what you then do for an encore." The real difference lies in craft, and writing for a larger audience, and being asked to write more stories. But because the skills come so easily to most computer-literate people (as one game producer said to my writing staff one dark and evil day, "What's so hard about it? All you have to do is type!" and yes, he was serious), the very, very difficult issue of what and how to write so as to achieve true intrinsic worth (to avoid being categorized in the "99 percent crap" bucket, as so eloquently phrased by Mr. Koster) is often ignored in the blush of false praise heaped upon young authors by their friends and social network.

Writing for quality over and over in such a manner that people will pay to consume more of that writing is a very rare skill – a skill that

Hollywood (to name but one funding source) pays top dollar to acquire. But the desire to have others see one's writing is very attractive, and the belief (as Mr. Koster stated) that one's writing is good is pervasive amongst the crowd of people that play games (at least it feels that way to me). Perhaps the cause rests in the observations of Henry Jenkins about the Web 2.0 generation; perhaps it lies in the easy self-publishing methods and the removal of traditional gatekeepers. I don't truly know. But what I do know is the evidence is in that the current generation of gamers *want* this type of media to respond to their desires, and they want this media to *hear* them. But, as we will delve into shortly, in what way do they want to be heard?

—Chris

---

[1] Rather than take it out of context, I'd like to give it full attribution: Mulligan, Jessica and Bridgette Patrovsky, *Developing Online Games: An Insider's Guide* (New Riders, 2003), pp. 145–146. ISBN 1592730000.

Do Players Know What They Really Want?

In the previous chapter, we talked about how giving players control of a story can actually lead to them unwittingly turning the story down a less enjoyable path, no matter how hard they try to create the best possible outcome. The example of a player-driven slasher story showed that often the "best" choice in a given situation doesn't lead to the most interesting or entertaining story. This brought me to an interesting question. Do players who say they want games with highly player-driven stories actually end up enjoying them more than games with more traditional stories? Perhaps, even if they like the idea of player-driven storytelling, they might unconsciously prefer more traditionally structured stories. For example, let's say we have a person who says that he thinks FPS is the best game genre there is. However, upon questioning him a bit further, we discover that his three favorite games of all time are RPGs. That's quite a big disconnect there. If he thinks FPS games are so amazing, shouldn't they dominate his top three list? This inconsistency suggests that although our subject may really like the style and concept of FPS games, he actually gets more enjoyment playing RPGs and therefore prefers them, albeit subconsciously.

Clearly, my research wouldn't be complete unless I checked whether players' stated storytelling preferences matched up with their actual ones. I was also very curious to see whether a large number of players demonstrated this type of mental disconnect or if I was merely overthinking things. Therefore, the question of whether players really know what they want became an important one as I continued to plan out my research methods.

The Survey

I decided that the simplest way to discover what types of stories players liked best was to ask them. To that end, I created and ran my first research survey in the summer of 2009. The survey focused on players' storytelling preferences in games, books, and movies and also contained questions designed to determine whether the players' stated preferences matched their actual ones. The results of that survey became an important part of my master's thesis, which laid much of the groundwork for this book. Though the results of that survey shed a considerable amount of light on what types of stories players enjoyed most and the stated vs. actual preference divide, it failed to consider how those preferences affected which games players buy. So in the summer of 2010, while writing *Interactive Storytelling for Video Games*, I conducted a second survey, this time focusing on how stories influence game purchasing decisions.

Both surveys were conducted using a targeted random sample of North American game players and can be considered a statistically valid and accurate representation of the opinions of American and Canadian gamers. We'll be covering the key findings and their implications here, but if you'd like more detailed information about the surveys' content and results, you can find it on this book's companion website, http://www.StorytellingForGames.com.

How Important Are Game Stories to Players?

The first thing the survey showed was that most players pay attention to and care about game stories. Nearly 70 percent of respondents said that they tend to pay close attention to dialog and cut-scenes in games. In contrast, fewer than 10 percent reported that they pay little or no attention. Furthermore, in their write-in comments, a large number of respondents said that their interest in and/or enjoyment of a game's story is the key factor when deciding whether to finish and/or replay most games. Clearly, the stories in games do matter.

We All Want to Know Why They Play

When we polled players in the *Earth and Beyond* audience during the game's live existence, we discovered that even in our MMO, more than 66 percent of the player base were aware of the ongoing story changes, even if they themselves hadn't actually partaken in the "story missions" we were delivering to the audience in our updates. If they hadn't actually played the missions, they had discovered the story changes by talking to fellow players or by spending time on player-created websites. This number surprised even the writing staff, as we had no idea that our story was penetrating so deep within our audience. We had not even come up with *WoW*'s brilliant idea of linking level advancement to completing every quest.

—Chris

That's not necessarily to say that story is more important than gameplay (opinions on that matter were rather evenly divided), but even most respondents who put gameplay above story were quick to point out just how much a good story adds to a game. It should be noted, however, that although respondents loved games with great stories and were generally okay with games that have no stories at all (provided that they enjoyed the gameplay), they were quick to point out that an uninteresting or poorly told story can easily ruin an otherwise good game. This further discounts the old notion that the story is a relatively unimportant game element that can be thrown together at the very end of the design process.

One last issue that came to light when studying the importance of game stories was that of demographics. With women accounting for more than 25 percent of respondents, and ages ranging from 13 to 60 across both genders, the surveys cover a very wide variety of gamers. Though, unsurprisingly, the "average" respondents were males in their late teens to mid twenties. Interestingly enough, there were no significant differences in storytelling preferences between respondents of different ages or genders. Although this goes against the common perception that men and women like different types of stories, it just goes to show something many writers have known for a long time: a good story can appeal to anyone, man, woman, or child. Of course, that doesn't mean that everyone will like any given story, no matter how good it may be, but it implies that individual likes and dislikes are based more on each player's personal preferences than age or gender.

What Players Say They Want

When asked to choose their three favorite genres of games, respondents listed games as shown in Figure 14.1 (averaged across both surveys).

Note that RPGs and adventure games, which are traditionally well known for their stories, are the most popular genres by far, and that fighting, sports, racing, and music games, which typically have little to no story, are the only mainstream genres to score less than 10 percent. Though gameplay preferences no doubt play a significant role in this breakdown, it backs up respondents' statements about the importance of stories in games. There's no other way to fully account for the massive gap between genres known for story-based games and those that focus almost exclusively on gameplay.

273

FIGURE
14.1

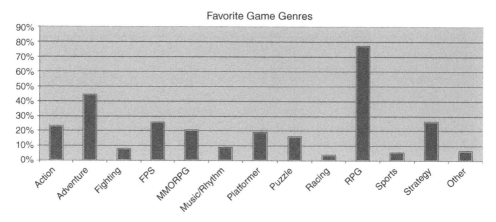

Respondents' top three favorite game genres.

Story Preferences by the Numbers

When asked directly which types of stories they preferred in games (show in Figure 14.2), 30 percent voted in favor of interactive traditional stories, 24 percent for multiple-ending stories, 20.5 percent for branching path stories, 6 percent for highly player-driven styles such as open-ended and fully player-driven stories, and 4.5 percent for no story at all. Most of the remaining 15 percent stated that as long as the story is well done, they have no real preference.

FIGURE
14.2

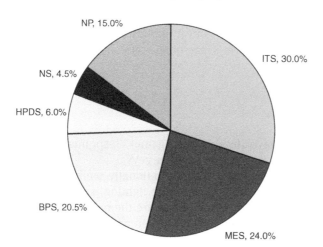

Respondents' preferred storytelling styles. Key: Interactive Traditional Stories (ITS), Multiple-Ending Stories (MES), Branching Path Stories (BPS), Highly Player-Driven Stories (HPDS), No Story (NS), No Preference (NP).

As you can see, interactive traditional stories – which are the most structured and least player-driven style – were the most popular answer, although multiple-ending and branching path stories score fairly high as well. Highly player-driven stories, however, scored extremely low among respondents, which casts a considerable amount of doubt on the argument that what players want most from stories is to take control and shape the plot to their own preferences. If this were true, highly player-driven stories would have a much higher rating. Although many respondents clearly like to have some control (as evidenced by the popularity of multiple-ending and branching path stories), they don't want to sacrifice a well-structured and well-paced story to get it.

When discussing what attracted them most to specific stories, respondents cited a variety of different factors, with the majority choosing either the characters or the setting. The overall plot was less of a concern, though in many games the characters and/or setting are tied so tightly into the main plot that it can be virtually impossible to separate them. Games such as *FINAL FANTASY XIII* and *Heavy Rain* contain perfect examples of highly character centric stories; *The Elder Scrolls III: Morrowind* and *Bioshock* stories are heavily tied into their settings. Many respondents also noted that particularly unusual or unique settings or story premises often pique their initial interest in a game, though their continued interest is entirely dependent on a combination of the gameplay and how the story plays out as the game progresses.

What Players Really Want

The next question to ask is whether those are really the types of stories that players most enjoy. If the respondents' actual preferences match up closely with their stated preferences, then the answer would be clear, but if there's a large disconnect between the two, it would strongly suggest that many players may not fully understand which types of stories they want and enjoy most.

The Best Game Stories

To try to solve this mystery, I asked my survey participants to name three games that they felt had exceptionally good stories. This yielded a list of 223 unique entries that included 199 games and 24 series (note that specific games from some of those series were also listed and are part of the 199). A complete list of these games and series can be found in Appendix B of this book. A breakdown of the storytelling styles used is shown in Figure 14.3, which focuses on only the 223 unique entries in the list. Figure 14.4 also accounts for how many respondents mentioned each specific game.

Note that six of those games (with one nomination each) were extremely obscure and I was unable to find enough information about them to identify their storytelling styles. Their storytelling style is listed as "unsure" in the charts and

FIGURE
14.3   Storytelling Methods in Favorite Game Stories (Unique Games)

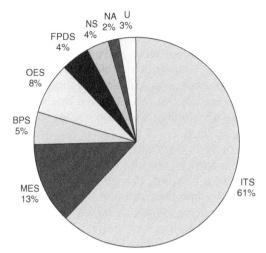

Respondents' best game stories (unique games). Key: Interactive Traditional Story (ITS), Multiple-Ending Story (MES), Branching Path Story (BPS), Open-Ended Story (OES), Fully Player-Driven Story (FPDS), No Story (NS), Not Applicable (NA), Unsure (U).

FIGURE
14.4   Storytelling Methods in Favorite Game Stories (All Games)

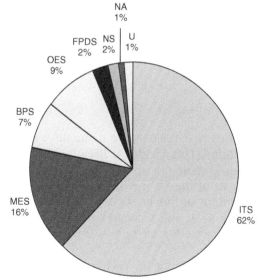

Respondents' best game stories (all nominations).

appendix. An additional four games (one of which received two nominations) are marked as not applicable, as three of them are board games (or digital re-creations thereof) and one is a tabletop RPG.

Surprisingly enough, the difference between the two graphs is minimal, with the percentages for most storytelling styles varying by only one or two percentage points. But, more importantly, these graphs show significant differences when compared to the chart of the respondents' stated preferences. First, it's clear that interactive traditional stories are still the most popular. However, though only 30 percent of respondents listed interactive traditional storytelling as their favorite style, more than 61 percent of the listed games have interactive traditional stories. In stark contrast to the massive jump in popularity experienced by interactive traditional stories, multiple-ending stories and branching path stories, both of which were the stated preference of more than 20 percent of respondents, dropped significantly. Multiple-ending stories fell from 24 percent to 13 percent in the first chart and 16 percent in the second. Branching path stories faired even worse, dropping from 20.5 percent to 5 percent and 7 percent. Open-ended stories scored 8 percent and 9 percent, showing a slight improvement, but fully player-driven stories received only 4 percent and 2 percent, putting them on the same level as games without stories.

As a note, the five games most frequently listed by respondents were

1. *FINAL FANTASY VII* (interactive traditional story)

2. *CHRONO TRIGGER* (multiple-ending story)

3. *XENOGEARS* (interactive traditional story)

4. & 5. (a tie) *FINAL FANTASY X* (interactive traditional story) and *Mass Effect* (multiple-ending story)

Further Analysis

So what does all of this mean? First, it shows that interactive traditional storytelling is the most popular game storytelling style among players, reflected by both their stated preferences and their favorite game stories. Second, in general, the more player-driven the storytelling style, the less popular it is among players. And although some types of player-driven storytelling – specifically, multiple-ending and branching path – proved to be moderately popular, it was extremely rare for players to list games using either style as having exceptionally good stories. Therefore, games using interactive traditional stories are not only the most popular among players, but are also the most likely by far to contain stories that players really enjoy.

So does this put an end to the debate? Maybe not entirely. When we take players' stated preferences into account, it's clear that a lot of them do like the idea behind multiple-ending and branching path stories, even though game stories using those styles rarely stack up to those using interactive traditional storytelling.

This seems to indicate that although many gamers do feel as if they want some control (though not an excessive amount) over the stories in their video games, they actually get more enjoyment out of well-structured stories, which provide them with a strong illusion of control instead. This result seems to indicate that traditional storytelling methods are superior.

However, it could be argued that the reason for these findings is that games using highly player-driven forms of storytelling are still relatively new and that players will come to enjoy them more as they become better accustomed to the style. You could also attempt to explain player-driven storytelling's lack of popularity by blaming the immaturity of the style itself, and say that it won't come into its true potential and gain the recognition it deserves until designers and writers become more experienced and skilled creating highly player-driven stories.

We Have to Find Our Own Way

Or you could say that it's just much, much harder to find a way to craft those kinds of stories in such a way as to make them as compelling as more traditional structures.

—Chris

It's quite possible that there's some truth to both of those claims. However, I can't imagine them accounting for the entirety of the massive gap in popularity found in the list of respondents' best game stories. If the second chart (the one that tracks how many times each game was listed by respondents) showed a significant increase in the popularity of games using highly player-driven stories when compared to the first chart, I'd be more inclined to agree, especially as there are far more games available which use traditional storytelling methods. But the fact that both charts are nearly identical shows that's not the case.

Do Stories Sell Games?

My first survey answered the question of which storytelling styles gamers prefer and enjoy the most, but the differences between their stated preferences and their actual preferences (as determined by their favorite game stories) made me wonder which of those two sets of preferences most affected which games they purchased. After all, game development is a business. Unfortunate as it may seem, whether or not people enjoy a game is often far less important than how many people buy that game to begin with. This is made quite clear by looking at games based on popular licenses (such as movies or TV shows), a good many of which receive strong sales despite rather abysmal reviews. So the fact that gamers tend to most enjoy games with interactive traditional stories would be far less important if they're more likely to buy games with highly player-driven forms of storytelling – assuming that stories play a significant role in the average gamer's purchasing decisions in the first place.

To solve this final puzzle, I focused my second survey on determining two things: what role, if any, story plays in deciding which games to buy, and whether gamers are more likely to buy games that use player-driven forms of storytelling.

Buying Habits by the Numbers

The first thing to establish was how large of a role stories have in which games people buy (Figure 14.5).

When asked to list the three most important factors when deciding whether to buy a game, more than 52 percent choose story, making it the most frequently chosen option over gameplay features (42 percent) and genre (37 percent). Furthermore, 40 percent of respondents said that they frequently buy games primarily for their story, 45 percent said they do so occasionally, and less than 14 percent said that they rarely or never do so.

Although this shows that stories do significantly affect which games players buy, it's not quite that simple. In their write-in answers, many respondents noted how difficult it can be to get a good feel for what a game's story is like before purchase. Some dealt with this problem by focusing on games that seemed to have particularly unique and interesting settings or characters; others choose games based on what they heard about the story from friends or read in reviews. However, the majority of respondents said that they tended to focus primarily on games

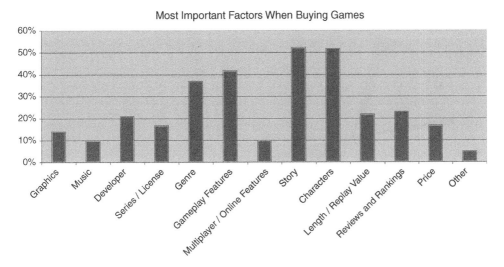

FIGURE
14.5

Respondents' most important factors when buying games.

by certain developers that they already knew – through personal experience – made games with excellent stories (such as Square Enix and Bioware).

As you can see in Figure 14.6, the majority of respondents specified the overall plot as the most important part of a story (28.5 percent), ahead of setting (24 percent), characters (15 percent), and interactivity (15 percent). Interestingly, series ranked fairly low, which could indicate that although many players look to specific developers and series in order to find good stories, they care much more about the quality of the story itself than they do about the series or brand.

At 15 percent, the interactivity score isn't amazing, but it does manage to tie characters for third place, so its impact on sales certainly can't be discounted. Furthermore, nearly 50 percent of respondents said that a high level of interactivity and freedom makes them more likely to buy a game. Of the remaining 50 percent, most don't care one way or the other (45 percent), and the remaining few (5 percent) say that a high degree of freedom makes them less likely to purchase a game. This seems to make player-driven storytelling a decent selling point, though it would likely need to be combined with other more important elements such as a strong plot (as evidenced by a respected brand and/or good reviews), an interesting setting, and good gameplay in order to make a significant impact on sales.

However, because I had already shown that players' stated preferences didn't always match their actual preferences, I wanted to see just how closely their stated preferences and game purchasing habits matched up. To do so, respondents were asked to list three games that they had purchased primarily for their story. The final list contained 191 unique entries composed of 174 games and 17 series (note

FIGURE
14.6

Most Important Story Elements When Buying a Game

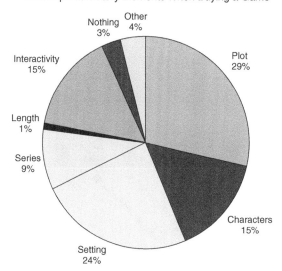

Respondents' most important story elements.

that specific games from some of those series were also listed and are part of the 174). It's important to keep in mind that respondents were questioned only about which games they bought primarily for their stories, not how much they ended up enjoying those stories later on. Figures 14.7 and 14.8 break down the storytelling styles used in those games. Note that Figure 14.7 focuses only on the 191 unique entries in the list and Figure 14.8 also accounts for how many respondents mentioned each specific game.

As you can see, despite the fact that 50 percent of respondents said that a highly player-driven story would make them more likely to purchase a game, games using interactive traditional storytelling still dominate when we look at both unique games and all nominations (71 percent and 65 percent, respectively) with multiple-ending stories remaining a very distant second (12 percent and 17 percent). Branching path stories did do slightly better than in the best game stories list (8 percent and 9 percent), primarily due to *Heavy Rain* and *Mass Effect 2* (both of which were released in early 2010, several months after the completion of my first survey). Once again, open-ended stories (6 percent and 8 percent) and fully player-driven stories (2 percent and 1 percent) scored very low. Interestingly enough, the list also contained a single fully traditional story, *Umineko no Naku Koro ni* (*When Seagulls Cry*), a Japanese visual novel by 07th Expansion, the same team behind *Higursahi When They Cry*.

Games Purchased Primarily for Their Stories (Unique Games)

FIGURE
14.7

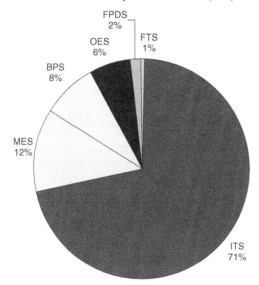

Respondents' games purchased primarily for their stories (unique games). Key: Fully Traditional Story (FTS), Interactive Traditional Story (ITS), Multiple-Ending Story (MES), Branching Path Story (BPS), Open-Ended Story (OES), Fully Player-Driven Story (FPDS).

FIGURE
14.8   Games Purchased Primarily for Their Stories (All Games)

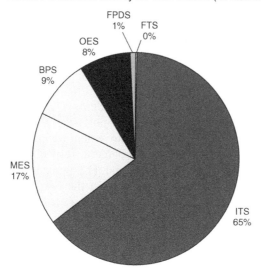

Respondents' games purchased primarily for their stories (all nominations).

The five games most frequently listed by respondents were

1. *Dragon Age Origins* (multiple-ending story)
2. & 3. (a tie) *Bioshock* (multiple-ending story) and *FINAL FANTASY XIII* (interactive traditional story)
4. & 5. (a tie) *Heavy Rain* (branching path story) and *Mass Effect* (multiple-ending story)

Further Analysis

As in the first survey, it's clear that there are a good number of gamers out there who like the idea of player-driven storytelling, or at least find it rather interesting. However, it's also clear that when deciding which games to buy, the amount of control and freedom given to the player isn't a big selling point, as the vast majority of games that are bought for their story use interactive traditional storytelling. In fact, the more player-driven a game's story is, the fewer people buy the game primarily for its story (which is not to say that a large number of gamers don't buy those games for other reasons, such as their gameplay). Although several multiple-ending and branching path story games did receive numerous mentions (as evidenced by the top five list), all of those titles were either created by developers with a reputation for telling excellent stories (such as *Dragon Age* and *Mass Effect*) or were the subject of numerous ads and positive coverage in the gaming press (such as *Bioshock* and *Heavy Rain*), so it seems likely that those factors had far more to do with those games' popularity.

In the end, stories do sell games. However, although the fact that a particular story is highly player-driven can increase peoples' interest in a game, it seems to have relatively little effect on sales, with things like the general content and theme of the plot and the reputation of the series and/or developer playing a much larger role.

Summary

It's clear that the majority of gamers prefer games with interactive traditional stories. Multiple-ending and branching path stories were fairly popular as well, though highly player-driven forms of storytelling such as open-ended and fully player-driven stories were not. However, when we looked at the respondents' actual preferences (as determined by the games they considered to have exceptionally good stories), interactive traditional stories dominated by an enormous margin, with multiple-ending stories trailing nearly 50 percentage points behind and other player-driven storytelling styles ranking even lower. There are a few possible reasons that could partially account for these results, but on the whole they strongly indicate that although gamers do have some interest in player-driven storytelling, they strongly prefer the stories in games using interactive traditional storytelling.

The second survey backed up the results of the first. Story is an important consideration for many people when purchasing games. However, due to the difficulty in gauging the quality of a game's story before purchase, a lot of gamers focus on games created by well-known developers or those with particularly unique-sounding plots or settings to help them decide. Highly player-driven storytelling does attract the interest of a fairly large number of gamers and rarely drives potential buyers away, but not many consider it to be an extremely important factor when deciding which games to buy. This conclusion is further supported by the respondents' buying habits, as games using interactive traditional storytelling are purchased primarily for their story far more often than those using any other storytelling style.

In the end, despite what many in the game industry say, what players seem to want and enjoy most in game stories is simply a well-told story, regardless of how much freedom and control they're given. To that end, interactive traditional storytelling is the most popular style by far, as it gives writers and designers free rein to control and fine-tune the pacing, characters, and plot progression in order to create the best possible experience for the players.

Things to Consider

1. Do you agree with the survey results and conclusions discussed in this chapter? Why or why not?

2. Was there anything in the survey results that you found particularly surprising? Why?

3. Did the information presented in this chapter change your opinion about which type of storytelling is best? Why or why not?

4. Look over your answers regarding traditional vs. player-driven storytelling from the previous chapters and discuss how and why your views on the matter have or haven't changed as you've read this book.

Fifteen

The Future of Storytelling in Games

By now, you should be familiar with the basics of story structure, character development, and the history of storytelling in video games. You should also have a clear understanding of the main types of interactive stories used in games and the strengths and weaknesses of each. Finally, you should have a better understanding of the traditional vs. player-driven storytelling debate, which stories players enjoy most, and why. All that's left is to take that information and use it to look ahead and see what game storytelling may be like in the future. But first, let's quickly recap what you've learned.

Stories Then and Now

Game storytelling has evolved considerably since the early days of *Donkey Kong* and *Colossal Cave Adventure.* The simplistic stories of early games have led to large, complex tales that can rival any found in books or movies. Furthermore, the importance of stories in games is continuing to grow. Though genres traditionally known for their strong storytelling, such as RPGs and adventure games, continue to lead the way, well-crafted stories have become a key part of many other types of games as well.

Over the years, writers and designers have experimented with many different ways to make the player a more integral part of the story. This experimentation has led to the development of several different types of game storytelling. Interactive traditional stories are more writer-focused and don't allow the player to significantly change the main plot in any way (though the player may have considerable freedom in other parts of the game). Multiple-ending, branching path, and open-ended stories, respectively, give the player greater degrees of freedom to affect and change the progression and outcome of the story; fully player-driven stories merely provide a setting and leave the player free to create a story of his or her choosing. However, there's considerable debate as to whether giving the player more control leads to better and more enjoyable stories.

285

The Key Arguments

Those who support highly player-driven storytelling say that traditional story-telling has long since reached its peak. However, the use of interactivity can grow and evolve the art form by allowing writers to explore many different paths and plot progressions while allowing each player to fulfill his or her greatest desires and become an active participant in the story. This power to change events and explore different possible outcomes lets players ensure that the story progresses in a way that they'll enjoy and helps strengthen the bond between the player and the character. Therefore, it's important that game writers and designers abandon their focus on more traditional storytelling methods and look toward the future.

Supporters of more traditional storytelling argue that storytelling has lasted so long in its current form precisely because of how perfect that form is. Games using highly player-driven forms of storytelling are difficult to make and require a consid-erable amount of time and money in order to create extra content that most players will never even see. Furthermore, what the player wants most isn't to be a part of the story, but to be entertained and/or engaged by the story. And the more control players have over events, the more likely they are to make a mistake and turn the story down a less interesting path. At the same time, the ability to go back and change the outcome of major events significantly reduces the emotional impact of those events, as players know they can always go back and try again for a better outcome. Because of this, it's better to give players a strong illusion of control (by granting them a large degree of freedom during exploration, battle, and/or other part of the game) rather than giving them any actual control over the story.

What Players Want

In the end, both sides' arguments are based on assumptions of what players want and enjoy most in a story. According to my own research and surveys, games' stories are very important to players, affecting which games they buy, how long they play their games, and their overall satisfaction with the games as a whole. Though a moderate number of gamers find the idea of player-driven storytelling interesting, it's rarely a deciding factor when purchasing games. Furthermore, the vast majority of players still prefer games that use interactive traditional storytelling. In fact, the more player-driven the storytelling style, the less popular it is among gamers. This lends considerable support to the arguments supporting more traditional storytelling in games and shows that, in the end, what players want most is simply a well-told story, even if they don't have any control over its outcome.

Looking Toward the Future

The game industry is always looking toward the future, which is necessary when many games require years of development time. So the big question is what game sto-rytelling is going to be like next year; three years from now; or five, ten, or twenty years from now.

First off, I should note that predicting the future – even the future of a single medium or technology – is difficult. Many brilliant minds have tried to do so, and although some predictions have held true, the vast majority have failed to hold up. Many people are simply either too optimistic or pessimistic to accurately judge how things will progress, and even the most realistic and well-researched predictions can be thrown off by an unexpected development or roadblock. So, with that in mind, let's take a cautious look at what the future of game storytelling might hold.

The Most Popular Types of Storytelling

Interactive traditional storytelling is currently the most popular form of storytelling in games, and this seems unlikely to change in the foreseeable future. Video games are certainly the most convenient way to tell many types of player-driven stories, but they're far from the only way. Writers have experimented with player-driven storytelling many times in the past, including things like the *Choose Your Own Adventure* books, interactive theater, and more recently, with video games and other digital media. But although some of those experiments did prove fairly popular, they in no way threatened the dominance of traditional storytelling. Storytelling in video games seems to be playing out in much the same way. Although more player-driven forms of storytelling have their supporters and have been used in some very successful games, they'll remain a relatively small part of the game industry. Due to the influence of games such as *Mass Effect*, *Heavy Rain*, and *The Sims* (all of which provide very different yet popular takes on player-driven storytelling), games using player-driven storytelling certainly aren't going to disappear anytime soon; in fact, it's quite likely that their popularity will continue to increase. However, their costs, challenges, and limitations aren't going to go away, either.

In the end, the carefully designed structure, characters, and pacing of interactive traditional stories will continue to dominate the industry and attract the attention of players. Just as Homer, Dickens, and others continue to enthrall us to this day, perhaps some of the best game stories of today will become the classics of future generations. Although it's quite possible that newer technologies like motion controllers and 3D displays will create some changes in the way that we interact with games, the basic foundations of storytelling itself will remain constant, just as they have throughout the thousands of years of change and developments that have come before.

The Most Important Thing

As Josiah and I were busy doing the last wave of edits on this book, I was attending a conference on the Digital Narrative. While there, I sat in on a discussion given by writers working in games as well as other interactive media, and the one thing they all agreed upon (amazing, actually, that there was even that singular thing – sometimes writers can be a bit opinionated) was that the limitations imposed on writers by the technology were finally for the most part a thing of the past. Budgets will always be an issue, of course, but these three writers agreed that for the first time in years, the technologists didn't need to sit in the story rooms putting the brakes on the writers any longer and that the technology was indeed now as flexible as the writers needed it to be, thus enabling them to tell the kinds of stories they wanted to tell. Additionally, these writers had also finally gotten their own technical chops up to speed, so they knew how to create within those technologies. And to their collective sigh of relief, *they* now once again had control over their stories instead of having the tech control the stories. But the questions remained, "What kinds of stories work best in this new interactive medium?" and "How do we tell those kinds of stories in the most compelling way possible?"

That's where this book comes in, and that's where my co-author's research and advice are so valuable. Writers have universally struggled with this new idea of handing over varying degrees of story control to the player, not because of an ego thing (well, not for the most part, anyway), but rather because they fear that certain types of story moments will be lost in translation. They fear that players – even the most well-intentioned players – will avoid painful story moments just because they are so painful (and because in the new paradigm they *can* be avoided). But often it is precisely those very painful story moments that give the story its power.

At the conference, a number of us were talking about this issue after dinner one evening. We mentioned the risk of writers in interactive media yielding authorial control too much; when they do so, the story tends to drift toward vanilla. Two examples immediately sprang to mind amongst our group: the ending David Chase crafted for the *Sopranos* series, and more recently, a small moment on the most recent episode of *Mad Men*.

We believed that both of these moments, as delivered by their authors, were not the kind of choice average audience members would have picked, had they been in the driver's seat; the first because the nature of the *Sopranos* ending prevents it from being a player choice (once that option exists for the players and is explained to them all, the power from that option would have been drained from the choice; it's a form of Catch-22). Can you imagine? ("You have the option to end the game now, right in the middle of the dialog, or continue.") The second was not a likely popular choice because the average *Mad Men* viewer roots for Don Draper (well, okay, if not "roots for" Don, then at least doesn't root *against* Don) and to see him make a decision that the viewer expects to end badly when an obvious better choice is right there in front of him is *so* painful to watch that the player, if playing Don, would almost always avoid that choice.

I mentioned to the group that for me, watching that moment in the episode, knowing that Don would screw up that opportunity, I literally fast-forwarded over that moment so that I didn't have to listen to him say those words. That story decision by the *Mad Men* staff was inevitable and painful and delicious, all at the same time. It was akin to watching someone you love fall back into addiction, even though that person has tried to kick the habit.

These kinds of moments are the ones that writers fear will be lost when we lose absolute authorial control. But let's examine that fear for a second. Is that true? Will we lose those moments? Or will they just morph into some other kind of equivalent game moment? In addition, does the player truly want to abdicate the writer's contribution?

Regarding the first point, there was a question in a session at the conference: "What about suspense? Where will suspense go when players control the story? If the players are making all the decisions, how will the writer surprise the players?" One way this seeming conundrum can be solved is through gameplay, substituting the suspense of fighting and trying to defeat, say, a boss, for the kind of suspense a story can bring. The player won't necessarily miss the feeling of suspense, because that visceral emotion is present in the story – just not in the traditional sense the questioner was thinking of. So, often the missing emotion morphs into something similar but different. And we writers must adapt; instead of twisting the plot in a way that ratchets up the surprises and the suspense, we build the stakes of the upcoming battle in such a way that when the battle finally arrives, the player is almost painfully aware of the rewards of victory and the perils of defeat. This challenge is on us to solve; the key is to be aware that players crave those kinds of emotions in their stories.

The second issue is where the players have indeed spoken, and Josiah has related their opinions. The conclusion of the survey for me is that what game players who love story really want most is to be the hero in a traditionally structured story, the kind of story they have seen and loved their whole lives – to take up a sword and slay the dragon, rescue the princess, solve the crime. Those archetypal stories have been told and retold for millennia because they have the kind of power that comes from emotional truth. They resonate with us now and have resonated with our parents and ancestors for the most important reason of all: they teach us how to live our lives. They contain these deep emotional truths, and we long to hear them again and again, helping to light our way as we struggle to understand the meaning of this life we all live. For that is what stories always do: illuminate our path, if even just a tiny bit.

Whether the story is read in a novel or is seen in a movie theater or comes echoing down the street to us from a puppet show in a nearby circus matters not. Games are just the latest wrapper for story; we writers can and must find new ways to deliver what the audience craves from us and not become distracted by the technology or abdicate our voice.

Writers: continue to be true to the heart of the story and honor your voice, for contained in your voice are the voices of Aeschylus, Shakespeare, Byron, and Miller. Your voice is their voice; it always has been and always will be. That is what the players want from us most.

—Chris

A Future for Everyone

How much do my predictions about the future of game storytelling really matter? Assuming that I'm right, and that interactive traditional stories will continue to dominate, does that mean the industry as a whole should forget about player-driven storytelling and focus entirely on interactive traditional stories, because they're the most popular? Or, if I'm wrong and player-driven storytelling experiences an enormous surge in popularity, should we forget about more traditional forms of storytelling? Of course not!

Unfortunately, many people in the game industry have a tendency to think that there's a best way to do everything, and that once we find that magical best game type, best story format, best graphical style, and so on, that will be all players will ever want anymore and every other type of game should go away. Over the years that I've followed the game industry, I've heard notable figures make many such claims, including that no one will play anything but RPGs; RPGs are a dead genre and no one will buy them anymore; players only want 3D games; big-budget games will be replaced entirely by small downloadable games; no one will want to play any game without motion controls; no one will want to play any game that's not online; and so on, ad infinitum. More recently, a lot of people have been saying how game consoles, big-budget games, and hardcore games are all going to go away because everyone will just be playing social networking games on Facebook. Game stories are no exception to this behavior. There are some, especially in the pro-player-driven-storytelling group, who are sure that any day now all players will suddenly decide that they like only stories of one type and will never play games using other forms of storytelling again.

Yet despite all these predictions, here we are today, and none of those things have even remotely come to pass. RPGs are still very popular, but so are many other genres. 2D games are still being released on every platform and many have sold millions of copies. Small downloadable games are a big market, but haven't hurt the sales of big-budget games in the least. Motion-controlled games helped expand the game market, and can be a lot of fun, but show no signs of taking over the industry as a whole. There are plenty of single-player games that lack online features entirely and still sell millions of copies. And, as popular as social networking games are, I haven't heard of any players throwing out their game consoles or high-end computer because they want to spend the rest of their lives playing nothing but *Farmville*.

Games, as do all entertainment industries, have their fads and new genres – that's just the way things go. As I write this, a certain series of teen novels has made vampire romance stories extremely popular, yet I don't hear any publishing executives or movie producers speaking out about how vampire stories will take over the entire industry and no other types of stories will matter anymore. It doesn't work that way. Vampires are currently selling a lot of books and movies and may even have drawn a lot of new people to reading or TV watching in general, but sometime over the next few years, the vampire craze will die down and everyone will be excited about mummies or time travel or something else. And just because so many people like vampire romance stories right now doesn't mean that all the millions and millions of fans of mysteries, sci-fi, fantasy, and other types of stories disappeared. They're still around and just as eager as ever to buy new books and watch new movies in the genres they like best. And, even after the next big fad starts, all those vampire fans aren't going to disappear, either.

The game industry is the same way. There are millions and millions of gamers out there with a wide variety of favorite genres, gameplay types, storytelling styles, and the like, and they're not going to suddenly abandon the kinds of games they love just because some other thing is the current "hot topic" in the industry. And that includes storytelling styles. Fans of interactive traditional stories certainly aren't going anywhere, and even though player-driven storytelling styles may be considerably less popular overall, there are still plenty of successful games out there that use them. So instead of arguing about which types of games or stories are going to dominate in the future, writers and designers should focus on what they do best: creating the kinds of games and stories they want to create. Chances are good that no matter what type of game and storytelling style they choose, there's an audience for it. There's a future out there for all gamers, no matter what types of games and stories they like. It's time to stop obsessing over the "best" way to do things and start enjoying the diversity.

Things to Consider

1. Do you believe that the game industry tends to become too fixated on a single "best" way of doing things? Why or why not?

2. What are some of the most important things you've learned from this book?

3. How will you use the things you've learned to improve your stories?

4. What are your own views on the future of storytelling in games?

Glossary

Archetype: A general character type such as the gambler or mentor that can be adapted for use in many different kinds of stories.

Branch: A chain of events in a branching path story.

Branching path stories: Stories structured around a series of specific choices that the player can make at various decision points. Depending on the option chosen, the story will branch off in different directions.

Decision point: A place in a branching path story at which the player is asked to choose between two or more options to advance the story.

FMV: Full-motion video. A prerendered video used in a game. It can't be interacted with, but features higher-quality graphics than the rest of the game.

FPS: First-person shooter.

Fully player-driven stories: Highly interactive stories in which the player is given an enormous amount of freedom to explore and do what he or she wants. There is often little to no main plot, with the primary focus being on the setting and the player's actions therein.

Fully traditional stories: Stories that adhere strictly to the traditional storytelling model and can't be changed or affected in any significant way.

Interactive storytelling: A form of storytelling in which the audience can interact with the story in some way, shape, or form, though the amount and type of interaction vary widely. All video game stories are interactive.

Interactive traditional stories: The most traditional form of player-driven storytelling. Though players have some control over the progression of the story, they can't change the main plot in any significant way.

Major/main branch: A branch that significantly alters the overall plot or breaks away from it entirely and starts its own unique story path.

Minor branch: A branch that quickly rejoins the main story with little to no effect on the overall plot.

MMO: Massively multiplayer online game.

Moderate branch: A branch that takes awhile to rejoin the main story, but has little to no lasting effect on the overall plot.

Multiple-ending stories: Similar to interactive traditional stories, except that the player is allowed to change the ending, either through a conscious choice or based on his or her actions throughout the story.

NPC: Nonplayer character. A game character who is not under the player's control.

Open-ended stories: Highly interactive stories with many branches and optional sections, some of which significantly affect the main plot. Progression is often based more on the player's actions than on obvious choices.

Pen-and-paper role-playing games: A form of RPG in which one person acts as the moderator or dungeon master, creates the story, and constantly modifies it based on the actions of the players.

Player-driven storytelling: A form of interactive storytelling in which the player is allowed to make one or more decisions that affect the main plot itself. Depending on the type of player-driven storytelling used, the results of those decisions could be minor or far-reaching.

RPG: Role-playing game.

Side-quest: A fully optional task that the player can choose to undertake in order to strengthen the hero and/or learn more about the story.

Traditional storytelling: The "classic" form of storytelling. Traditional stories have a clearly set beginning, progression, and ending and remain exactly the same no matter how many times they're read or watched.

Game Writing Groups and Other Useful Resources

Game Writing Groups

IGDA Writing SIG

http://www.igda.org/writing/

A special interest group of the IGDA (International Game Developers Association) focused on all things related to game writing and stories. It contains several sub-groups and features a group blog, online chat sessions, and an email discussion list.

LinkedIn Game Writing Group

http://www.linkedin.com/groups?home=&gid=89330

LinkedIn is a business-focused social networking site used by many in the game industry. Its game writing group features discussion boards and job listings. Note that you need to join the group before you can access its home page.

Additional Resources

Gamasutra

http://www.gamasutra.com

Featuring articles, blogs, news, and special features covering every aspect of the game industry, Gamasutra is an excellent resource for anyone who is or wants to be part of the industry. It also features an extensive job board with listings from many top game developers and publishers.

Game Developers Conference
http://www.gdconf.com
The Game Developers Conference is a yearly gathering focusing on the creation and advancement of video and computer games. Key features include a large number of lectures, presentations, and roundtables by notable industry figures, an expo showcasing the latest game-related technology, and a career fair. Aside from the main conference in San Francisco, California, the GDC also hosts yearly conferences in Austin, Texas (which features the annual Game Narrative Summit), Canada, Europe, and China.

IGDA
http://www.igda.org
The International Game Developers Association is a nonprofit, membership-based group for people in the game industry. It hosts local meetings in many cities, contains numerous special interest groups, and publishes various game-related articles and white papers. Its mailing lists and meetups are excellent opportunities to get to know other people in the industry.

The *Interactive Storytelling for Video Games* Website
http://www.StorytellingForGames.com
The official companion site of this book. Features include a complete classroom-ready Microsoft PowerPoint lecture for every chapter, additional research data, links to movies and demos of many of the games discussed, and links to other useful sites and resources.

Survey Data

Top Game Stories

Key

x *X* = Number of people who cited the game
(ITS) = Interactive Traditional Story
(MES) = Multiple-Ending Story
(BPS) = Branching Path Story
(OES) = Open-Ended Story
(FPDS) = Fully Player-Driven Story
(NS) = No Story
(NA) = Not Applicable (a nonvideo game title such as a board game or tabletop RPG)
(U) = Unsure

Games

.hack Series *(ITS)*
.hack//G.U. Series *(ITS)*
Prototype *(ITS)*
Age of Mythology x 2 *(ITS)*
Animal Crossing *(FPDS)*
Another World x 2 *(ITS)*
Ar Tonelico *(BPS)*
Assassins Creed x 2 *(ITS)*
Baldur's Gate Series *(ITS)*
Baldur's Gate *(ITS)*
Baldur's Gate 2 *(ITS)*
Baten Kaitos Series *(ITS)*
Baten Kaitos Origins x 3 *(ITS)*

Battle Moon Wars *(U)*
Battlefield: Bad Company *(ITS)*
Big Brain Academy *(NS)*
BioShock x 10 *(MES)*
Blue Dragon *(ITS)*
Braid x 2 *(ITS)*
Brain Age *(NS)*
Brain Age II *(NS)*
Breath of Fire II
Breath of Fire V: Dragon Quarter *(ITS)*
Brothers in Arms: Hell's Highway *(ITS)*
Call of Duty 4 x 2 *(ITS)*
Carcassonne x 2 *(NA)*
CHRONO TRIGGER x 14 *(MES)*
Chronos *(U)*
Command & Conquer: Tiberian Sun *(ITS)*
Conquests of the Longbow: The Legend of Robin Hood *(MES)*
Custom Robo *(ITS)*
Dark Cloud 2 *(ITS)*
Dark Messiah of Might and Magic *(MES)*
Day of the Tentacle *(ITS)*
Dead Space *(ITS)*
Deus Ex x 6 *(MES)*
Devil May Cry *(ITS)*
Disgaea x 2 *(MES)*
Donkey Kong Country *(ITS)*
Doom 3 *(ITS)*
Dragon Warrior VIII *(ITS)*
Dragon Fable *(ITS)*
Duck Hunter *(NS)*
Dungeons and Dragons *(NA)*
Earthbound *(ITS)*
Elder Scrolls II – Daggerfall *(OES)*
Elder Scrolls III – Morrowind x 2 *(OES)*
Elder Scrolls IV – Oblivion x 2 *(OES)*
Elder Scrolls Series *(OES)*
Eternal Darkness *(ITS)*
Evergrace *(ITS)*
Fable x 2 *(OES)*
Fable 2 x 2 *(OES)*
Fable Series *(OES)*
Fallout 2 x 3 *(OES)*
Fallout 3 x 7 *(OES)*
Fate/Stay Night x 2 *(BPS)*

FINAL FANTASY Series x 3 *(ITS)*
FINAL FANTASY *(ITS)*
FINAL FANTASY III *(ITS)*
FINAL FANTASY IV x 4 *(ITS)*
FINAL FANTASY VI x 9 *(ITS)*
FINAL FANTASY VII x 16 *(ITS)*
FINAL FANTASY VIII x 4 *(ITS)*
FINAL FANTASY IX x 5 *(ITS)*
FINAL FANTASY X x 13 *(ITS)*
FINAL FANTASY X-2 *(ITS)*
FINAL FANTASY XII x 4 *(ITS)*
FINAL FANTASY TACTICS x 7 *(ITS)*
FINAL FANTASY TACTICS A2 *(ITS)*
Fire Emblem Series x 2 *(BPS)*
Fire Emblem: Genealogy of the Holy War *(BPS)*
Fire Emblem: Path of Radiance x 2 *(BPS)*
Fire Emblem: The Sacred Stones *(BPS)*
Freelancer *(ITS)*
Frogger *(NS)*
Gears of War *(ITS)*
Gears of War 2 *(ITS)*
God of War x 2 *(ITS)*
Golden Sun Series *(ITS)*
Gothic *(ITS)*
Gothic II *(OES)*
Grand Theft Auto Series *(OES)*
Grand Theft Auto IV x 5 *(OES)*
Grand Theft Auto: San Andreas x 2 *(OES)*
Grim Fandango *(ITS)*
GrimGrimoire *(ITS)*
Growlanser Generations *(MES)*
Guilty Gear X2 *(ITS)*
Half-Life Series *(ITS)*
Half-Life 2 x 2 *(ITS)*
Halo Series x 2 *(ITS)*
Halo x 3 *(ITS)*
Halo 3 *(ITS)*
Harvest Moon *(FPDS)*
Hotel Dusk *(ITS)*
Ico x 5 *(ITS)*
Indigo Prophecy x 2 (MES)
Inuyasha: Secret of the Cursed Mask x 2 *(MES)*
Jak 3 (ITS)
Killer7 *(MES)*

KINGDOM HEARTS x 9 *(ITS)*
KINGDOM HEARTS II x 3 *(ITS)*
King's Quest VI *(ITS)*
Klonoa Door to Phantomile *(ITS)*
Legacy of Kain: Soul Reaver 2 x 2 *(ITS)*
Legend of Dragoon x 2 *(ITS)*
LEGEND OF MANA *(ITS)*
Legend of Zelda Series x 3 *(ITS)*
Legend of Zelda Ocarina of Time x 6 *(ITS)*
Legend of Zelda: Twilight Princess x 5 *(ITS)*
Lineage II *(FPDS)*
Lost Odyssey *(ITS)*
Lord of The Rings Online *(OES)*
Lufia 2 *(ITS)*
Lunar 2: Eternal Blue x 2 *(ITS)*
Lunar Knights *(ITS)*
Mabinogi *(FPDS)*
Mario Cart Wii *(NS)*
Mary Kate and Ashley Olson's Great Adventure *(U)*
Mass Effect x 13 *(MES)*
Max Payne x 3 *(ITS)*
Metal Gear Series *(ITS)*
Metal Gear Solid x 8 *(MES)*
Metal Gear Solid 2 x 2 *(ITS)*
Metal Gear Solid 3 x 3 *(ITS)*
Metal Gear Solid 4 x 3 *(ITS)*
Monkey Island *(ITS)*
Monster Rancher 3 *(FPDS)*
Mother Series *(ITS)*
Mother 3 x 2 *(ITS)*
Myst x 2 *(MES)*
Neverwinter Nights *(OES)*
Neverwinter Nights 2 *(OES)*
Oddworld: Stranger's Wrath *(ITS)*
Odin Sphere *(MES)*
Off Road *(U)*
Ogre Battle 64 x 2 *(MES)*
Okami x 4 *(ITS)*
Paper Mario Series x 2 *(ITS)*
Paper Mario: The Thousand-Year Door x 2 *(ITS)*
Perihelion: The Prophecy *(U)*
Phoenix Wright Series *(ITS)*
Phoenix Wright: Ace Attorney x 2 *(ITS)*
Phoenix Wright: Justice for All *(ITS)*

Phoenix Wright: Trials and Tribulations *(ITS)*
Planescape Torment x 8 *(OES)*
Pokemon Series x 2 *(ITS)*
Pokemon Crystal *(ITS)*
Pokemon Mystery Dungeon *(ITS)*
Pokemon Ranger 2 *(ITS)*
Pokemon Silver x 2 *(ITS)*
Portal x 5 *(ITS)*
Prince of Persia: Sands of Time x 2 *(ITS)*
Psychonauts x 2 *(ITS)*
Ragnarok Online *(FPDS)*
Resident Evil 5 *(ITS)*
Resistance *(ITS)*
Riven *(MES)*
Runescape *(FPDS)*
Seiken Densetsu 3 *(BPS)*
Serious Sam *(ITS)*
Settlers of Catan *(NA)*
Shadow Complex *(ITS)*
Shadow Hearts Series x 2 *(ITS & MES)*
Shadow of the Colossus x 5 *(ITS)*
Shadows over Camelot *(NA)*
Shaun White Snowboarding *(NS)*
Shin Megami Tensei: Digital Devil Saga *(ITS)*
Shin Megami Tensei Nocturne *(MES)*
Shin Megami Tensei: Persona 3 x 4 *(ITS)*
Shin Megami Tensei: Persona 4 x 3 *(MES)*
Siege of Avalon *(ITS)*
Sigma Star Saga *(MES)*
Silent Hill *(MES)*
Silent Hill 2 x 4 *(MES)*
Sims x 2 *(FPDS)*
Skies of Arcadia *(ITS)*
Sonic Adventure *(ITS)*
Sonic Adventure 2: Battle *(ITS)*
Sonic the Hedgehog *(ITS)*
Soul Calibur II *(ITS)*
Soul Nomad *(MES)*
Splosion Man *(ITS)*
STAR OCEAN *(MES)*
STAR OCEAN: SECOND STORY *(MES)*
Star Wars: Knights of the Old Republic Series x 2 *(BPS)*
Star Wars: Knights of the Old Republic x 8 *(BPS)*
Star Wars: Knights of the Old Republic 2 *(BPS)*

Star Wars Tie Fighter x 2 *(ITS)*
Steambot Chronicles *(OES)*
Suikoden Series *(MES)*
Suikoden 2 x 6 *(MES)*
Super Mario Series x 2 *(ITS)*
Super Mario 64 x 2 *(ITS)*
Super Mario RPG *(ITS)*
System Shock 2 x 2 *(ITS)*
Tales Series *(ITS)*
Tales of Phantasia *(ITS)*
Tales of Symphonia x 6 *(ITS)*
Tales of Symphonia: Dawn of the New World *(MES)*
Tales of the Abyss *(ITS)*
Terranigma *(ITS)*
Tetris *(NS)*
The Hitchhiker's Guide to the Galaxy *(ITS)*
The Way *(U)*
THE WORLD ENDS WITH YOU x 8 *(ITS)*
Thief x 2 *(ITS)*
Uncharted: Drake's Fortune *(ITS)*
Vagrant Story x 2 *(ITS)*
Valkyria Chronicles *(ITS)*
Voodoo Vince *(ITS)*
Wild ARMS 2nd Ignition *(ITS)*
Warcraft Series *(ITS)* *(FPDS)*
Warcraft 3 x 3 *(ITS)*
World of Warcraft *(FPDS)*
XENOGEARS x 14 *(ITS)*
Xenosaga Series *(ITS)*
Xenosaga x 2 *(ITS)*
Xenosaga 3 *(ITS)*
Ys Book I & II *(ITS)*

Games Purchased Primarily for Their Story

Key

x X = Number of people who cited the game
(FTS) = Fully Traditional Story
(ITS) = Interactive Traditional Story
(MES) = Multiple-Ending Story
(BPS) = Branching Path Story
(OES) = Open-Ended Story
(FPDS) = Fully Player-Driven Story

Games

.hack Series *(ITS)*
.hack//Infection *(ITS)* x 3
Ace Attorney: Miles Edgeworth Investigations *(ITS)*
Adventure Quest *(ITS)*
Alan Wake *(ITS)* x 4
Alundra *(ITS)*
Apollo Justice: Ace Attorney *(ITS)*
Ar Tonelico Series *(BPS)*
Ar Tonelico II *(BPS)*
Assassin's Creed *(ITS)* x 2
Assassin's Creed 2 *(ITS)* x 2
Baldur's Gate *(ITS)*
Baldur's Gate 2 *(ITS)*
Baten Kaitos *(ITS)*
Baten Kaitos Origins *(ITS)*
Bioshock *(MES)* x 12
Borderlands *(ITS)*
Breath of Fire V: Dragon Quarter *(ITS)*
Broken Sword Series *(ITS)*
Broken Sword: Shadow of the Templars *(ITS)*
Call of Cthulhu: Dark Corners of the Earth *(ITS)*
Call of Duty Modern Warfare *(ITS)*
Call of Duty Modern Warfare 2 *(ITS)*
Castlevania: Dawn of Sorrow *(MES)*
Castlevania: Lament of Innocence *(ITS)*
Chibi Robo *(ITS)*
CHRONO CROSS *(MES)*
CHRONO TRIGGER *(MES)* x 5
Clannad *(BPS)*
CRISIS CORE – FINAL FANTASY VII *(ITS)*
Dawn of War 2 *(ITS)*
Deadly Premonition *(ITS)*
Disgaea: Hour of Darkness *(MES)*
Dragon Age: Origins x 13 *(MES)*
DRAGON QUEST *(ITS)*
DRAGON QUEST V *(ITS)*
DRAGON QUEST VII *(ITS)*
Drawn to Life *(ITS)*
Dues Ex *(BPS)*
Elder Scrolls III: Morrowind *(OES)* x 4
Elder Scrolls IV: Oblivion *(OES)* x 5
Fable *(OES)* x 3

Fable: The Lost Chapters *(OES)*
Fable 2 *(OES)* x 3
Fallout Series *(ITS & OES)*
Fallout *(ITS)*
Fallout 2 *(OES)*
Fallout 3 *(OES)* x 6
FINAL FANTASY Series *(ITS)* x 2
FINAL FANTASY *(ITS)*
FINAL FANTASY IV *(ITS)* x 2
FINAL FANTASY IV: THE AFTER YEARS *(ITS)*
FINAL FANTASY VI *(ITS)* x 3
FINAL FANTASY VII *(ITS)* x 9
FINAL FANTASY VIII *(ITS)* x 8
FINAL FANTASY IX *(ITS)*
FINAL FANTASY X *(ITS)* x 4
FINAL FANTASY X-2 *(ITS)*
FINAL FANTASY XII *(ITS)*
FINAL FANTASY XIII *(ITS)* x 12
FINAL FANTASY TACTICS *(ITS)*
Fire Emblem x 3 *(BPS)*
Fire Emblem: Genealogy of the Holy War *(BPS)*
Fire Emblem: Path of Radiance *(BPS)*
Fire Emblem: Shadow Dragon *(BPS)*
Gears of War 2 *(ITS)*
Glory of Heracles *(ITS)*
God of War *(ITS)*
Golden Sun *(ITS)*
Golden Sun: The Lost Age *(ITS)* x 2
Grand Theft Auto III *(OES)*
Grand Theft Auto IV *(OES)* x 2
Guild Wars *(ITS)*
Guild Wars Nightfall *(ITS)*
Half-Life Series *(ITS)* x 2
Half-Life *(ITS)*
Half-Life 2 *(ITS)* x 3
Halo 2 *(ITS)*
Heavy Rain *(BPS)* x 10
Hoshigami: Ruining Blue Earth Remix *(BPS)*
Hotel Dusk *(ITS)*
Ico *(ITS)*
Indigo Prophecy x 3 *(MES)*
Infamous *(MES)*
Katamari Damacy *(ITS)*
KINGDOM HEARTS *(ITS)* x 2

KINGDOM HEARTS II *(ITS)* x 4
KINGDOM HEARTS 358/2 *(ITS)* x 4
KINGDOM HEARTS CHAIN OF MEMORIES *(ITS)* x 2
KINGDOM HEARTS RE: CHAIN OF MEMORIES *(ITS)*
Knights in the Nightmare *(ITS)*
Legacy of Kain Defiance *(ITS)*
Legend of Dragoon *(ITS)*
Legend of Heroes VI: Sora no Kiseki *(ITS)*
Legend of Zelda Series *(ITS)* x 2
Legend of Zelda *(ITS)*
Legend of Zelda: Majora's Mask *(ITS)*
Legend of Zelda: Ocarina of Time *(ITS)* x 4
Legend of Zelda: Twilight Princess *(ITS)* x 7
Lost Odyssey *(ITS)*
Lufia 2 *(ITS)*
Luminous Arc *(ITS)*
Lunar Knights *(ITS)*
Lunar Silver Star Story Complete *(ITS)* x 2
Magna Carta: Tears of Blood *(ITS)*
Mario & Luigi: Superstar Saga *(ITS)*
Mass Effect *(MES)* x 10
Mass Effect 2 *(BPS)* x 9
Metal Gear Solid Series *(ITS)* x 5
Metal Gear Solid *(MES)*
Metal Gear Solid 2 *(ITS)*
Metal Gear Solid 3 *(ITS)*
Metal Gear Solid 4 *(ITS)* x 5
Metroid Prime: Corruption *(ITS)*
Mother 3 x 2 *(ITS)*
Neverwinter Nights 2 *(OES)*
Nier *(MES)*
NiGHTS *(ITS)*
Ogre Battle 64 *(MES)*
Okami x 2 *(ITS)*
Overlord *(MES)*
Paper Mario: The Thousand Year Door *(ITS)* x 2
Patapon 2 *(ITS)*
Phoenix Wright: Ace Attorney Series *(ITS)* x 2
Phoenix Wright: Ace Attorney *(ITS)* x 3
Pikmin x 2 *(MES)*
Planescape: Torment x 3 *(OES)*
Pokémon Series *(ITS)* x 2
Pokémon Diamond *(ITS)*
Pokémon Emerald *(ITS)* x 2

Pokémon Mystery Dungeon Explorers of Darkness *(ITS)*
Pokémon Mystery Dungeon Explorers of the Sky x 2 *(ITS)*
Pokémon Platinum *(ITS)* x 3
Pokémon Ranger Shadows of Almia *(ITS)*
Pokémon Soul Silver *(ITS)*
Portal *(ITS)* x 5
Prince of Persia *(ITS)*
Prince of Persia: Sands of Time *(ITS)*
Professor Layton Series *(ITS)*
Professor Layton and the Diabolical Box *(ITS)*
Radiata Stories *(BPS)*
Ratchet & Clank Series *(ITS)*
Ratchet & Clank: A Crack in Time *(ITS)*
Red Alert Series *(ITS)*
Red Dead Redemption x 3 *(ITS)*
Rise of the Argonauts *(ITS)*
Riviera: The Promised Land x 2 *(MES)*
Resident Evil Series *(ITS)*
Resident Evil 4 *(ITS)*
Resistance: Fall of Man *(ITS)*
Romancing Saga *(BPS)*
Rule of Rose *(MES)*
Scribblenauts *(FPDS)*
Shadow Hearts: Covenant x 2 *(MES)*
Shadow of the Colossus *(ITS)* x 2
Shadow the Hedgehog *(BPS)*
Shenmue *(ITS)*
Shin Megami Tensei: Digital Devil Saga 2 *(ITS)*
Shin Megami Tensei: Persona 3 FES *(ITS)*
Shin Megami Tensei: Persona 4 *(MES)*
Silent Hill Series *(MES)*
Skies of Arcadia x 2 *(ITS)*
Spore Creatures *(ITS)*
Starcraft *(ITS)*
STAR OCEAN: FIRST DEPARTURE *(MES)*
STAR OCEAN: TILL THE END OF TIME *(MES)*
Star Wars: Knights of the Old Republic *(BPS)* x 2
Star Wars: Knights of the Old Republic 2 *(BPS)*
Strong Bad's Cool Game for Attractive People *(ITS)*
Suikoden V *(MES)*
Summon Night: Swordcraft Story *(ITS)*
Super Smash Brothers Brawl *(ITS)*
Tales of Monkey Island *(ITS)*
Tales of Hearts *(ITS)*

Tales of the Abyss x 2 *(ITS)*
Tales of Symphonia *(ITS)* x 7
Tales of Symphonia: Dawn of the New World *(MES)* x 2
Tales of Vesperia *(ITS)*
The Longest Journey Series *(ITS)*
The Longest Journey *(ITS)*
The Saboteur *(ITS)*
The Sims 3 *(FPDS)*
The Witcher x 2 *(ITS)*
THE WORLD ENDS WITH YOU *(ITS)* x 4
Uncharted: Drake's Fortune *(ITS)* x 2
Umineko no Naku Koro ni *(FTS)*
Warcraft III *(ITS)*
Warhammer Online *(FPDS)*
Wild ARMS Series *(ITS)*
World of Warcraft *(OES)* x 2
XENOGEARS x 4 *(ITS)*
Xenosaga *(ITS)*

Books and Journals

Barth, J. (1967). The literature of exhaustion. In *The Atlantic*. Boston: Atlantic Monthly Group.

Campbell, J. (1949). *The hero with a thousand faces*. San Francisco: New World Library.

Charles, F., Mead, S. J., & Cavazza, M. (2002). From computer games to interactive stories: Interactive storytelling. *The Electronic Library*, *20*(2), 103–112.

Cowden, T., LaFever, C., & Viders, S. (2000). *The complete writer's guide to heroes & heroines*. Hollywood: Lone Eagle Publishing Company.

Danielewski, M. Z. (2000). *House of leaves*. New York City: Random House.

DeMaria, R., & Wilson, J. L. (2004). *High score! The illustrated history of electronic games*. Emeryville: McGraw-Hill/Osborne.

Desilets, B. J. (1989). Reading, thinking, and interactive fiction. *English Journal*, *78*(3), 75.

Edelstein, L. (1999). *The writer's guide to character traits*. Cincinnati: Writer's Digest Books.

Freeman, C. (2004). *Creating emotion in games*. Berkeley: New Riders Publishing.

Glassner, A. S. (2004). *Interactive storytelling: Techniques for 21st-century fiction*. Wellesley: A. K. Peters, Ltd.

Guinness World Records. (2008). *Guinness World Records Gamer's Edition 2008*. Vancouver: The Jim Pattison Group.

Guinness World Records. (2009). *Guinness World Records Gamer's Edition 2009*. Vancouver: The Jim Pattison Group.

Kent, S. L. (2001). *The ultimate history of video games*. New York City: Three Rivers Press.

Kohler, C. (2005). *Power-up: How Japanese video games gave the world an extra life*. Indianapolis: BradyGames.

Lancy, D. F., & Hayes, B. L. (1988). Interactive fiction and the reluctant reader. *English Journal*, *77*(7), 42.

Laramee, F. D. (2002). *Game design perspectives*. Hingham, MA: Charles River Media.

Lebowitz, J. (2009). *Do modern stories need interactivity? A comparison of storytelling methods in media*. Tempe: The University of Advancing Technology.

McCarthy, D., Curran, S., & Byron, S. (2005). *The art of producing games*. Boston: Thomson Course Technology.

Miller, K. (2008). Grove Street Grimm: Grand Theft Auto and digital folklore. *Journal of American Folklore*, *121*(481), 255–285.

Montfort, N. (2005). *Twisty little passages*. Cambridge, MA: MIT Press.

Montgomery, R. A. (1978). *Choose your own adventure: Journey under the sea*. New York City: Bantam Books.

Montgomery, R. A. (1986). *Choose your own adventure: Beyond escape!* New York City: Bantam Books.

Mulligan, J., & Patrovsky, B. (2003). *Developing online games: An insider's guide.* Upper Saddle River: New Riders.

Pinhanez, C. S., Davis, J. W., Intille, S., Johnson, M. P., Wilson, A. D., Bobick, A. F., et al. (2000). Physically interactive story environments. *IBM Systems Journal.*

Rollings, A., & Adams, E. (2003). *Andrew Rollings and Ernest Adams on game design.* Indianapolis: New Riders Publishing.

Rowling, J. K. (1997). *Harry Potter and the sorcerer's stone.* New York City: Scholastic.

Ryan, M. (2001). Beyond myth and metaphor: The case of narrative in digital media. *The International Journal of Computer Game Research, 1*(1), 1–13.

Ryan, M. (2004). *Narrative across media.* Lincoln: University of Nebraska Press.

Spierling, U., & Szilas, N. (2008). *Interactive storytelling.* Cambridge, MA: Springer.

Tavinor, G. (2005). Videogames and interactive fiction. *Philosophy and Literature, 29*(1), 24–40.

The Gamepros. (2006). The 55 greatest moments in gaming. *Gamepro Magazine, .*

Vogler, C. (2007). *The writer's journey* (3rd ed.). Studio City: Michael Wiese Productions.

Wizards of the Coast. (2008). *Dungeons & Dragons* (4th ed.). Renton, WA: Wizards of the Coast.

Web Resources

Adams, E. (2004, December 22). *The designer's notebook: How many endings does a game need?* Gamasutra. http://www.gamasutra.com/view/feature/2179/the_designers_notebook_how_many_.php.

Amazon.com sales rankings and reviews. (2002–2009). Amazon.com. http://www.amazon.com.

Amazon.com Bestsellers in video games. (2002–2009). Amazon.com. http://www.amazon.com/gp/bestsellers/videogames/ref=pd_zg_hrsr_vg_1_1.

Boyer, B., & Cifaldi, F. (2006, November 3). *The Gamasutra quantum leap awards: Storytelling.* Gamasutra. http://www.gamasutra.com/features/20061006/quantum_01.shtml.

Jerz, D. G. (2001, May 3). *Dennis G. Jerz's Site.* http://jerz.setonhill.edu/if/adams/intro.html.

Katz, D. (2008). *Damian's Gamebook Web Page.* http://www.gamebooks.org/index.php.

Kumar, M. (2008, February 20). *GDC: Deconstructing the best interactive storytelling.* Gamasutra. http://www.gamasutra.com/php-bin/news_index.php?story=17537.

Noyle, J. (2006, April 26). *Techniques of written storytelling applied to game design.* Gamasutra. http://www.gamasutra.com/view/feature/2677/techniques_of_written_storytelling_.php.

NPD Group. (2002–2008). *Video game industry sales data.* NPD Group. http://vgsales.wikia.com/wiki/Video_Game_Sales_Wiki.

Video Games

07th Expansion (Developer). (2002). *Higurashi When They Cry* [Video Game PC]. London: MangaGamer.

Advanced Microcomputer Systems (Developer). (1983). *Dragon's Lair* [Video Game Arcade]. El Cajon: Cinematronics.

ArenaNet (Developer). (2005). *Guild Wars* [Video Game PC]. Seoul: NCSoft.

Bethesda Game Studios (Developer). (2002). *The Elder Scrolls III: Morrowind* [Video Game Xbox & PC]. Rockville: Bethesda.

Bethesda Game Studios (Developer). (2008). *Fallout 3* [Video Game Xbox 360, PlayStation 3, & PC]. Rockville: Bethesda.

Bioware (Developer). (2007). *Mass Effect* [Video Game Xbox 360 & PC]. Red Wood City: EA Games.

Bioware (Developer). (2010). *Mass Effect 2* [Video Game Xbox 360 & PC]. Red Wood City: EA Games.

Blizzard Entertainment (Developer). (2004). *World of Warcraft* [Video Game PC]. Irvine: Blizzard Entertainment.

Career Soft (Developer). (2001). *Growlanser II: The Sense of Justice* [Video Game PlayStation 2]. Redding: Working Designs.

CCP Games (Developer). (2003). *EVE Online* [Video Game PC]. Reykjavik: CCP Games.

Crowther, W., & Woods, D. (Developers). (1977). *Colossal Cave Adventure* [Video Game PC].

Cyan Worlds (Developer). (1993). *Myst* [Video Game PC]. Eugene: Broderbund.

Game Arts (Developer). (2009). *Lunar Silver Star Harmony* [Video Game PSP]. Torrance: Xseed Games.

Garriott, R. (Developer). (1981). *Ultima I: The First Age of Darkness* [Video Game Apple II]. California: California Pacific Computer Co.

Gearbox Software (Developer). (2009). *Borderlands* [Video Game PC, PlayStation 3, & Xbox 360]. Novato: 2K Games.

Irrational Games (Developer). (2007). *Bioshock* [Video Game Xbox 360, PlayStation 3, & PC]. Novato: 2K Games.

Konami (Developer). (1998). *Metal Gear Solid* [Video Game PlayStation]. Tokyo: Konami.

Konami (Developer). (2004). *Metal Gear Solid 3: Snake Eater* [Video Game PlayStation 2]. Tokyo: Konami.

Konami (Developer). (2005). *Castlevania: Dawn of Sorrows* [Video Game Nintendo DS]. Tokyo: Konami.

Konami (Developer). (2008). *Metal Gear Solid 4: Guns of the Patriots* [Video Game PlayStation 3]. Tokyo: Konami.

Konami (Developer). (2009). *Love Plus* [Video Game Nintendo DS]. Tokyo: Konami.

Lionhead Studios (Developer). (2008). *Fable II* [Video Game Xbox 360]. Redmond: Microsoft Game Studios.

Lucasfilm Games (Developer). (1990). *The Secret of Monkey Island* [Video Game PC]. San Francisco: Lucasfilm Games.

Maxis (Developer). (2008). *The Sims* [Video Game PC]. Redwood City: Electronic Arts.

Monolith Soft (Developer). (2004). *Xenosaga Episode II: Jenseits von Gut und Böse* [Video Game PlayStation 2]. Tokyo: Namco.

MumboJumbo (Developer). (2008). *Samantha Swift and the Hidden Rose of Athena* [Video Game PC]. Dallas: MumboJumbo.

Nintendo (Developer). (1981). *Donkey Kong* [Video Game Arcade]. Kyoto: Nintendo.

Nintendo (Developer). (2001). *Animal Crossing* [Video Game Gamecube]. Kyoto: Nintendo.

Nippon Ichi Software (Developer). (2007). *Disgaea: Afternoon of Darkness* [Video Game PSP]. Gifu: Nippon Ichi Software.

Number None Inc (Developer). (2008). *Braid* [Video Game Xbox 360, PlayStation 3, & PC]. San Francisco: Number-None Inc.

Nutting Associates (Developer). (1971). *Computer Space* [Video Game Arcade]. Mountain View: Nutting Associates.

PopCap Games (Developer). (2009). *Plants vs. Zombies* [Video Game PC]. Seattle: PopCap Games.

Quantic Dream (Developer). (2010). *Heavy Rain* [Video Game PlayStation 3]. Tokyo: Sony Computer Entertainment.

Rockstar North (Developer). (2008). *Grand Theft Auto IV* [Video Game Xbox 360 & PlayStation 3]. New York City: Rockstar Games.

Russell, S. (Developer). (1962). *Spacewar!* [Video Game PDP-1].

Silicon Knights (Developer). (1996). *Blood Omen: Legacy of Kain* [Video Game PlayStation]. Redwood City: Crystal Dynamics.

Softmax (Developer). (2005). *Magna Carta: Tears of Blood* [Video Game PlayStation 2]. Tokyo: Atlus.

Sony Computer Entertainment (Developer). (1995). *Arc the Lad* [Video Game PlayStation]. Redding: Working Designs.

Sony Computer Entertainment (Developer). (1996). *Arc the Lad II* [Video Game PlayStation]. Redding: Working Designs.

Square Co., Ltd (Developer). (1991). *FINAL FANTASY IV* [Video Game Super Nintendo]. Redmond: Nintendo of America Inc.

Square Co., Ltd (Developer). (1994). *FINAL FANTASY VI* [Video Game Super Nintendo]. Redmond: Nintendo of America Inc.

Square Co., Ltd (Developer). (1995). *CHRONO TRIGGER* [Video Game Super Nintendo]. Tokyo: Square Electronic Arts LLC.

Square Co., Ltd (Developer). (1997). *FINAL FANTASY VII* [Video Game PlayStation]. Tokyo: Sony Computer Entertainment, Inc.

Square Co., Ltd (Developer). (1998). *SAGA FRONTIER* [Video Game PlayStation]. Foster City: Sony Computer Entertainment America, Inc.

Square Co., Ltd (Developer). (1999). *FRONT MISSION 3* [Video Game PlayStation]. Tokyo: Square Electronic Arts LLC.

Square Co., Ltd (Developer). (2001). *THE BOUNCER* [Video Game PlayStation 2]. Tokyo: Square Electronic Arts LLC.

Square Co., Ltd (Developer). (2001). *FINAL FANTASY X* [Video Game PlayStation 2]. Tokyo: Square Electronic Arts LLC.

Square Enix Co., Ltd (Developer). (2005). *KINGDOM HEARTS II* [Video Game PlayStation 2]. Tokyo: Square Enix, Inc.

Square Enix Co., Ltd (Developer). (2007). *CRISIS CORE – FINAL FANTASY VII* [Video Game PSP]. Tokyo: Square Enix, Inc.

Square Enix Co., Ltd (Developer). (2007). *FINAL FANTASY TACTICS: THE WAR OF THE LIONS* [Video Game PSP]. Tokyo: Square Enix, Inc.

Square Enix Co., Ltd./Jupiter (Developer). (2007). *THE WORLD ENDS WITH YOU* [Video Game PSP]. Tokyo: Square Enix, Inc.

Square Enix Co., Ltd (Developer). (2009). *FINAL FANTASY XIII* [Video Game PlayStation 3 & Xbox 360]. Tokyo: Square Enix, Inc.

Square Enix Co., Ltd (Developer). (2009). *STAR OCEAN: SECOND EVOLUTION* [Video Game PSP]. Tokyo: Square Enix, Inc.

Team Ico (Developer). (2005). *Shadow of the Colossus* [Video Game PlayStation 2]. Tokyo: Sony Computer Entertainment.

Telltale Games (Developer). (2010). *Sam & Max: The Devil's Playhouse* [Video Game PC, PlayStation 3, & iPad]. San Rafael: Telltale Games.

thatgamecompany (Developer). (2009). *Flower* [Video Game PlayStation 3]. Tokyo: Sony.

Type-Moon (Developer). (2004). *Fate/Stay Night* [Video Game PC]. Tokyo: Type-Moon.

Ubisoft (Developer). (2008). *Prince of Persia* [Video Game PlayStation 3, Xbox 360, & PC]. Paris: Ubisoft.

Valve Corporation (Developer). (2002). [Video Game Xbox 360, PlayStation 3, & PC].

Westwood Studios (Developer). (2002). *Half-life* [Video Game PC]. Los Angeles: Sierra, Earth and Beyond. Redwood City: Electronic Arts.

Zynga (Developer). (2009). *FarmVille* [Video Game PC]. San Francisco: Zynga.

Other Resources

Lucas, G. (Director). (1977). *Star Wars: Episode IV* [Motion picture]. San Francisco: Lucasfilm.

Edwards, B. (Director). (1965). *The Great Race* [Motion picture]. Burbank: Warner Bros.

Index

Note: Page numbers followed by *b* indicate boxes; *f* indicate figures.

Printed and bound by CPI Group (UK) Ltd, Croydon, CR0 4YY

21/10/2024

01777093-0003